BODY PIERCING SAVED MY LIFE

BODY PIERCING

Inside the Phenomenon
of Christian Rock

SAVED MY LIFE

Andrew Beaujon

DA CAPO PRESS
A Member of the Perseus Books Group

Designed by Brent Wilcox
Set in 11-point New Caledonia by the Perseus Books Group

Library of Congress Cataloging-in-Publication Data
Beaujon, Andrew.
    Body piercing saved my life : inside the phenomenon of Christian rock /
Andrew Beaujon.
        p.   cm.
    Includes bibliographical references (p.   ) and index.
    ISBN-13: 978-0-306-81457-0 (pbk. : alk. paper)
    ISBN-10: 0-306-81457-9 (pbk. : alk. paper)
    1. Christian rock music—History and criticism.   2. Rock music—Religious
aspects—Christianity.   I. Title.
    ML3187.5.B43   2006
    781.66—dc22

                                                                                2006006254

First Da Capo Press edition 2006

Published by Da Capo Press
A Member of the Perseus Books Group
http://www.dacapopress.com

Da Capo Press books are available at special discounts for bulk purchases in the
U.S. by corporations, institutions, and other organizations. For more
information, please contact the Special Markets Department at the Perseus
Books Group, 11 Cambridge Center, Cambridge, MA 02142, or call (800) 255-
1514 or (617) 252-5298, or e-mail special.markets@perseusbooks.com.

1 2 3 4 5 6 7 8 9—09 08 07 06

For Ewa and Cameron

How is it that in matters concerning the flesh we have so many fine poems and hymns but that in those concerning the spirit we have such sluggish, cold affairs? Why should the devil have all the good music?

—Martin Luther, *Tischreden* 5:5603

Can't you see? You're not making Christianity better—you're making rock 'n' roll worse!

—Hank Hill, *King of the Hill*

CONTENTS

Acknowledgments   ix

1 *I Swear*   1

2 *No More LSD for Me (I Met the Man from Galilee)*   19

CHRISTIAN ROCK LIFERS #1: Doug Van Pelt   45

3 *More Than Just a Song*   55

4 *The Baffled King Composing Hallelujah*   75

CHRISTIAN ROCK LIFERS #2: Steve Taylor   95

5 *Clarity*   105

6 *Drinking Blood Out of Skulls, Living High in the
Kingdom of Death, and a New Way to Be Christian*   115

CHRISTIAN ROCK LIFERS #3: Jay Swartzendruber   139

7 *Salt and Light, Inc.*   149

8 *If We Are the Body*   169

CHRISTIAN ROCK LIFERS #4: Bill Hearn   179

9 *Black and White in a Gray World*   187

CHRISTIAN ROCK LIFERS #5: Mark Salomon   217

10 *To Be Mad for My King*   225

11 *Just Like Heaven*   247

Afterword   269
Notes   273
Bibliography   275
Index   277

ACKNOWLEDGMENTS

Thank you, thank you, thank you:

Ewa Beaujon. Ben Schafer at Da Capo. Jim Fitzgerald and Anne Reid Garrett at the James Fitzgerald Agency. Peter Kaufman at the *Washington Post*. Andy Greenwald. Sia Michel, Charles Aaron, Jeanann Pannasch, Doug Brod, Jon Dolan, Dave Itzkoff, Melissa Maerz, Caryn Ganz, Phoebe Reilly, and Chuck Klosterman at *Spin*. Leonard Roberge at the *Washington City Paper*. Chip Porter. Scott DeSimon. Carrie Nieman at *Style Weekly*. Mark Mobley. Doug Van Pelt. Jim and Beth Coe. Mark Nelson. The Bazan family. Amanda MacKinnon at Tooth & Nail. Rich Guider at Word. Shelly Jennings at Mars Hill, Seattle. Tricia Whitehead. Jeff Jackson. Leigh Ann Hardie and Shawn Green at EMI Christian Music Group. Jay Swartzendruber at *CCM*. Desiree Flores at the Ms. Foundation. Marjorie Signer at the Religious Coalition for Reproductive Choice. Jenny Toomey at the Future of Music Foundation. Mark Allan Powell. Shawn Young. Nathan Lamb. Scott Crowder. Keri and Tim Baughman. Richard and Janet Couch. Ewa Golabek. Ben Riley and Vicky Navarro. Isobelle Aitkenhead Beaujon, R.I.P.

I Swear

The three thousand kids jammed into this tent on a former pig farm in Bushnell, Illinois, look like the audience you'd see at any rock show. Some have decorated their bodies with all sorts of foreign materials—metal, ink, even giant earlobe-hole stretchers made from wood. Others have wildly colored hair. A lot of them have adopted a look that could best be described as "renaissance nerd"—thick glasses, tight T-shirts, thrift-store trousers—and wouldn't be out of place at a Dashboard Confessional concert.

Instead of the jaded resignation that seems to pump out of the vents at rock clubs, however, the air underneath the tent's soft peaks is electric with anticipation, because Dave Bazan is playing, and you never know what he'll do. He just might . . . cuss out loud. The singer for Pedro the Lion cuts a schlubby figure in a faded red T-shirt and cutoffs, with a bushy beard that makes his head seem too large for his body, more like the bobble-head doll of an antiglobalization activist than the bad boy of Christian rock.

But this is the annual Cornerstone Festival, and expectations are different here. And tonight, Bazan seems heck-bent on defying as many of those expectations as possible. I'd talked to him before the show, when he was gaily swigging from a milk jug full of vodka and water in defiance of the festival's no-alcohol policy, and now, onstage, as his band launches into "Foregone Conclusions," his decision as to whether to flout Cornerstone's unwritten ban on profane language seems to have been made.

"You were too busy steering/The conversation toward the Lord," he sings. "To hear the voice of the Spirit/Begging you to shut the fu-uck up." Squeals of delight fill the empty pagoda of air, joined quickly by a pair of panties flying toward the stage. Then, three more pairs follow.

This was not the scene I'd expected to find at a Christian rock festival. I'd done enough research to know that Christian music was far better than when I was in high school and "saved" friends tried to get me to come to a Christian youth group called Young Life by dangling ski trips and the work of groups like Stryper and Petra, whom they assured me were "just as good" as the hard rock groups I liked. At the time, I was hardly a discerning listener, but even then I remember thinking the Christian bands were okay at best. Why settle for a copy when you can have the original?

Then there was the small matter of not being a Christian. It's not that I'm a Jew or a Muslim or a Unitarian. In fact, I consider atheism to be too much of a commitment. Aside from an annually renewed belief that the Washington Redskins have a shot at the playoffs, I'm not religious, and I haven't put in much time trying to work out whether I'm wrong, or maybe just lack the right gene.

That's not to say I'm antireligion—in fact, I'm kind of a fan. Probably because of my own inability to sense the eternal, I love talking to people who can and comparing their takes on God. On the block I live on in Richmond, Virginia, I have neighbors who are Muslims, Jehovah's Witnesses, Baptists, nondenominational Christians, and Unitarians. My wife is British (and a disaffected Catholic, if you're wondering), and it kind of freaks her out how vocal people here are about their faith, but I love it. There's something so beautifully American about this country's crazy-quilt religious landscape, where you can find a hundred different views of God within a five-minute walk.

A year before I went to Cornerstone, I went to Denver to interview the rock band P.O.D. for *Spin* magazine. I knew the members of P.O.D. were born-again Christians, but their lyrics were so much background noise to me, just more chest-beating rap-metal. On the plane on the way out, however, I finally *listened* to P.O.D. Every song, and I mean every song, referred to the band's spirituality. And this was no niche act—P.O.D.'s last record had sold three million copies, and they played concerts with groups like Linkin Park and Korn. At the time I went out to meet them, they were the biggest-selling group on Atlantic Records not named Led Zeppelin.

The interview was kind of a wash—the band's publicist demanded that *Spin* rent a conference room for the main interview, a move that perhaps works with *Rolling Stone.* My editor countered with a suggestion that we use my hotel room instead. That apparently wasn't good enough, so someone in the P.O.D. camp paid for a conference room in the basement of the hotel where we were all staying. It was a good interview, but I suspect *Spin*'s unwillingness to pony up for the conference room worked against me. That was mostly it for access to the band—I spent the rest of the evening watching them from behind a curtain of security dudes before they played at Red Rocks and utterly, completely failed to capture any of the atmosphere that makes such stories readable.

But that's neither here nor there. What fascinated me about P.O.D. was a bonus track on one of the band's early independent albums, *Snuff the Punk* (the punk in question being the Devil). The song is called "Abortion Is Murder," and it seemed like the type of territory a mainstream band wouldn't touch with someone else's career.

The lyrics go, "Abortion is murder/There's nothing you can say or do/To justify the fact/That there's a living breathing baby inside of you."

The band had already expertly batted away my fumbling questions about their religion—"We just wanna make music that'll continue to affect people" was a typical gloss—when the group's singer, Sonny Sandoval, started talking about the difficulties of maintaining street cred in their hardscrabble San Diego neighborhood after the word got out that they had become Christians.

"Dude, no one's gonna tell me what I can and can't believe!" he said of his attitude then, adding that in the early days of their conversions, the group sang about issues a lot more specific than they addressed now. "Before it was like, you could do a pro-life song," Sandoval said.

"Which you did," I said.

Spines stiffened around the table.

"It was more like gangsta cred," said drummer Wuv Bernardo.

"We don't do that stuff anymore," said Sandoval, "'cause that's not where we're at. You know, we're not about stepping on people's toes."

Now, a more cynical person might detect a marketing calculation in this live-and-let-live attitude, but after an hour with P.O.D., I think the group's reticence is sincere. They see themselves as people saved by Jesus Christ, and they'd love for you to come to Him through their music; what they'd like most of all, however, is for everyone to feel comfortable at a P.O.D. concert.

I certainly did; I'd seen the band twice before I met them and, like I said earlier, hadn't even noticed that the lyrics, which seemed like typical modern rock fare—"I feel so alive for the very first time/I can't deny you," for example—were about a different kind of relationship than that normally covered by, say, Limp Bizkit.

And here's something else that was interesting about P.O.D.: They got hot under the collar chatting about people who "burn the flags and then they sip their lattes" and wrote a song called "Freedom Fighter," which is not about Che Guevara at all—it's a salute to

U.S. soldiers in the Middle East. "I just appreciate my blessings in America," Sandoval told me. "I'm not one of them Hollywood celebrity–type people that are, like, antigovernment and antiwar and all that stuff. I'm about my freedoms, man."

"That's not a popular stance in the music world," I ventured.

"You'd be surprised," bassist Traa Daniels replied.

This flies in the face of conventional wisdom. Pop musicians are supposed to be politically liberal, just like their audiences. But what if a significant number of fans *were* turned off, for instance, by the sight of rock stars like Dave Grohl and Bruce Springsteen stumping for John Kerry in 2004? What if Traa Daniels was right?

What else would those socially and politically conservative fans have in common?

Lasting social change isn't neatly contained within a generation. There's a ripple effect; just look at how a 1973 Supreme Court case that effectively legalized abortion is still debated in statehouses, schools, and, yes, rap-metal songs.

I began to think a bit about the ripples that might have helped form P.O.D.'s worldview. At the show, they were hanging out with members of Korn—coincidentally, I assume, the latter's Brian "Head" Welch converted to Christianity two years later—but they also spent time with the folks from Evanescence. Tim Cook, P.O.D.'s manager, told me that he knew all the Evanescence folks from when he was booking Christian clubs in his native Oklahoma. There's a very well-organized Christian underground rock scene, he told me, one every bit as developed as the indie rock/punk circuit that burst into the mainstream in the '90s, making stars of groups like Green Day, Nirvana, and, more recently, Modest Mouse.

This interested me, too. I grew up going to indie and punk shows and remember well how weird it was to see bands I'd once seen play to twenty people accepting MTV Video Music Awards. It wasn't just processing the fact that major corporations were putting out records by artists whose previous albums had sold in the ten to thirty thousand range; it was also watching as singers like Liz Phair and Nina Gordon become adult-contemporary artists and Courtney Love became first a movie star, then an internationally famous punch line.

After I finished the P.O.D. story, I started paying attention to other Christian artists that had crossed over to the mainstream or were bubbling just underneath it. In 2003 and 2004, there were quite a few: Switchfoot; Sixpence None the Richer; Stacie Orrico; MercyMe; Yellowcard; Further Seems Forever; Chevelle; Underoath.

What if, I wondered, these artists, almost all in their early to mid-twenties, represented the first flowering of a movement that began thirty years ago, when evangelical churches began reaching out to disillusioned hippies? Had born-again Christians finally managed to trade the image of old men in blue polyester suits with bad toupees for one of hipsters with nose rings?

Making Christianity cool is a tall order. When I started researching this book, the reaction of most of my colleagues was "better you than me." Christian rock has an arguably deserved reputation as the least fashionable music on earth. "Oh my God, you may just be the most deeply unhip person I've ever met," said *Six Feet Under*'s Claire Fisher when she found out her boyfriend listened to Christian rock. And on *Seinfeld*, when Elaine expresses similar horror that her boyfriend likes Christian music, George says, "I like Christian rock. It's very positive. It's not like those *real* musicians who think they're so cool and hip."

Anything this uncool, I figured, was probably worth investigating. I couldn't put my finger on it at the time, but I felt there was something so quintessentially American about the idea of religious people creating an alternate version of popular culture. If nothing else, Christian music, as has been noted by better critics than myself, exists in a parallel universe. And who's not up for the occasional trip into a parallel universe, especially one that exists so close to the one we know?

I named this book after a T-shirt I kept seeing at Cornerstone, the back of which showed Jesus' hands with holes in them. It seemed like a suitable metaphor for the way Christian music imbued the language and symbols of the rock world with unexpected, ultimately subversive meaning. Plus, it sounds kind of badass.

I guess this would be a good time to talk about what words like *Christianity* and *Christian* are going to mean in the context of this book. They're shorthand for a particularly American strain of Christianity. Despite the fact that a significant number of early American settlers came here to worship freely, by the turn of the eighteenth century, the centripetal force tethering Americans to religious life was weakening. The Puritan insistence on demonstrable "conversion experiences" resulted in rapidly declining numbers in the pews, as children raised in the church didn't really have anything to convert *from*.

An influx of Scotch-Irish immigrants to the frontier, where they were joined by an exodus of second-generation fortune seekers, made for similarly rocky ground for religious experiences. There were neither many preachers nor parishioners in most parts, and the dangers and stresses of frontier life were rather time-consuming. Plus, the predominant Calvinist theology of the time, which taught that only a few "elect" were going to heaven anyway, wasn't perhaps the best recruitment tool.

But with the entrepreneurial derring-do that soon came to be a hallmark of American character, a few men saw not a rapidly growing spiritual wasteland but an opportunity. The first "Great Awakening" in America occurred in the 1730s, when traveling evangelists such as Jonathan Edwards and George Whitefield, employing not a little bit of showmanship, began to hold "revival" meetings that encouraged self-directed Bible study.

Whitefield was a prototype of a modern evangelist; the classically trained British actor even sent an employee ahead to arrange advance publicity for his American meetings. He preached in a theatrical style, often crying when emotion overcame him.[1] Whitefield was particularly popular with rural audiences and held vast meetings in fields, much to the disapproval of genteel city types. When the dust settled, though, the "Great Awakening" he helped to spark was credited with producing more than fifty thousand converts when fewer than a million people lived in the colonies.[2]

There were two further Great Awakenings in America, starting in 1801 with "camp meetings" in the South and switching into high gear in 1820 when preachers such as Charles Grandison Finney began holding massive revival meetings. Finney capitalized on the growing Protestant taste for a faith that could be measured in personal terms—one's own relationship with Christ. This idea would really blossom at the turn of the twentieth century with, among other events, the political ascendancy of William Jennings Bryan, who mixed fundamentalist Christianity with political populism and was a key player in battles over prohibition and the teaching of evolution in schools.

Nowadays, as anyone not living under a rock or in New York City knows, evangelical Christianity is perhaps the most powerful social, political, and, of course, religious movement in the United States. Much of evangelical Christian belief derives from the charismatic, Pentecostal traditions of American churches that themselves sprang from the third Great Awakening.

There is now a well-established, evangelical Christian subculture in America. Don't let me confuse you too much with the term—I'm referring to the primarily white, primarily conservative and rural (in spirit if not residence), Protestant Christian culture that accounts for 23 percent of all Americans, according to a 2004 poll.[3] While about 48 percent of Americans consider themselves born-again, for our purposes, evangelical Christians are the smaller percentage who try to incorporate their religion into every aspect of their daily lives, who believe that the simplest reading of the Bible—which they believe is inerrant—is the only correct one, that a personal relationship with Jesus is the key to salvation, and that they are called by God to bring others to the same salvation that awaits them. Great numbers of them also believe their values are under attack by the mainstream media.

Let's dispel a couple of secular stereotypes right away, then: Only about a third of Evangelicals are Southerners, and about a quarter of them have college degrees, numbers that compare well with the population at large. Seventy-five percent don't attend megachurches. And only about one-third considers "moral values" the most important issue in American politics.

Then, there are less-than-surprising facts: nearly 70 percent of evangelical Christians vote Republican. More evangelicals are concerned more about sex and violence on TV (65 percent) than about being affected by terrorism (25 percent). And less than 1 percent of American evangelicals believe that mankind had anything to do with writing or translating the Bible.[4]

With strongly held beliefs regarding the hostility of the outside world to their religion, Evangelicals are indeed an attractive market for alternative entertainment. According to that same 2004 poll, 76 percent of evangelical parents restrict their kids' TV and movie viewing habits. And sales of Christian music—which exceeded 47.1 million albums in 2003, more than classical, jazz, and New Age music combined—continue to grow, rising 10 percent over the last five years. Over the same period, mainstream record sales have declined by the same percentage.

There are few words in music that scare people more than "Christian rock." There's a Time-Life commercial that I think epitomizes what many people think Christian rock is. It's for the *Worship To-gether Collection*, and it shows a bunch of dorky concertgoers freaking out like Beatles fans at Shea Stadium in 1964 as some of the worst music you'll ever hear blasts out of the arena's speakers. The songs are a blend of folk-rock, country, and singer/songwriter blahness spiced up with the odd sampled beat. The first time I saw it, I wondered if the audience had been paid.

Those rock-based tunes are in fact part of contemporary Christian music—the proper term is *worship music*, and we will get to it later. But Christian rock itself, like the American exurbs in which it thrives, has sprawled so widely that it's hard to define with any grace. And I'm not just talking about stylistic diversity, though the term *Christian rock* now covers everything from dippy folk-rock to throat-shredding emocore. There are Christian bands that view their music as ministries or evangelical tools and many more whose members consider themselves "just Christians in a band," even though they play primarily on the well-worn Christian rock circuit. And quite a few who wish very much that the term *Christian rock* would disappear altogether.

One of the latter is Switchfoot, who played Cornerstone's first night. Setting up an interview with Switchfoot was not easy. The band's publicist was concerned that I would portray them as Christian rockers, which seemed like a curious concern when the band in question was playing at a Christian rock festival, but it's quite a serious matter when that same band has crossed over to what Christians call the "general market."

And Switchfoot has crossed over big. The band, also from San Diego, formed in the mid-'90s and signed to Christian music pioneer Charlie Peacock's label re:think, an imprint of Sparrow. Early on, singer Jonathan Foreman displayed a talent for the universal, writing lyrics about being caught somewhere between this world and the next that sounded like they might translate to a wider audience.

Singer and actress Mandy Moore gave Switchfoot an opportunity to test that theory. Moore, a Christian and a fan of the group, asked Switchfoot to contribute several songs to the soundtrack of her 2002 film *A Walk to Remember.* The soundtrack's success led to a contract with Sony, a competitor with Sparrow's corporate parent EMI, in the general market (the band remains on Sparrow in the Christian market).

This synergistic strategy paid off. Switchfoot's next album, *The Beautiful Letdown,* yielded two Top 100 singles and sold two million copies. Their biggest hit was a song called "Meant to Live," a crunchy rock tune on that perennial rock 'n' roll theme: feeling dissatisfied. "We were meant to live for so much more," sings Foreman in his appealingly raspy voice. "Have we lost ourselves?" They're brilliantly malleable lyrics—an expression of spiritual yearning that also works quite nicely as a drive-time sentiment for anyone with a crappy job.

One of the funny things about being a rock journalist is that you quickly find out that the most restricted areas of venues are usually dumps. Dressing rooms, tour buses, and the wings of a stage are all stark exceptions to the glamour we assume cossets our rock stars. Switchfoot's trailer at Cornerstone was no exception. The stairs swayed ominously as you entered, and the interior was a spartan, wood-paneled reminder that this room would be someone else's home tomorrow. Some of the band members sat on aluminum chairs talking on their cell phones; others perused the card table piled high with snacks courtesy of well-wishers from earlier days: JON, TIM, CHAD & JEROME, WE'RE SO PROUD OF YOU! GOD BLESS YOU! read a note affixed to a cellophane-wrapped plate of cookies.

The group's manager introduced me to the fellows in the band, and I had a few moments of amusing banter with guitarist Andrew Shirley, who offered to tell me "the truth about these guys." And then, suddenly, I was whisked into an adjoining room where Foreman was sitting in a folding chair.

Immediately, I sensed this interview wasn't going to go well. Foreman was anything but hostile, but he was maddeningly vague about his relationship with the festival and Christian music. Keyboardist/guitarist Jerome Fontamillas had told me he'd been to Cornerstone thirteen times, but Foreman kept trying to steer away from questions about his own history at the festival with nonanswers like, "I dunno. It's a unique experience."

Then, I asked if this was the only Christian event Switchfoot played.

He lowered his eyes.

"You have to be—the thing is, when you're talking about Switchfoot, you're talking about music that we've fought really hard to keep out of boxes," he said.

"I'm not interested in 'proving' you guys are a Christian rock band," I told him. "But this *is* a Christian festival."

"That's the thing," he replied. "If we're gonna stay out of the box, we're gonna have to be very conscientious of what everything is saying. Even opening up for Kid Rock [which they had done earlier that year] says something. Like everything in life, any relationship is a compromise. But where we're at right now, we're fortunate enough to pick the shots, and this is one of the festivals that, for the most part, it's a lot of people that are, you know, searching spiritually. It's actually a bunch of people that want to see the world change for the better. I don't know, that's important to me."

Later, he told me that most of the kids at Cornerstone "can relate to being treated by how they look, and maybe they can band together and be part of changing that."

Now, I'm willing to grant him a bit of room on the idea of Cornerstone being filled with "spiritual seekers" rather than Christians who were stuck in their ways. The crowd here was young, and fire-and-brimstone was definitely at a minimum. But I'd never seen such a clean-cut crowd in my life. For every punk kid with piercings or tattoos, there were ten who looked like they'd come straight off the set of *Everwood*. Overwhelmingly below twenty, well-scrubbed, fresh-faced, and good-natured, if anything, these were the kids school administrators wished all their students looked like.

Foreman's insistence that Switchfoot came to Cornerstone to connect with these radicals was beginning to sound more and more like cognitive dissonance. Especially in light of the fact that the same summer, Switchfoot played at two other Christian festivals and showed up for the Dove Awards—the Christian Grammys—where they took home three statues. It's easy to understand why Switchfoot would want to avoid being known as a Christian rock band, but they also seemed to want to have it both ways.

Later on, as Switchfoot played, Foreman introduced his songs using terms not entirely unfamiliar to the crowd. "This is about the war that goes on inside," he said, introducing "Ammunition." "I'm burning for something beyond what we have in a physical sense" led into "On Fire." "You can never get comfortable here," he told the audience after finishing "The Beautiful Letdown," with its gospel music–like chorus "I don't belong here." The concert, like Switchfoot's records, was terrific. But I had to wonder how Foreman could play his cards so close to his chest and still achieve the connection he repeatedly told me he longed for with his audience.

If you take away the reasonably priced food, the utter lack of security concerns, and the sober teenage virgins, Cornerstone is just like any other rock festival. The pathways leading between its seven main stages take two forms—blinding dust or shoe-sucking mud. The toilets are a challenge to city-softened sensibilities. And most of the attendees are white, middle-class kids in their late teens or early twenties—many sporting Mohawks and henna tattoos that one suspects will not be making the trip back home—who are here to see rock bands and meet people their own age.

Being at Cornerstone is a bit like being in *Logan's Run,* in fact, with so few people over thirty in attendance that anyone who looks like he or she might remember the first President Bush is probably working. Employees also often have golf carts, and after repeatedly sucking their dust clouds on the twenty-minute hike between the main stage and the exhibition area (where all the other stages are), I began to think decidedly unchristian thoughts about the folks whizzing past me.

Cornerstone is organized every year by the Jesus People USA, JPUSA for short. The Jesus People began as a traveling ministry in 1971, as legend has it, decided to stay in Chicago when the school bus that served as its headquarters broke down there. Now, inspired by the second chapter of Acts ("All who believed were together and had all things in common; they would sell their possessions and goods and distribute the proceeds to all, as any had need"5), the five hundred or so members of JPUSA live communally in a gritty neighborhood on Chicago's North Side, where they operate, among other things, a senior-citizens' home, a carpentry business, a recording studio, a print shop, and a self-storage facility.

The Cornerstone Festival began as an outgrowth of JPUSA's rock magazine of the same name, an early champion of the burgeoning Christian music scene. Today, it's grown into an institution, especially among young Christians. The festival's willingness to book bands that don't necessarily fit in with the evangelical scene is a big draw—unlike at many Christian festivals, artists at Cornerstone don't have to sign statements that they haven't engaged in "unbiblical" activities over the past three years.

Most of the twenty-five thousand attendees camp on the sprawling festival grounds, and more than a few bring their own musical equipment for impromptu concerts on the informal stages (basically a generator truck and a PA system) distributed throughout. It is not a place conducive to "quiet time."

In the exhibition tents, outfits with names like Onetruth.com, Something Sacred, and Teen Mania had some of the catchiest displays. Black T-shirts ringed the tents at eye level, boasting slogans with plenty of attitude: MOSHING FOR JESUS, REJECT RELIGION, EMBRACE JESUS, and NOTW (NOT OF THIS WORLD).

Antiabortion shirts abounded. A group called Rock for Life appeared to be doing a brisk business selling tees warning an undefined "you" to STOP KILLING MY GENERATION. Its booth was staffed by a guy who wouldn't have looked out of place on Carnaby Street in 1977, sporting a ceiling-scraping Mohawk and a leather jacket festooned with patches from punk bands who'd probably have had coronaries if they saw where he was working.

There was also a table selling *The Word on the Street,* a hip retelling of the Bible by Rob Lacey, a Welsh performance artist. Lacey was a frequent performer between main-stage bands: one of his bits was a three-minute version of the entire Bible; he also performed an update of the story of the Prodigal Son, in which "Sam Aritan" stops to help an injured stranger.

"Rewind!" Lacey shouted, after setting up the premise. Then, he recast the role of the Good Samaritan: an illegal immigrant, a Welshman, a homosexual (who minced and lisped and called the man's wounds "just beastly"), and, to loud boos, a Frenchman. ("Boot I em a pacifeest!" he protested.)

I was standing next to a photographer from Agence France Press during this particular display. He didn't seem too disturbed. "We're still asking the same question," he told me when I asked if French people knew that they'd often been portrayed in this way over here since withholding support for the Iraqi war. "Where are the weapons?"

By the third day of Cornerstone, I'd already seen more decent metal and hardcore punk bands—and more god-awful singer/songwriters—

than I could count. I'd sat in on a nuanced discussion of Christian film criticism. And I'd even met some Christian Goth rockers, who'd constructed a little refuge for their lonely breed. People who wear black on the outside because black is how they feel on the inside need to stick together in situations like this.

"A lot of people can identify with being really low," said Liz, a Christian Goth from Cedar Rapids, Iowa (the epicenter of Christian Gothdom, apparently), after I stumbled into their campsite one morning trying to figure out just what a bunch of people in robes and chain mail were doing at a Christian festival. Much of her friends' dark finery was drying on clotheslines around their neat encampment.

Liz, a short blonde who, in her non-Goth gear, looked strikingly normal, got saved in 1999 and was into what she called "dark music" long before then. She used to find comfort and community in fellow appreciators of the thudding beat, reverbed guitars, and cryptic lyrics of Goth music. Now she still thinks the world is dying, still feels misunderstood by normal people, and still finds security in the company of fellow outcasts. But her motivation has changed: her alienation now stems from the realization that bigger battles are raging than whether kids with surgically implanted fangs will be admitted to the shopping mall.

"Once you connect with God, only then can you see the colossal struggle that's going on in the world," she said. "We see the drama in a lot more things. Asylum"—the tent she and her Goth buddies had set up as a meeting place for fellow children of the night—"has become an asylum in a true sense."

Asylum offered vegan food, coffee, and tea. At midnight on this last night of Cornerstone, Liz and her friends had scheduled a fashion show and, later, a Renaissance parade (there is some crossover between Goths and medieval reenactment types). Amid the muddy, dusty festival grounds, Asylum was an oasis of cleanliness and order.

Their fondness for stage blood notwithstanding, Goths, I learned, are scrupulously clean. Liz and her friends proudly showed me their portable shower, a small nylon tent with a solar-heated bag of water ever at the ready. Liz said she showers "only" twice a day, which makes her quite slatternly by Goth standards. Her friend Skye, after some prompting from her fellow children of the night, showed me her tent, the inside of which looked as pristine as the traveling quarters of a Victorian general—except that the mosquito netting surrounding her bed had big black cloth spiders sewn into it.

Early Christians in Rome used to meet furtively, painfully aware that exposure of their beliefs was a death sentence. These Goth kids' spiritual convictions, however, were perfectly in line with those of the people giving Asylum the stinkeye as they headed over to the main arena to see bubbly, bouncy bands like Relient K. Any friction that existed was because of the Goth kids' sartorial nonconformity.

"There's no denying that this world is hurting us," said Saj, a Christian Goth from New Haven, Connecticut, as I said good-bye. "Sometimes saying hello makes a total difference."

It wasn't until after I'd left that I realized I should have asked whether he was talking about the world I knew or the one I had just started learning about.

CHAPTER 2

No More LSD for Me
(I Met the Man from Galilee)

In the beginning was the funk.

No, not the style of music. The early days of Christian rock music were notable for the smell emanating from the musicians, reconstructed hippies crammed into a station wagon, lying on top of amps as they traveled from church to church. They loved Jesus. They didn't shower much. They scared the bejeezus out of 90 percent of their audiences. But the remainder found something in these hairy wandering prophets that they'd been lacking—people talking about God in a language they understood.

But before we learn how hippies got into the church, we've got to understand how the church got inside hippies. And to do that, we need to travel to—where else?—California.

There are differing accounts of how what came to be known as the Jesus Movement started. Significantly, most of the narratives start with communal living experiments—the House of Acts in Marin County, the Lighthouse Ranch in Eureka County, the Topanga Community House, and the Salt Company in Hollywood, plus communities in less sun-blessed areas like Milwaukee and upstate New York—places where people disillusioned with both American society and the counterculture could find a sense of community and purpose in salvation through the grace of Jesus Christ, which evangelist Arthur Blessitt called the "eternal rush."

The House of Acts spawned a "street ministry" in San Francisco called the Living Room. Blessitt opened a coffeehouse called His Place on Hollywood's Sunset Strip. Between them, they brought thousands of hippies, called Jesus Freaks or Jesus People by the press, to a brand of Christianity rooted in conservative evangelical theology but updated with the language of the day.

One resident of the House of Acts, a charismatic street preacher named Lonnie Frisbee, was recruited by Chuck Smith, the pastor of a small, nondenominational church called Calvary Chapel in Costa Mesa, to do outreach to the freaky youths crowding the town's streets. Frisbee's preaching proved wildly successful, and Calvary's flock began to grow rapidly as folks who came because of Frisbee got hooked on Smith's plain-language sermons and end-times theology.

Calvary has since become a minidenomination, spawning more than a thousand rock-friendly churches worldwide, but its most germane contribution to Christian music may be Maranatha, the record label it founded to release rock 'n' roll and later praise-and-worship albums with a contemporary, rock-based sound.

You see, while it was one thing for these former flower children to step away from what they saw as the hollow core of the counterculture, it was an entirely different proposition to expect them to listen to Southern gospel. Or, to put it another way, how could you expect 'em to love Pat Boone after they'd heard *Led Zeppelin II*? A lot of people rejected rock music as a trapping of their past lives, but a few hardy souls began to wonder if the music's animal beat and brain-rattling volume couldn't be put into the Lord's service.

There's no consensus on who made the world's first Christian rock album. Some say the Concrete Rubber Band. Some say Wilson-

McKinley or Myron LeFevre, or Azitis. But there's really only one first that counts in music—the record that most people heard. And that album was made by a deeply weird man from San Francisco named Larry Norman.

Upon This Rock wasn't Norman's first record, nor did it commemorate his conversion to Christianity. Norman's group People had debuted in 1968 with an LP whose title its record label, Capitol, changed from *We Need a Whole Lot More of Jesus and a Lot Less of Rock and Roll* to simply *I Love You*—not coincidentally the name of People's Top 40 hit.

Norman quit the group when he saw what Capitol had done with his concept and—as one does in these situations—wrote a couple of musicals. Then, a year later, he reemerged as a Christian solo artist (still on Capitol) with *Upon This Rock*. "I Wish We'd All Been Ready" is a creepy classic that imagines the Rapture—the belief among some fundamentalist Christian groups that Jesus' return will be preceded by the instant ascension to heaven of the faithful. "Two men walking up a hill," he sings over backing music that makes David Bowie's "Space Oddity" sound like a Sousa march. "One disappears and one's left standing still." Its coda, "You've been left behind," would lend a title to a wildly successful series of books about the Rapture a few decades later.

The singer's end-times rock jibed perfectly with the eschatological leanings of the Jesus People, who were increasingly returning the welcoming embrace of the conservative evangelical churches. It's almost impossible to overstate Norman's importance to putting a cohesive face on the Jesus Movement—he invented the Jesus Freak equivalent of the peace sign, one finger raised upward toward the heavens, in his song "One Way." His rollicking "Sweet Sweet Song of Salvation" was instantly adopted by churches and youth groups as a modern hymn. And he revived Martin Luther's famous quotation "Why should the Devil have all the good music?" as a boogie-woogie manifesto.

But Larry Norman's most important contribution was that he was good at his job. Early Jesus People bands were long on inspiration but short on self-editing—a problem that would prove endemic in Christian music in the years to come—but Norman's productions were at least as good as anything on the radio at the time, and he is an excellent songwriter and vocalist, as willing to cast a critical eye on the church as he was to society at large.

Norman later estranged himself from Christian music, the inevitable result of a personality that could charitably be described as "unpredictable." His business practices at Solid Rock, the record label he founded after leaving Capitol, alienated many of the artists he signed, some of whom became Christian music legends in their own right. He's railed against "liberal journalists," whom he says conspire against him, and refuses most interviews. He lives in Salem, Oregon, issuing and reissuing fascinating documents of Jesus Movement music in limited quantities and suffering from health problems that have curtailed his recording and performing activities. In 2005, he announced his retirement from performing with a farewell concert at Salem's Elsinore Theatre, where Frank Black of the Pixies, a fan from childhood, backed him.

"I think we should read the Bible for personal reasons and not say, Well, I'm going to put God into the meat grinder and come out with something that will be printed on sheet music, sung by choirs and have synchronization rights," Norman told the Salem *Statesman-Journal*'s Angela Yeager on the eve of his farewell show. "I just think it's about a personal relationship with God, the Bible. Not an easy thing to do. But not impossible."

Nearly as important as Norman to the burgeoning movement was the band Children of the Day, whose fall from grace presaged the awkward manner in which the Christian music scene still handles controversy. Marsha Carter, a sixteen-year-old from Southern California, became a Christian at a beachside service and brought her sister Wendy and her friend Peter Jacobs to Christ as well. With Jacobs' bandmate Russ Stevens—whom Marsha married—on board, the newly formed Children of the Day became a favorite at Calvary Chapel, and their debut record, *Come to the Waters,* on the church's Maranatha label, sold half a million copies.

"It absolutely established this genre of Christian pop as a viable, marketable thing," says Mark Allan Powell, a professor at Trinity Lutheran Seminary in Ohio, whose book *The Encyclopedia of Christian Contemporary Music* is an indispensable guide. "It sold 500,000 copies in Christian bookstores. You couldn't buy it at the mall!"

Come to the Waters, which has a gentle folk-rock sound reminiscent of the Seekers, or maybe the Carpenters, yielded a genuine worship hit, Stevens' "For Those Tears I Died." Many of the churches that incorporated the tune into their songbooks, however, tore out the pages and mailed them to her after what Powell describes as "Christian music's first official scandal"—Marsha Stevens' divorce from Russ and the announcement that she was a lesbian.

Marsha Stevens has been written out of Christian music history as a result. Maranatha excluded Children of the Day from its twenty-fifth anniversary collection. Marsha Stevens still maintains a ministry named Born Again Lesbian Music, or BALM. As Powell notes in his entry about Stevens, "The exclusion of Martha Stevens from participation in the contemporary Christian music scene reveals a tacit endorsement of particular doctrines far more specific than anything that is officially stated."[1] Stevens may have the support of her particular church and write songs exclusively about her love of Jesus, but as far as most Christian music institutions are concerned, she has never existed.

There were, of course, many important artists a lot less controversial than Norman and Stevens. Love Song, a band that got saved en masse at Calvary Chapel (and, not quite understanding what was expected of them, reportedly got high to celebrate), fused the happy-go-lucky folk-rock of Children of the Day with the country-rock (Byrds, Flying Burrito Bros.) popular at the time and seeded the sound of what would later be known as contemporary Christian music (CCM).

Gospel singer Andraé Crouch was not a product of the Jesus Movement, but he sure was appreciated by Jesus Freaks. Crouch brought the crunch and backbeat of rock and the slow burn of Motown and Philly Soul to his barn-burners, essentially creating the sound of what most people associate with gospel music today. With his band the Disciples, Crouch made a string of stone classic albums that no self-respecting Jesus Person's crash pad was without—*Keep on Singin'* (1971), *Soulfully* (1972), *Live at Carnegie Hall* (1973), *Take Me Back* (1974), *This Is Another Day* (1976), and *Live in London* (1978).

If the appeal of emotional worship has always been lost on you, let Andraé Crouch show you the way. You can practically feel the sweat flying off the speakers as he takes band and audience alike on a voyage through ecstatic, unapologetic adoration.

In 1972, the Jesus Movement had its coming-out party, a concert called Explo '72 held in Dallas that featured Crouch, Norman, Johnny Cash, and then-Christian artist Kris Kristofferson. Billy Graham, one of the festival's speakers, called it a "religious Woodstock," which wasn't too far off the mark. Explo drew a crowd of one hundred fifty thousand—believers and curious alike.

These numbers couldn't be ignored for long. That same year, Billy Ray Hearn, a music minister from Waco, Texas, founded a record label called Myrrh under the auspices of a small local gospel record company called Word. Hearn had left full-time ministry a few years earlier after working on a musical called *Good News* with a Christian promoter named Ralph Carmichael.

"He realized that these kids would listen to Christian music if it just existed," says Billy Ray's son Bill Hearn, now president of EMI

Christian Music Group. "Young church people realized that there was good music out there that also had lyrics that affirmed their faith, that was consistent with their lifestyle. They said, 'Hey, we didn't realize that we needed this, but we really like this, and we want it.'"

Billy Ray Hearn signed Jesus Movement veterans 2nd Chapter of Acts and Randy Matthews to Myrrh, then quickly added Barry McGuire—who'd had a secular hit with "Eve of Destruction"—to the roster.

"He built the first national [Christian] record company," says Bill Hearn. "There were church-based ministries and bands and artists putting out their own records, but Myrrh was the first full-blown contemporary label that recorded and produced and promoted and distributed albums."

At the time, Bill Hearn says, Word was predominantly a Southern gospel label. "They could make live Southern gospel records for $5,000 and sell thirty thousand albums," he says. "My dad wanted to spend $20,000 to make a real quality record in the studio, and it would sell only twenty or twenty-five thousand copies. [Word was] like, 'Wait, this doesn't make sense.' He said, 'Trust me, it does.' Within a year, it was the highest-volume label at Word."

That was due as much to the dedication of Myrrh's artists, whom Bill Hearn remembers as "people who had a real heart to communicate the Gospel through music." The musicians toured incessantly, he says, "not for money and to be successful. They'd get in minivans, trucks, anything they could get in. Mobile homes, whatever. They would stay in people's homes, not in hotels. It wasn't about production and sound and lights—it was what they had to do. They toured because it was what God told them to do."

Barry McGuire's most lasting contribution to the Christian rock canon may not be his 1975 live album *To the Bride* (though that's awesome) or his 1979 novelty hit "Cosmic Cowboy." As John Thompson notes in his book *Raised by Wolves: The Story of Christian Rock*

& *Roll,* McGuire's 1978 song "Bullfrogs and Butterflies," from a children's album of the same name, "developed a taste for basic rock instrumentation in children and parents alike." Christian music's first million-selling LP, *Bullfrogs* was in nearly every hip evangelical's home and may well be the first piece of music that made an impression on today's generation of Christian rockers.

The group 2nd Chapter of Acts bears mentioning, too. *With Footnotes,* the group's 1974 debut, is a sine qua non of Jesus Music, and its lead track, "Easter Song," is easily one of the best, most audacious songs to emerge from that era. The tune rocks to a rhythm all its own, a loping, imprecise waltz time over which the group's three singers blast barely in-tune harmonies. It is over in two minutes.

In 1975, Billy Ray Hearn left Word and started his own label, Sparrow, taking most of his artists with him and also making visionary signings at his new home.

One of those was a transitional figure in contemporary Christian music named Keith Green. Green wasn't the most original singer or songwriter of his generation—much of his early output outright mimics Elton John and David Cassidy—but he had an uncanny ability to be in the right place at the right time, which, as any veteran of the music industry will tell you, is worth its weight in gold. A precocious songwriter, Green signed his first record contract in his early teens but never became the teen idol Decca groomed him to be. Washed-up before he could legally drive, he went deep into hippie culture, ferociously embracing sex, drugs, and rock 'n' roll before becoming a Christian at nineteen.

Green soon took the fervor he brought to debauchery to his faith. His 1978 LP *No Compromise* is, as its title implies, a strident call to the barricades for those who agree with his fundamentalist view of faith and a literal "see you in hell" for everyone else.

Two years later, Green decided it was wrong to charge money for the Gospel and embarked on a financially risky program in which he'd mail a copy of *So You Wanna Go Back to Egypt* to anyone who requested one, with the understanding that people would send back whatever payment they could afford. Incredibly, Sparrow went along with this plan. It may have helped that a recent Christian convert and friend of Green named Bob Dylan played a harmonica solo on the record, but even under this slightly wacky business plan, the album sold well.

With his wife, Melody, Green established Last Days Ministries in Texas, and it was while touring the ministry's compound with some friends in an overloaded sightseeing plane that Green was killed, along with two of his children, the pilot, and a family of eight. It was an end, as Powell puts it, "both unnecessary and horrific," but, as is so often the case in popular culture, in death Green has become an even more important artist than he was when he ruled the burgeoning Christian music scene.

"Where are the Keith Greens of today's music world?" asked *HM* magazine's Doug Van Pelt in a 2004 editorial. "The type of person who can walk up to you and deliver the truth that hits you right in the chest and brings you to your knees. . . . Reveal yourself, please!"

I called Green a transitional artist because he was the last significant Christian artist for a long time to be both a critical favorite and a bestseller. After Green, music that some unkind souls call "Christian mush" began to dominate the Christian mainstream, while a loosely organized underground of misfits began to haunt the corners of the '80s Christian experience.

There are a lot of reasons for this, the major one being that corporations had realized that this music was becoming an essential accessory to new Christians' lifestyles, creating a viable market, and those companies soon had sizable investments to protect. ABC bought Word in 1974. Sparrow, which Billy Ray Hearn founded after leaving Myrrh in 1976, became part of the MCA system in 1981, and CBS started its own Christian label, Priority (*definitely* not to be confused with the later hip-hop label that introduced the world to

N.W.A). Also, joint ventures like Exit and What? Records were distributed by Island and A&M, respectively, in the general market.

But just as important as this infusion of corporate capital was the emergence of the Christian bookstore as gatekeeper. Christian bookstores had existed for years, but the '60s saw an explosion in their numbers, and in 1969 the Christian Booksellers Association's annual confab outgrew its usual hotel ballroom and took over an entire convention center in Cincinnati.

Bookstore buyers are extremely sensitive to the needs of their customers. For example, I live in a reliably "red" state, one that last went to a Democratic presidential candidate in 1964, and during the 2004 presidential election, my local Barnes and Noble had what seemed like thirty anti–John Kerry books up front as you entered the store. Though my research methods are a tad on the empirical side (skulking by the magazines and hoping no one noticed me snooping), it sure didn't seem like an unpopular move (the anti-Bush books moldered in the back).

Let's face it—like many Americans, Christians can be touchy. Evangelicalism had its genesis in Martin Luther's call for individualism, and, today, the only rough equivalent to Americans' many different takes on interpreting the Bible is the myriad allegiances French people have to that country's thousands of locally produced cheeses. Depending on whom a Christian looks to for spiritual guidance, smoking, drinking, cursing, dancing, and even songs that use minor chords are all potentially forbidden.

Larry Norman perhaps felt the sting of this retail sensitivity first, when Christian bookstores refused to stock his album *So Long Ago the Garden* because of its trippy cover art, which shows Norman sitting behind a lion with what looks like a sub-Saharan veldt superimposed over both of them. Norman, whose skin is on the light side of albino, appears almost naked, and there were whispers that one patch of grass near the bottom of the photo is in fact pubic hair. As unlikely as this scenario may have been, the album was basically killed by the controversy, even after MCA, Norman's label, rushed out a cropped version of the cover.

And it's not like the situation has eased up over the years. Christian stores refused to carry P.O.D.'s 1999 major-label debut, *The Fundamental Elements of Southtown,* because the cover shows a figure sitting cross-legged with open cavities in his head and body (one stores the sacred heart of Jesus, and a dove is dropping a symbol of the Trinity into another). The group changed the artwork for the Christian market to a black cover with a small square showing only the seated figure's face. The band refused, however, to change its 2003 album, *Payable on Death,* which sports a drawing of a woman with butterfly wings, a crown, arms crossed over her naked chest, and the word *sanctus* written on a banner that floats across her waist. The problem with this one was, according to the *Christian Post,* "the visibility of the woman's pubic bone."[2]

Christian bookstores, reasonably, decided to take the path of least resistance—to sell music and artwork that couldn't possibly offend any of their customers—and the Christian music industry was relieved to give the bookstores what they wanted. Christian singers like Dallas Holm and Cynthia Clawson took nonthreatening stances to new heights. Their pleasant music had lyrics that rarely strayed from safe themes like gratitude toward Jesus and was an ideal soundtrack for evangelical Christianity's new place in the culture—a refuge from a morally ambivalent world where doubt and relativity ruled. By 1980, when Christians were key to the election of Ronald Reagan, the face of Christian music was no longer a hairy ex-hippie with a thatch on his face and a song in his heart. It was a woman with gigantic hair and way too much makeup or a man who looked about as countercultural as Johnny Unitas.

For Glenn Kaiser, life as a Christian musician was a bit grittier than that. Kaiser's group, the Resurrection Band (later renamed Rez Band and then just Rez), had begun playing muscular, blues-based rock 'n' roll in the spirit of secular groups like Led Zeppelin and Jefferson Airplane.

Resurrection Band began as an attempt to bring young people to revivals led by Jesus People USA, the traveling commune mentioned in chapter 1. In the early days of the Jesus Movement, Kaiser says, "you could probably count all the bands on two hands, maybe three. A lot of us had been musicians before we became Christians. All of a sudden, there were a stack of bands that nobody had ever heard of. I suppose the proverbial look would be a whole bunch of folks with long hair and bell bottoms, and you know, smelling like patchouli."

Concerts in those days, he says, were done on a shoestring budget, usually with the hope that the band would be paid enough to make it to the next town. "You were literally praying that there'd be enough money showing up in the offering," he says. "Somebody'd pass a chicken bucket or literally a hat—and there'd be enough cash to put gas in the station wagon."

The venues weren't glamorous either. "It was playing in parks, it was playing in parking lots of the local Piggly Wiggly," he says. "Churches, little by little, opened the doors to bands like ours."

This transition was not without its bumps. Kaiser remembers one huge Midwestern church where the "pastor had left a bunch of deacons in charge," and Rez was booked to play at a revival meeting. The deacons, he says, were "very nice gray-haired old guys with the Fonz's old hairdo, a real Southern Pentecostal vibe even though it's in the North." A traveling evangelist was in charge of the revival, and he'd booked the band, telling them the church had given him free reign for the whole week.

"Now at this point," Kaiser says, "we'd still throw in stuff like [the gospel standard] 'Oh Happy Day.' It didn't sound anything like they'd heard it; it was more like AC/DC doing it. Well, the kids of course all jumped up, went nuts, and started dancing."

At this church, dancing was not allowed.

"So, we got several hundred kids going absolutely crazy," Kaiser says, "and a couple of them spilling out in the aisles. Somewhere in the middle of the third song—I'll never forget it. I mean, it was a long, long aisle. I remember these two white-haired old deacons with their pink sport coat thingies on, their faces were red, veins popping out of their necks, and they're literally running to the stage. I yelled over the amps, 'I think we're through!' It was like, 'Thank you, God bless,' and everybody grabbed everything they could and went out the back door. I mean, we were *gone,* man."

But after a few years of terrorizing their elders, Kaiser says "an awful lot of people started to bring [Rez] back. I had so many people come up and say, 'I hate your music but I love your preaching.'"

Resurrection Band "really spoke to me," says Anthony Barr-Jeffrey, a writer for *CCM*, a magazine so integral to Christian music that its name serves as shorthand for the genre. "I didn't really hear anybody talking about anything that seemed significant to me and sounded like it matched what I was hearing people say in churches. Speaking to me on an emotional level."

Barr-Jeffrey strongly identified with the band's "dirty rotten bluesy classic rock" and its willingness to address the harder side of life on albums like 1981's *Mommy Don't Love Daddy Anymore*, about divorce. "If you've ever heard it, the title track will kill you," Barr-Jeffrey, a former latchkey kid himself, says. "You ain't gotta have no parent problems, that song will kill you."

The fact that Rez took on such topics, however, did little to endear them to the Christian music business, even after they managed to find a label willing to put out their albums. The group started touring in 1972—Kaiser says they were "way too controversial" to play Explo '72—but didn't release its first proper album until 1978. They were too hard for the Christian market and too Christian for the general market. "Everybody turned us down," Kaiser says. "Even secular labels. They were like, 'Okay, cool, but you gotta change the lyrics.' The Christian labels went, 'Cool, but we can't take the heat.' They didn't want the flak. They were afraid of conservative folks in the church freaking out and boycotting their label and preaching against them in church on Sunday."

Finally, StarSong, which Kaiser describes as "a custom label, it wasn't a true label," decided to take a chance on the band. *Awaiting Your Reply* is a classic of Christian rock and one of the few albums from the movement's early days that was as good as anything in the general market. But because of Rez's subject matter, the group remained a cult band in the Christian scene, foreshadowing the way Christian music would treat its square pegs in the future.

"Life isn't always fair," Kaiser says to criticisms that the group was too depressing. "The biggest category of God's word" in the Psalms, he says, "has to do with pain, struggle, suffering. Christians get cancer, and they get healed, but they also get cancer and die. We get flats on the freeway just like everyone else. God doesn't answer every one of our prayers; nor should He. It's His grace, His compassion, His mercy. Back in the day, a lot of Christian churches freaked because we looked like and sounded like 'the world.'"

And so began a subculture within a subculture, that of artists ignored by "mainstream" Christian music, itself barely noticed by the larger pop culture. Meanwhile, the big Christian labels, faced with a new generation that wasn't connecting with the big hairs, began putting out music that closely echoed whatever the pagans were listening to, but with a "better message." Take DeGarmo and Key, the Christian Hall & Oates, for example, or Petra and WhiteHeart, Christian bands that constantly fiddled with their sound and personnel to reflect musical trends in secular radio. Christian bands were making money, but, artistically, they were often a joke.

"And the joke is funny because it's true," says Mark Allan Powell. "Everything was like something popular but not as good."

In the '80s, fundamentalist Christians made ideal political partners for economic conservatives for a number of reasons, not least that they were vociferously anticommunist due in part to the persecution of evangelicals behind the Iron Curtain. But the Soviet Union and evangelical Christian pop culture had some ironic similarities: a centrally planned, monolithic approach to entertainment that cleansed popular music of subversive messages and elicited tearful confessions from citizens who went off-message.

Petra and WhiteHeart were the logical extension of a culture that considered music to be simply one of many useful evangelistic tools and a song's message to be more important than its quality. And possibly more important than either of those notions was that serious money was involved by the mid-'80s—thanks to the teenage daughter of a Nashville doctor.

Amy Grant was sixteen when her self-titled debut album was issued by Word and sold fifty thousand copies. In his *Billboard Guide to Contemporary Christian Music,* Barry Alfonso says, "you could say—at the risk of using a pagan metaphor—that Amy Grant's popularity opened a Pandora's box of troublesome issues that the Christian music industry has wrestled with to the present day."[3]

Amy Grant is one of the more accomplished singers and songwriters working in pop music today. But her first three albums, frankly, are treacly confections that hold little appeal outside Grant's good looks and incongruently sensual vocals. They sold very well in the Christian market. It wasn't till 1982's *Age to Age* that Grant came into her own as a performer—songs such as "El Shaddai" and "I Love a Lonely Day" connected on a level beyond what Glenn Kaiser calls "happy-clappy" Christianity. *Age to Age* was Christian music's first gold record (five hundred thousand sold), and Amy Grant was no longer a secret—she was poised to be its first genuine success story within and beyond the subculture.

That promise was fulfilled with 1985's *Unguarded*, Grant's commercial breakthrough, which went to No. 4 on the *Billboard* albums
chart and gave Grant her first Top 40 single, "Find a Way." The following year, a duet with ex-Chicago singer Peter Cetera, "The Next
Time I Fall," went all the way to No. 1. It took eight years, but Amy
Grant became a star to believers and unbelievers alike.

The Christian music world had long awaited such general-market
validation. So, of course, it began to completely freak. As Powell
says, "Conventional wisdom held that Christian singers would be os-
tracized from secular radio. . . . If such things [as Grant's general-
market success] were possible, why did there have to be separate
Christian radio stations or charts or record companies?"[4]

Christian critics went after the one thing Grant couldn't necessarily control—how attractive other people found her. She was criticized for dancing onstage, for her clothes, for telling *Rolling Stone*
that she liked to sunbathe nude. Even now, one website purports to
prove that Grant's on a mission from Satan himself because of a hand
gesture she made at a concert.[5]

"When Amy Grant crossed over, she was definitely demonized in
some circles," says Pedro the Lion's David Bazan, who grew up in
what he calls a "Sandi Patty household." ("My mom loved Sandi
Patty," he explains, "so we didn't have any Amy Grant records.")

Bazan says Michael W. Smith's 1991 Top 10 hit "My Place in This
World" (cowritten by Grant) likewise upset a lot of Christians he
knew because the song's content wasn't explicitly Christian. "People
said, 'Oh they're appealing to a bigger audience,'" he says. "There's
this whole subtle idea behind Christian music that you always have
to be telling people about Jesus. It's ludicrous because no one who
isn't a Christian would ever want to listen to that music."

Eventually, the Christian music biz reconciled itself to Grant's
success, which neither proved to have coattails long enough to carry
many other CCM artists to the Top 40 (as Bazan notes, CCM didn't

have a particularly deep bench) nor shuttered the rapidly coalescing industry, which was beginning to center around Nashville. Bill Hearn thinks the move to Music City was not necessarily a retreat, rather a recognition that Christian music's seat-of-the-pants days were over.

"I think [artists and record companies] gravitated more toward the commercial reality of the industry," he says. "I think that's why Nashville became the place—because that's where the songwriters and publishers were."

Contrary to the memories of anyone exposed to early CCM by a well-meaning friend, there *were* good Christian artists in the '80s— it's just that few people heard them. In addition to Resurrection Band, groups like the Seventy Sevens and Daniel Amos made waves among the growing, albeit tiny, pool of Christian rock snobs who hated CCM with a passion.

Anthony Barr-Jeffrey describes *Doppelganger,* the fifth album by Daniel Amos (a band, not a person), as *"Pilgrim's Progress* on crack."

"I mean, this stuff was bizarre," he says. "The music to the first song is kind of a spoken word thing, and [singer] Terry Taylor is talking over this backward-masking song, and you find out that it's actually the last song on the previous record, played backwards."

The Seventy-Sevens, Vector, and Vector's keyboardist, Charlie Peacock, all made impressive bows in the '80s, but ironically, their forward-thinking way of doing business—signing with a record label, Exit, that partnered with Island to distribute records in both the Christian and the general markets—was their undoing. As it turned out, a three-quarters Christian band from Ireland overloaded Island's promotional bandwidth when its 1987 album, *The Joshua Tree,* became a generational touch point.

U2 had nothing to do with the American Christian music scene. Three of its four members—Bono, the Edge, and Larry Mullen Jr.—were regulars at a Dublin Christian fellowship group called

Shalom in the late '70s. But Shalom had turned against U2 by the time the group's second LP, 1983's *War*, was released. According to Steve Stockman, a Northern Irish minister who chronicled the group's faith in a book called *Walk On: The Spiritual Journey of U2*, a member of Shalom claimed to have received a prophesy that U2 should split up.

"When the band members returned to the fellowship, which at that time they craved and thrived upon," Stockman writes, "they entered a tense situation where the fellowship was split over whether God wanted U2 to carry on or pack up their instruments."[6] Had they followed that advice, he notes, "the rock world would have missed one of the most influential bands of the latter part of the twentieth century."[7]

Perhaps because of this experience, U2's members have always been wary of aligning themselves with any religious institution, and they've always kept the American Christian music business at an especially great distance, even as their work has explored issues of faith, doubt, and Christianity-inspired social justice for three decades.

So, when U2 became a world-beating phenomenon, Christian music's "legalistic" tendencies—the strict adherence to what many fundamentalists consider biblical law—again emerged. To this day, many Christian radio stations will play covers of U2 songs by other Christian artists, but not by the band itself, as the Christianity of its members is considered to be in doubt. The evidence? Bono swears, smokes, and drinks. The band's music often evinces ambiguity about truth ("I Still Haven't Found What I'm Looking For") and its stage shows can play with challenging imagery (Bono's "MacPhisto" and "The Fly" guises from the '90s). U2 refused to break bread with the American evangelical mainstream—on the band's live album *Rattle and Hum*, for instance, Bono extemporaneously describes seeing a thinly veiled Jerry Falwell "stealing money from the sick and the old," then shouts, "Well, the God I believe in isn't short of cash, mister!"—and, as a result, the Christian subculture spent the next two decades insisting that it had never wanted anything to do with the Irish band anyway.

U2's members weren't the only "artists of faith" in the mainstream in the '80s. The Alarm, After the Fire, the Call, the Innocence Mission, the Ocean Blue, Mr. Mister, the Violent Femmes, and Lone Justice all made reference to their Christian beliefs on vinyl, cassette, and MTV. With a few exceptions, though, these artists weren't products of the subculture. Christian music was in danger of becoming irrelevant, despite the presence of such talented artists as Steve Taylor, who attacked the church's eagerness to let the bland lead the bland in songs like "I Want to Be a Clone."

Plus, all of evangelical Christianity, which had become a formidable political and economic force by the late '80s, was tainted by scandal when two televangelists, Jim Bakker and Jimmy Swaggart, fell from grace in 1987 and 1988, respectively. These somewhat spectacular flameouts, *Billboard*'s Alfonso notes, were "black marks on the reputations of evangelicals across the board—musicians included."[8]

That wasn't fair, but it was understandable. Nonevangelical Americans had been tolerating triumphant broadsides from preachers like Jerry Falwell and Pat Robertson for years, and here were two of the biggest names in evangelicalism felled by extremely tawdry and arrogant behavior. "These are the people who think they're so much better than us?" folks wondered.

Christian music's flirtation with the mainstream, it seemed, was over, and its status as a world apart seemed set in stone.

In 1991, Sparrow moved to Nashville. Word followed the next year. EMI bought Sparrow in 1993, and Word was purchased by Gaylord Entertainment Company in 1998, which sold it to the Warner Music Group in 2001. Longtime fans and artists grumbled about the

Christian mainstays' joining hands with "the world," but, as Bill Hearn puts it, the labels had very little choice.

"The bottom line is we needed the resources in order to grow," he says, "in order to fulfill our vision. A lot of times, I've said we sold the company for [the recording artist] Steven Curtis Chapman. We needed the distribution. We knew that we had something with Steven—we were selling three hundred, three hundred fifty thousand albums. And we knew if we were ever gonna get him to a million or more, we needed to get his records out further."

Far from Nashville, musicians and labels were exploring the fertile artistic and commercial possibilities opened up by alternative artists. Seattle's Poor Old Lu, a band named for a character in a C. S. Lewis book—evangelicals love C. S. Lewis, whose books offer a defense of Christianity using a form of theology called apologetics— was influenced more by general-market alternative acts like the Cure and the Smiths than by Petra and the Lost Dogs.

"They liked bands that were true, that were expressing themselves in a way that wasn't based on commercial demands, necessarily," says David Bazan about Poor Old Lu. "They believed in the creative process in a way that was antithetical to the culture that they were part of. They were definitely influenced by that culture, but there was this element that they were trying to do things that were new and different."

"I had a three-song demo of theirs from 1998 that I listened to over and over again," he says. "There was a song called 'This Theater' that talked about the exploitation of the small town. I remember listening to that demo, thinking, 'This is real, this is true.' At that point, deep in my mind it even transcended my understanding of Christianity, which was still very reactionary and very clichéd. It was very in line with what was going on."

What was going on was a rich underground scene centered, again, in the Los Angeles suburbs, especially Orange County. Beginning in the early '80s, a Christian hardcore scene had sprung up around bands such as the Crucified, Scaterd Few, and the Altar Boys. The Crucified's singer, Mark Salomon, was heavily influenced by the Washington, D.C., band Minor Threat, whose singer, Ian MacKaye, outlined a way of living called "Straight Edge"—no drugs, drinking, or meaningless sex.

The members of Minor Threat weren't exactly fans of Christianity; their song "Filler" features the lyrics "Your brain is clay/What's going on?/You picked up a Bible/And now you're gone." But their no-compromises ethos proved eminently translatable to Christianity's more strident forms. The Crucified left a big footprint in Southern California Christian punk and metal, influencing, among others, a multiracial rap-metal group from San Diego called Payable on Death, or P.O.D. for short.

Christian heavy metal came into its own in the '80s as well, with bands such as Holy Soldier, Whitecross, and a hair-metal group called Stryper, which almost immediately became a media sensation—the novelty of a group of Christians in black-and-yellow spandex with poodle haircuts playing hard rock being a bit too much for the mainstream press to resist.

"When Stryper happened, holy cow!" says worship music artist David Crowder, who wasn't allowed to listen to secular music growing up. "Finally we had somebody who rocks and wears tight clothes!"

Stryper signed to Enigma, a division of Capitol, without telling the label that they were a Christian band. They changed their lyrics once the ink was dry on the contracts, and the resulting *The Yellow and Black Attack* is a milestone of Christian hard rock. Stryper camped it up, throwing New Testaments out into the crowd at shows and giving their albums titles like *In God We Trust* and *To Hell with the Devil.* They took a lot of guff from secular critics, as well as from people within the church, especially Jimmy Swaggart, for whom they became something of a white whale. (Ironically, Michael and Robert Sweet, the brothers who founded Stryper, reportedly got saved by watching Swaggart on TV.)

And Stryper sold a lot of records. Their first three LPs charted, and their power ballad "Honestly" went to No. 23 in 1987. Metallica and Poison *opened* for Stryper. And for some reason, Stryper was enormous in Japan. None of this helped the band within the Christian music scene, though, when a 1990 *Rolling Stone* piece claimed its members drank, smoke, and would no longer be singing about God.

The band disowned the interview, but the damage was done. Benson, which distributed the group's records in the Christian market, refused to carry the group's new LP, *Against the Law*, and the group broke up in 1992. It has since reformed and put out a new album, *Reborn*, in 2005. Stryper may have been a knowing joke, but the group embodied a street-level evangelism that put the work of many of its peers to shame. And they did it all dressed like bumblebees, which come to think of it, may be why they were so popular in Japan.

The Southern California label Frontline was an early standard-bearer for Christian alternative music, signing bands such as Mad at the World, the Altar Boys, and Bloodgood. In 1993, a hyper recent University of Oregon graduate named Brandon Ebel founded his own record label while interning at Frontline. Tooth & Nail would grow into a powerhouse of Christian alternative music, selling hundreds of thousands of copies of records by the Third Wave ska group O.C. Supertones and the Washington state pop-punkers MxPx.

But this energy was lost on Nashville, which, by the early '90s, had fallen into an inspirational-music rut. It would take three young, outspoken Christian nerds who attended Jerry Falwell's Liberty University to lead Christian music back to relevance.

D.C. Talk wasn't the first group to fuse hip-hop and rock. Its members weren't the first pretty-boy lightweights to transform themselves into a vital rock band (those would be, in order, the Beatles and the Beach Boys). But, by gum, they were the first Christian band to do both.

"There were two things going on there," says Jay Swartzendruber, editor of *CCM* magazine, about D.C. Talk. "You had this group that was merging rap with pop and rock from the get-go. Combining rap with singing was really rare and unusual, to the point where people who really knew music in the mainstream would comment on it. But then, at the same time, you had some really, really cheesy stuff on their first album. From there, they went on to become one of the most innovative, creative, boundary-stretching bands in Christian music."

In my opinion, Toby "Toby Mac" McKeehan, Michael Tait, and Kevin "Kevin Max" Smith's first *two* albums—1989's eponymous debut and '90s *Nu Thang*—are pretty horrendous, but they sold very well, probably because, as Powell notes, D.C. Talk "offered kids a sanitized-for-your-protection version of the dangerous new hip-hop sound that had become established in the world at large."[9]

The group's third LP, 1992's *Free at Last*, demonstrates a considerable leap in quality, and its rapped verses with sung choruses became a formula for mainstream hip-hop a decade later. *Jesus Freak*, which followed in 1995, turned the band into a legend.

The album's title track did what rap music is supposed to do: it made a supposedly undesirable upbringing—Christian evangelicalism—something to be worn with pride. With one song, Christian rock was saved. "I don't really care if they label me a Jesus Freak," the band sings. "There ain't no disguising the truth." And it is a flat-out great song, combining grunge guitars, a rapped bridge, and a chorus that could knock down walls.

Jesus Freak sold 1.6 million copies and even cracked the Top 40 with the ballad "Just between You and Me." D.C. Talk's celebration of multiculturalism, great hooks, and unapologetic apologetics revived an artistically moribund industry, which would soon take chances on relatively edgy bands like Jars of Clay, whose self-titled 1995 album spawned a No. 1 Christian single, "Flood," which even scraped the general-market Top 40.

These groups' successes hardly set off a revolution of great songwriting in mainstream Christian music—how else to explain the continued popularity of Point of Grace, 4 HIM, and Avalon?—but they made it okay to innovate musically, a not insignificant development in a style of music better defined by its lyrics than its sound.

The past decade has seen an impressive number of Christian artists crossing over into the general market, from the aforementioned P.O.D. to Stacie Orrico, MercyMe, Switchfoot, Third Day, Chevelle, and Relient K. Some of these artists are more or less slumming in the mainstream, but others are determined to forge a new path.

"The artists have gotten more sophisticated," says Swartzendruber. "I think for so long in the Christian music community and, as well, the church, music was seen as a tool either for evangelism, for praise or teaching Christians something. And as time has gone on, artists have come to see music as an expression of worship, whether it's an instrumental or whatever."

Swartzendruber saves special praise for Switchfoot, whom he credits with a "frankly groundbreaking" quote in a 2003 interview with *Rolling Stone*. "I've seen other bands latch on to it since," he says. "*Rolling Stone* says, 'Are you a Christian band?' and Tim Foreman, the bass player, says, 'We're Christian by faith, not by genre.' Boom! There it was. The first person to ever put that in one sentence. It didn't sound like they were being defensive, or running from the church, or ashamed of the church."

Kaiser doesn't exactly see it that way. "I gotta say, with the explosion of Christian bands, and with the explosion of Christians in bands, they look at what they do as not so much ministry as art, as entertainment, and the message often has gotten very watered down or even left out entirely."

Music or message? Christian band or Christians in a band? Christian music has spent the past three decades between Jesus Freaks and "Jesus Freak" wrestling with these questions as it's perched precariously between a subculture that's never been entirely comfortable with what used to be seen as the Devil's music and a mainstream that's never been entirely comfortable with what it sees as a recruiting tool for the other side.

This book isn't about those questions, though they'll come up again and again in its pages. It's about whether Christian music can figure out how to transform itself from being simply a lifestyle accessory to becoming an enduring part of American culture. The doors of the church are finally open to rock 'n' roll. But is Christian rock music—which traces its origins to a bunch of misfits stinking up the Devil's music—going to remain as tough a lock to pick for Christians who just don't fit in? And furthermore, is the mainstream ready for Christian rock that's actually good?

When I first met Doug Van Pelt at the 2004 Cornerstone Festival, I was astonished that he was older than me. I'd been reading the magazine he edits, *HM,* for a few months, and just from the way his writing swung from ecstatic fandom to bitter disillusionment, I had expected a twenty-five-year-old with a backpack full of CDs, an iPod fused to his hip, and perhaps a neck beard.

Well, he has a beard, anyway: a small soul patch. Van Pelt is one of the mellowest, friendliest people I've ever met. Through the course of my researching this book, he's been an invaluable resource, always happy to point me to a Christian punk band from the '80s that I absolutely "have to know about" or to run interference when I couldn't get past a skeptical publicist, or just to go for a beer when we're in the same city.

Doug Van Pelt started *Heaven's Metal* in 1985 as an outlet for three of his loves: Jesus, hard rock, and music journalism. At first, it was simply a mimeographed fanzine, but with the concurrent success of Stryper, "Christian heavy metal was really starting to explode, and I kind of blew up with it," he says.

With the ascendance of alternative rock in the early '90s, the word *metal* became more and more of a hindrance commercially, and Van Pelt marked the magazine's tenth anniversary by changing the name to *HM: The Hard Music Magazine* and shifting its focus to include Christian alternative music.

My favorite monthly feature in *HM* is "So and So Says," where Van Pelt or another writer interviews a rock star from outside of the Christian market and asks what he or she thinks of Jesus Christ. Sometimes it leads to fascinating discussions (as with Tom Morello of Rage Against the Machine and Sammy Hagar), sometimes *HM* discovers Christians in bands you wouldn't expect (Social Distortion, the Misfits), and sometimes the interviewer is dismissed, angrily or otherwise (Henry Rollins, Godsmack).

Some of the best of these interviews are collected in Van Pelt's book *Rock Stars on God.* Van Pelt's commitment to printing every word of an interview can make for slow going at times—those uh's, kind of's, and you know's add up—but I appreciate the underlying philosophy: this is the conversation as it happened, not dolled up or airbrushed.

In 2004, *HM*'s ran a cover essay by Van Pelt called "The Ugly Truth about Christian Rock," which he calls "19 years of frustration coming out in one article." Lambasting sound-alike bands, shady business practices, and a tolerance of mediocrity on the part of both artists and consumers, Van Pelt issued an impassioned call to Christian bands to try to surpass general-market bands, not just aim to be as good.

Doug Van Pelt lives in Austin, Texas, with his wife, Charlotta, and two kids. This interview (edited—sorry, Doug!) took place at the Cornerstone Festival in July 2004, which Van Pelt has attended faithfully since 1987.

How did you come to Christian music in the first place?

DOUG VAN PELT: The story of my life is kind of a prodigal-son story. My granddad brought a personal faith in Jesus to our whole family. And first it was my oldest sister, and then my dad, and during the time that he was going to Southern Methodist University—we were living in Richardson, by Dallas, we went to this big thing in 1972 called Explo 72 that Campus Crusade [for Christ] put on—

Explo?

Yeah. Explo '72. Teenagers from all over the country and probably all over the world came to Dallas for this free concert where all these freeways intersected. The headliners were Kris Kristofferson, Johnny Cash, and Larry Norman. Kris Kristofferson was a Christian artist at the moment. I was nine.

Music's always been really big for me. When I was six and seven years old, I was calling up radio stations and requesting the Grass Roots' "Temptation Eyes" or Deep Purple's "Smoke on the Water" or Led Zeppelin.

And then, in high school, when I was a young rebellious teenager, I was reading *Creem* and *Circus* magazine all the time, kind of learned the ropes of life by Ted Nugent and Steven Tyler. I credit a lot of my attitudes to those guys just from interviews. So, I had a deep love for music, and I had a healthy respect for music journalism. I had to read it, felt compelled to read it, and just absorbed it like an encyclopedia. I enjoyed keeping facts in my head.

So, you were a student at the University of Texas when you became a Christian?

Yeah. I was home for the summer. I used to try not to think about God. Not consciously, but, subconsciously, I always tried to avoid the subject because, deep down inside, I probably believed that it was the truth, and my lifestyle didn't equal to that, and I didn't want to have to face that, so I didn't. So, I just kind of distracted myself with whatever I could.

That's very common. People who are in a lot of debt try to avoid thinking about living above their means.

Yeah. They don't want to face the music, so to speak.

So, you weren't facing the music.

Yeah, though throughout this time, I was always involved with music, and I knew from my experience as a little kid that Christians had rock 'n' roll music, and, so, I knew that although my lifestyle would change, I wouldn't have to forsake my love for music. Which, by that time, as a young adult, was really expanding. All kinds of classical music and jazz. So, quickly, when I came back to Christ, I didn't want to listen to some of my favorites, you know, the Black Sabbaths, even some Led Zeppelin, Pink Floyd.

Because of what the music represented to you?

It just reinforced attitudes. I always likened it to going shopping with a buddy, and the whole time you're at the mall, he's like, "Let's rip this off. Let's steal this. Let's snatch this. Let's steal. C'mon let's shoplift." It's kind of annoying to always be saying no to him.

I knew just to reinforce my faith that having Christian rock music would help. A lot of people talk about music being evangelistic; I think the biggest gift of Christian music is pastoral. Just the day-to-day upkeep and encouragement to keep on, to make it through your teenage years. Whether it's a faith-based teenage years or not. Just having uplifting encouragement along the way—so positive and helpful.

When I came back to faith in Christ, I started gobbling up all the Christian rock music I could find, especially stuff that catered to my taste. A lot of times the music was subpar, like, some of the early Christian heavy metal and rock couldn't hold a candle to the Scorpions, Pat Travers, and Ted Nugent. But that's how Christian music became a big part of my life. And then, of course, just like high school, I wanted to start reading about it.

When did you start HM?

The winter of '84, '85. I was reading an underground fanzine called *ACME,* which was an acronym for Alternative Christian Music Enthusiasts. It mostly focused on alternative and punk, and it had a little bit of news in there about Christian heavy metal, and it said, "With the advent of Christian heavy metal, somebody should start a Christian metal fanzine/newsletter." And—bing!—a light bulb went off in my head, and it said, "You could even have fun doing it!"

I got permission from this campus fellowship at UT to use their mimeograph machine, a blue-ink thing, and I had a friend who was going to Cornerstone '85, and he said, "Why don't you print your first issue, and I'll hand it out?" So, that was the kind of shove out the front door. It was just a little six-page, folded-over fanzine thing.

What do you see as the strengths of this kind of music? You mentioned its encouraging aspects.

Well, like I mentioned before, pastorally, encouragement, reinforcing a faith. And from there, you can get into some interesting discussions about propaganda and art, and the classic fusion of faith and art, like Michelangelo.

What about challenging faith?

Yeah. Some of the early pioneering bands, like Larry Norman, Resurrection Band, they would always preach during their shows. Sometimes a good fifteen, twenty minutes. And it was usually a challenge. Like the cliché "comfort the afflicted, and afflict the comfortable," they would often do that. They would really challenge the believers not to just have an easy believism, American Western consumerism viewpoint of Christianity, but to look around them at the bigger picture and to live out their faith.

One strength is the whole safety factor. I'm a parent, so I understand how parents are concerned about what kind of media intake their kids are having. Because Christian rock has a sanitized seal of approval from the church or Christian leaders, for some kids, that's such a liberating thing, because rock 'n' roll epitomizes parts of humanity. Wonderful parts, you know, passion, emotion, angst, and even aggression and anger that can be channeled in positive ways.

Having an art form that can help express that, both as a participant and a creator, can be very healthy. So, if the kid actually gets approval from mom and dad to listen to an album, they can go in their room, put their headphones on, go to a concert, jump around in a mosh pit, and just go crazy and have fun in a supervised environment but still feel like they're doing what they wanna do. Like, even if their parents weren't watching with their arms crossed in the back, they can just go nuts and have a blast. It's not superspiritual, necessarily, but I think that serves a great purpose.

Okay, we've talked about strengths. Let's go to weaknesses.

Believe it or not, I was the starting inside linebacker at my high school. It was a 1A school in Southern California. I weighed 162; I was 5'10"; I ran a 5:34. Slow as a donkey, you know. If I were to have tried out at a 5A school, third string at best, maybe.

In the same way—I go to the Calvary Chapel in Austin, Texas—if I called my pastor up, who's a good friend, and said, "Hey, my daughter just painted some really neat things, like Noah's Ark or whatever, can we put it in the hallway?" he might say yes. 'Cause he's my friend; 'cause it's a church; it's a small thing.

But if I go to the Chicago Institute of Art carrying my daughter's pastel drawings, they're just gonna say, "Security! Get this guy out of here!" In a small goldfish bowl, it's easier to rise to the top or get noticed. But in the bigger marketplace of ideas, it gets harder.

So, a weakness of Christian music is that it's a subculture, and it's a smaller goldfish bowl, so mediocrity can be perceived as excellence.

I read a quote from somebody saying for a long time, if, say, Weezer got popular, the Nashville labels would rush to sign the "Christian Weezer."

Yeah, it sure seems like it in hindsight, that they're following trends. In the hard music genre, there's some bands that have been innovators. Fourteen years ago, King's X, which I wouldn't necessarily call a Christian-market band, they were doing something brand-new.

On balance, do you think it makes sense for kids to listen to only Christian music? What's your thought on a sensible diet?

Well, I think "diet" is a good way to put it. In high school, there were certain albums I'd listen to getting ready, getting home, and at night, so maybe two three times a day, I was listening to the same album. And that's like a form of meditation in a sense.

That's often how kids listen to music.

I think there can be a balance. The classic example is, some kid gets born again, some time within the next couple of weeks, he burns his whole music collection, he goes out and buys Christian rock records. And I think that happens so often because the transformation that takes place in a person, they kind of see the world with new eyes, and they see old lifestyle as bad, this new lifestyle that they're learning about as good.

I think a lot of times, God honors it. It's like baby steps. A lot of times, years later, as they mature, they're like, "You know, that Neil Young song really speaks a truth to me that I can handle."

And I went through that phase, where I felt like I was sitting down with the guidance of the Holy Spirit saying, "What albums should I get rid of?" and I knew my albums pretty well and got rid of three hundred and something albums. A few of which, like my Led Zeppelin collection, ten years later, I bought the box set on CD when it came out.

There's a big difference between once every six months and once every day. Even if it's the most negative message you can think of, even if there were backwards masking, you can have your defenses up, but if it's an everyday occurrence, you're always around it; your defenses kind of wear down.

The extreme would be mind control. That some kid is gonna kill themselves, or go murder somebody because they hear a song. That's ridiculous, I think. I don't even want to comment on how that could be feasible. It probably has to do with a mental disorder.

Lots of people listen to Ozzy Osbourne without killing themselves.

Exactly. So, moderation in all things. A little bit of wine is actually a biblical prescription. Overdrinking wine can lead to a wrecked family, wrecked lives, and whatnot. A little moderation is wise for the diet.

I understand that some people, they have kind of a narrow focus that usually widens later on. But I think Christians don't have a monopoly on truth. You can learn about truth from any other religion, or any artist that's out there. So, it's good to distill that and pull truth from various sources.

It takes some maturity—some twelve-year-old kids go to the museum and see the naked sculptures, and they giggle and snicker. But an eighteen-year-old can go to the same museum and really learn something from that sculpture.

There was a really thoughtful discussion about Christian film criticism earlier today, and one of the critics said he wasn't a fan of much Christian art, that he looks for truth in all art. A kid in the audience who's studying screenwriting at a Christian college asked him how he should write, and the guy said, "Just write what you know." What do you look for when you're listening to music?

Your discussion prompted something I wanna answer first, before I answer the question. A brilliant guy who lives in Houston named Kemper Crabb, he used to write a column called "The Christian and Art," and one of the things he pointed out was the influence of the Gospel and the influence of Christ on all of Western civilization. That even the simple narrative has been altered due to the story of the Gospel. The problem-resolution thing. Even the sitcom.

So, I think it's neat that the imprint of the Gospel—even though I don't think we're a Christian nation—the imprint of Christianity is all over this country and Western civilization. So, yeah, in all stories there's truth to be found. I think it's good to be open to that.

So what do I look for in music? Well, when I'm reviewing an album, if it comes out on Tooth & Nail or Sparrow or Forefront, I'm pretty much assuming these are Christian or faith-based artists that are infusing that into their art. But more and more these days, Christians are going out of the small subculture and into the marketplace of ideas, which means that I've got to look at albums more carefully because some of the artists aren't being blunt; they're not looking at their art as ministry tools but as art.

So, I'll look at the song titles; I'll look at the photo of the band; I'll look at the artwork. If God, or Christ, or "my pastor" is thanked, then I'll have some clues. I look at the lyrics if they're printed. This is just to answer the question, Should I be writing about this in my magazine?

One thing that my magazine's done as far as having a track record is being kind of a filter for those parents as to what music is safe. You know, whether it's from the mainstream or Christian world, we've written about predominantly Christian art, especially album reviews and whatnot. We have a reputation for that; we kind of maintain that because if we ever cross that line, it wouldn't be the worst thing in the world, but the simplistic person who uses *HM* for that purpose would have to think a little more analytically, and we wouldn't be serving them the way we do now.

How about personally? Once you've gone through the artwork and the lyrics, what gets you most of all?

Gosh, so many things. The most would be emotional impact, something I could identify with. A common emotion. Even a sappy country song like [Tim McGraw's] "Don't Take the Girl."

Oh man, I can't be with you on that.

Thank my wife for that. She grew up in Houston and doesn't hate country like I do. Sometimes the subject matter, the story impacts me—

Do you cry during movies?

Yeah.

What about commercials?

I probably have before, but I can't think of a single time that I have.

So, you're basically a grown-up emo guy.

Yeah. 'Cept I have a wife. So, I don't have that to complain about. And live performance–wise, some things connect. Certain melodies, and even rhythms, there's certain areas emotionally that music can touch. Especially when coupled with a story.

CHAPTER 3

More Than Just a Song

Brandon Ebel tried to kill me. That's the only conclusion I can draw in retrospect, remembering the way he whipped me around the curving streets of Seattle's Magnolia District in his Mini Cooper. Moments before the murder attempt, we'd seen a vintage sports car a few hundred yards ahead of us. "Dude, look at that old Ferrari," he said.

"I think that's an old Z," I idly parried as the car disappeared around the curve of a hill.

Ebel immediately floored the Mini, dusting the well-manicured yards of Magnolia's streets with a certain authority. My back felt like it was going to go through the seat. Knuckles white, I hung on to the little handle over my head, trying not to think about how little protection the Mini's tiny front end would afford me in the event of a crash, nodding as much in terror as politeness while Ebel told me about the driving courses he's taken and pointed out landmarks whizzing by us—Magnolia is where he lives.

A minute later, we caught up to the car in question, just as its no doubt freaked-out driver realized he was in fact being tailed and fled down a side street. There was a familiar logo on the car's back.

"I *thought* it was a Ferrari," Ebel said. We slowed, and I felt the blood return to my fingers. I resolved to keep any future disagreements with Brandon Ebel to myself.

Tooth & Nail records, the label Ebel founded twelve years ago, isn't far from where we chased the Ferrari, ten minutes north of Seattle's center. It's almost always a slight letdown to see the offices of a record company—while you'd expect maybe a Gothic castle with flames shooting out of the top, outside New York and L.A. (where they resemble law firms) they look mostly like chiropractor's offices. And Tooth & Nail is no exception.

It was 10 AM, a little early by music-biz standards, when I arrived at Tooth & Nail, so I walked around the building for a while, knocking on doors to no avail. Eventually, I just opened one and walked in, through a ground-floor warehouse sporting—kleptomaniacal Christian rock fans, take note!—thousands of CDs on rows of metal shelves. Finally, I found someone who brought me upstairs to Tooth & Nail's main floor.

Amanda MacKinnon has been Tooth & Nail's publicist for five years. The diminutive, bubbly twenty-five-year-old grew up in a Christian family in Indiana, where she got radicalized early on by a seminar called "Kiss Dating Good-bye" led by a guy named Josh Harris, who argued that dating was a one-way road to bitterness and regret and that Christian singles should focus on old-fashioned courtship instead.

MacKinnon got serious with Christian music when her brother Adam took her to a show by a Christian ska group called the O.C. Supertones. By her last year at Indiana University, where she was studying journalism, she'd decided she wanted to work at Tooth & Nail instead, and a coincidence soon made that possible—a friend of a friend was looking for someone to sublet his apartment in Seattle. MacKinnon hadn't told anyone about her plans but decided to take the apartment, even though doing so meant bailing on an internship that summer at the Associated Press in Washington, D.C., and her plans to attend law school after graduation. Her parents were furious, but MacKinnon came out to the other Washington, dropped by the Tooth & Nail offices, and asked for an internship. Three months later, she was hired full-time. And her brother? He works downstairs in the warehouse.

MacKinnon's cubicle is dotted with Smurfs dolls, Elvis figures, and clipped headlines like "Explore Regional Mexican" (her mom is Mexican) that friends have sent her. There are also a few pictures of the squeaky-clean '60s beach-movie character Gidget, which is MacKinnon's nickname. She'd recently moved into doing A&R—signing bands and shepherding them through the recording process—as well as publicity and gave me a copy of the new album by the Tooth & Nail band Norma Jean, which she'd helped produce.

Before this trip, I'd hung out with Amanda a couple of times, first at Cornerstone, then when she accompanied Underoath to Richmond, where I live. We'd had a beer at a nearby bar, and she'd made some affectionate jokes about how serious Underoath were about saving themselves for marriage, so I felt a little more comfortable with her than I had with some of the less humorous Christians I'd met so far, like the guy who told me his band nailed a full-size cross onstage at Cornerstone to protest the commercialization of Christian rock. (Oddly, they weren't asked to return.)

But there's often a hint of border tension when you've got a lot in common with someone whose core beliefs are nonetheless quite different from yours—maybe that's what it's like to be a Canadian in the United States, come to think of it. Still, I had to know. I asked her if she thought God had engineered her move to Seattle.

"Totally," she replied. We went to find Brandon.

A boyish-looking thirty-four-year-old with dark, almond-shaped eyes and short dark hair, Ebel was swiveling in his chair and talking on a headset phone when Amanda swung me by his office. He signaled that he'd be out in a minute, and she showed me around some more.

Ebel's a serial remodeler, she told me, pointing out all the improvements he'd made—new carpets, new lighting—when the staff was at Cornerstone the summer before. He had more changes in mind. "Is that a personality trait?" I asked her.

"More like a disorder," she said laughing.

"All the staffers collect toys," MacKinnon said, taking me into director of A&R Chad Johnson's office, where some rare Kubrick-brand *Star Wars* figures occupied a shelf alongside work-related tchotchkes such as jars of Norma Jean barbecue sauce and an Underoath skateboard.

Ebel appeared, and the three of us went downstairs to see the label's new Mini Cooper. Inside was a stereo system that could shake small trees out of the ground and a video screen on the dash connected to, among other things, a camera in the rear bumper. A silly extravagance on a car twelve feet long, but Ebel got the Mini for a song. "I bought this from two guys who owned a car-audio shop and were feuding," he explained.

At Chinook's restaurant in the Fisherman's Terminal, Ebel negotiated with the waitress, giving up first his fries, then the coleslaw that came with his tuna burger so he could get a salad instead. We shot the breeze for a few minutes, and when I mentioned a jam-band festival I'd attended the year before in Tennessee, Ebel told me the first of many things he didn't want me to publish.

"I wanna tell him my jam-band story, but I'm afraid it'll go in the book," he said to MacKinnon.

"Why are you worried about that?" I asked him.

"It kind of compromises . . . "

He paused.

"Do you feel like you have an image to maintain?" I asked.

"Well, only so much," he said. "Tooth & Nail's been different from a lot of labels—we don't hide anything. But there's a lot of stuff that goes on in the Christian music industry that's pretty hidden."

"Such as?"

"Well, like, if an artist is divorced or has an affair, labels try to cover it up," he said. "It's bad imaging."

I asked whether Tooth & Nail had ever had to deal with scandals.

"A few times," he said. "But it's never been like some of the national pop artists that'll sell a million records. A lot of our stuff might happen because somebody might say something onstage or smaller stuff.

"A lot of our artists are successful in the general market," he said. "In a weird way, the more we've had success in the general market, the less our artists are probably in a lot of scrutiny. The scrutiny comes more from the Christian side."

We talked a little more about the strictures of the Christian rock scene, what Ebel called being "under the microscope." A few years back, Tim Owen, who co-owns the general-market indie label Jade Tree, was visiting his girlfriend at Tooth & Nail and stopped by to say hey to Ebel, who was reading his mail, which he shared with Owen. "Just by coincidence, I got two of the worst letters ever back-to-back," Ebel said. The first, he related, said something like "How dare you right-wing Christian faggots try to shove your views down our throat? We're coming to nail your effing Christ to a cross!"

"And then I opened up another letter," Ebel said, "And a guy goes, 'I'm a pastor at a church—how dare you use God to make money and infiltrate the Christian market? We know you're not really Christians; how dare you put out your devil heavy metal music blah blah blah.'"

"Tim was like, 'How can either of those letters be right, man? All you're doing is putting out records. I thought it was hard enough just dealing with bands. You have to deal with this stuff, too.'"

Ebel said he felt a lot less resistance from the general market these days—in fact, 50 percent of Tooth & Nail's sales are outside Christian outlets. "Our number one account is Best Buy," Ebel said proudly. "And our records aren't in the Christian section; they're in the normal section."

This isn't the only time Ebel used the word *normal* to describe non-Christian music. ("Most of our bands play with normal bands," he said at one point, explaining Tooth & Nail's growing traction in the mainstream underground.) It's kind of a curious adjective, but I think it sums up some of the forces in play. Christian bands have to worry about a lot of things that aren't, by popular standards, "normal": letting a cussword fly when they stub their toes onstage; defending their theology, their ministry, or their lack of theology or ministry; making their album artwork acceptable to Christian bookstores; having the number of times they do or don't mention Christ in their lyrics determine how much airplay they'll get; having to make a conscious decision whether to play shows in clubs, in churches, or in both; choosing their tourmates; deciding whether to do an "altar call." . . .

When I first started thinking about writing this book, I lurked on a few Christian rock fansites. One message board featured a healthy debate on whether U2's Bono could possibly be a Christian because (a) he swore at the Golden Globe Awards in 2003; (b) he smokes. These may seem like trivial vices to anyone outside evangelical Christianity, but they are deathly important to the people inside.

Which is one reason, Ebel says, Tooth & Nail bands avoid smoking when they play church shows and why he himself is so careful about his public image—he told me some frankly pretty mild stories on the day we spent together, which were always followed quickly with an admonition to keep them out of this book. But this isn't baseless paranoia: Ebel's the face of Tooth & Nail and, therefore, the face of a revolution in Christian music.

Brandon Ebel was born in Dallas in 1970 and moved around the West and Northwest with his father, a pastor named Dale Ebel, until the family settled in the suburbs of Portland, Oregon in 1978. That year, Dale began a church in his basement that grew into Rolling Hills Community Church, which now has more than five thousand congregants. "I think a lot of Tooth & Nail's success has been because I didn't really know any better," Ebel said. "I thought, 'I'll just start this company, and it'll get big, like my dad's church! I just grew up thinking, 'Oh, I can do that,' not really knowing that's not normal."

Ebel grew up listening mostly to church-approved music, though he still remembers his first non-Christian album, by Shaun Cassidy, with affection. At Oregon State University, he developed into a full-fledged music nut. "I was always going to shows, everything from Def Leppard to the Ramones," he said. "I wasn't really genre-specific; I just loved music."

A broadcasting major, he had the keys to KBVR, the college radio station, where he feasted on the record library, especially releases by the Seattle indie label Sub Pop. Sub Pop records in the late '80s and early '90s all had a recognizable look, as well as a certain standard of recording quality. But more important, they had style, a lesson not lost on young Brandon.

"It was the first time I wanted to buy all the releases on a label," he said. "That's how I tried to market Tooth & Nail, to be honest."

But first Ebel had to learn the ropes. He began at Frontline, a Southern California Christian label then home to Mad at the World, the Altar Boys, and Daniel Amos. Ebel set about learning what everyone at Frontline did and started pitching bands to the A&R staff with little success. So, on November 23, 1993, Tooth & Nail was born with the release of Wish for Eden's *Pet the Fish*. Records by Minor Threat–worshiping hardcore band the Crucified, cinematic bedroom popster Starflyer 59, and somewhat generic alternative bands like Plankeye followed, but Ebel didn't begin to taste success until two years later, when he put out the debut album of a bunch of Christian skater kids from Seattle.

MxPx's *Pokinatcha* wouldn't sound unusual to anyone familiar with Blink-182, Green Day, or any of California's zillion other pop-punk bands that prize speedy riffs over searing originality (though for Christian kids forbidden to listen to general-market music, MxPx might as well have invented the stuff). But MxPx also pulled off a trick that's eluded so many of their peers—they managed to come off as a rock band full of Christians rather than a Christian rock band. *Pokinatcha* sold a hundred thousand copies, a lot of them outside normal Christian rock channels and, as the band's later major-label deal suggested, to kids who weren't Christians.

In 1997, Tooth & Nail made a deal with Caroline, an "independent" distributor owned by EMI. Ebel decided to create two imprints: Solid State, which specializes in hardcore punk, noise, and metal, and BEC, which markets primarily to the Christian mainstream. Tooth & Nail would continue to showcase alternative acts with general-market appeal. Diversification proved to be an incredibly savvy move.

Jay Howard and John Streck's book *Apostles of Rock: The Splintered World of Contemporary Christian Music* divides Christian music into three camps: Separationist, Integrationist, and Transformational. It's a useful way to look at a genre that, as Ebel is fond of pointing out, "doesn't sound like anything."

Separationist artists, by Howard and Streck's definition, create Christian music primarily for other Christians. It's the stuff of the Gospel Music Awards, the sound of family-friendly radio formats like "The Fish" and the bread-and-butter of the Nashville-based Christian music industry.

Separationist music's sonic palette is largely that of adult contemporary, with strong vocals set against shimmering acoustic guitars, gigantic drum sounds, and symphonic flourishes—think of the stylistic common ground between Celine Dion, Faith Hill, and Maroon 5. And one of its biggest stars is Jeremy Camp, who's signed to BEC.

Ebel met the thirteen-year-old Jeremy Camp when he'd hitchhiked to Cornerstone by himself and asked a family—the Camps, as it turned out—if he could share their campground. He and Jeremy hit it off. "I kept up with him for the last ten years, and then he started doing music, and I heard his stuff and was into it and signed him." Camp's three CDs have since sold over a million copies combined.

While there is crossover potential for Separationist artists, Integrationist musicians are the ones who try to translate their faith into mainstream music or, at the very least, offer a wholesome alternative to what's in stores and on the radio. Amy Grant is the most obvious example of an artist who's enjoyed success in both the Christian and general markets, but you could include Switchfoot, P.O.D., and even the modern rock group Chevelle in that category. Tooth & Nail's no slouch in this department either, selling, as I noted above, half its records outside of Christian bookstores, with some artists—Underoath, Demon Hunter, and Mewithoutyou—routinely selling tens, sometimes hundreds, of thousands of copies of their records to kids down with the program and kids who just came to mosh.

What Howard and Streck call "Transformational" music is the most difficult to define. It's music for misfits, people who struggle with their faith but still attempt to bring "salt and light" to the world. "Salt" because, in the Sermon on the Mount, Jesus admonishes his followers not to lose their "taste" lest they be "trampled under foot." Some artists take this as a call to liberally season their work with accounts of personal struggles and failures. "Light" because, in the same sermon, Jesus encouraged people to set a good example, to be a "city built on a hill."

This is the philosophical space where most Christian punk and indie music comes from, and artists such as Starflyer 59, Denison Witmer, and Pedro the Lion are some of its most notable practitioners. And they've all, at one point or another, recorded for Tooth & Nail.

It's no wonder Brandon Ebel is a rising star at EMI, which frequently flies him out to corporation-wide conferences to try to figure out what he's doing right. Even so, this powerhouse of Christian music is barely known in its hometown. It would be a little more understandable if Tooth & Nail were, say, a bluegrass label, but it's really quite astonishing how few of Seattle's hipsters know that there's a local independent rock label that routinely sells hundreds of thousands of CDs and isn't named Sub Pop or Barsuk.

Here's what Michaelangelo Matos, the music editor of the *Seattle Weekly,* wrote me when I e-mailed him looking for local perspective on Tooth & Nail: "I'm afraid I'm about the last person who could offer any insight on T&N. We've never covered them in any substantial way, and I'm not very familiar w/either their output or their mission." Steve Manning, Sub Pop's publicity director, told me he doubted the label was even interested in cozying up to the local music scene. "I've heard of them," he said. "But I think half the people in the office would be surprised to find out they're in Seattle." A Nexis search of all three of Seattle's newspapers turned up exactly three references to Tooth & Nail. "Low profile" doesn't begin to cover it.

"We're not a local label," Ebel said flatly when I brought this up. "It's nothing that we've tried to do; we've just never signed a lot of local bands."

"I think we're getting more involved locally," said MacKinnon. She'd recently reached out to KEXP, the University of Washington's powerhouse college station. "They were like, 'It's weird that we're not involved with you; you're, like, down the street,'" she said. "I don't know if that's something no one's really tried to do or we haven't put out the right albums." She's probably a bit too kind. It's quite likely that Tooth & Nail's records aren't played by local radio stations or reviewed by the local press due to one of the last politically correct prejudices: it's okay to ignore or denigrate records issued by a Christian label simply because they were issued by a Christian label.

One of those three mentions of Tooth & Nail that I noted above was in a 2000 review of a Starflyer 59 album that referenced: (1) "those ugly bastards from Stryper"; (2) "that woman with bright purple hair on the religious channel, sitting in her $25,000 gold chair and singing about the fact that she needs $50 million for God's satellite network because without it no one is getting into heaven"; (3) a member of Black Sabbath who found God after "he'd slept with 4,000 groupies." Then the reviewer turns somewhat objective and decides that the record, which he'd originally thought was okay, is still okay. "It's not right for me to judge a band by its religious beliefs, just as it's not right for those bands to beg me to find God."[1]

Okay, but how many pieces have you read taking Coldplay's Chris Martin to task for stumping for fair trade? Starflyer 59 have nothing to do with Stryper (who, I'm sorry, had some good tunes), television evangelists, or the conversion experiences of Jeff Fenholt, the Black Sabbath singer in question—whose membership in Black Sabbath, incidentally, is disputed by the band. All Starflyer 59 did to offend this writer was put out a record on a Christian label.

But there's more than simpleminded bigotry at play here. One of the unintended consequences of American evangelical Protestantism is that a sense of community is often a casualty of the demands of an intensely personal relationship with Jesus Christ, resulting in a music scene that regards attempts to reach beyond its borders with suspicion. As Howard and Streck put it in *Apostles of Rock*, "In focusing on individual belief, evangelicals have necessarily focused on individuals. . . . Poverty, hunger, abortion, drug abuse, and other such issues are thus approached as personal failings rather than social problems. Systemic elements simply aren't included in the equation."[2]

Certainly Brandon Ebel's personal politics are long on emphasizing personal responsibility. "I'm almost libertarian in how conservative I am," he told me. "I'm for lesser government period. You know, this really has nothing to do with my record company."

I assured him I would make that clear.

"I know some of my staff voted for Kerry and Ralph Nader," he continued. "I think more of us voted for Bush than ever before. I definitely don't think you have to vote one way or another to be a Christian."

He told me why he didn't want to talk about his views several more times—he thinks most of his artists are liberals, he said, as is his best friend—then charged ahead, as, I was beginning to note, is his style.

"If I had it my way, there would be no public education, and people would make their own decisions on everything. Pat Buchanan says that we should have almost no foreign policy. I'm not saying I agree with Pat Buchanan on a lot of things, but I think we should not be the world's policemen. At home, I think we should have lower taxes, and people should be responsible for themselves. That doesn't mean I don't care about people. I give 10 percent of all the money I make away to churches and charities."

"What about Tooth & Nail?" I asked him. "Does the label do charity work?"

"No, we've done banner ads for different things, like the tsunami. I've never told anybody in an interview that I give 10 percent away. I don't know why I did that. I don't want to do it, like, 'Look at me.'"

"Christians aren't supposed to make a big deal about their charity," I prompted.

"There's many Scriptures about that," Ebel agreed. "I just want to be careful that it's not like, 'Look how great Tooth & Nail is. We're *so* trying to help everyone.' I think it would be kind of funny to do, you know, a compilation for five bucks and 10 percent of the proceeds go to the victims, which is, like, a thousand dollars. I just wrote a check personally for many thousands of dollars for that, which I've never told *anybody* till you right now. Please don't print that."

After lunch, Ebel offered to drive me over to see the studio Tooth & Nail owns in Seattle's Capitol Hill district. On the way over, I noticed that Brandon Ebel had a story that related to anything I brought up.

For instance, we started talking about illegal drugs on the drive to the studio (I don't remember why, though possibly because we were cruising through Courtney Love's old stomping grounds). Ebel told me he'd never tried marijuana but doesn't think it should be illegal. Inevitably, the conversation turned to Miami Dolphins running back Ricky Williams, who famously left the NFL to smoke more pot.

Ricky Williams crashed at Ebel's sister's house for a couple of days once.

When he asked me about my trip to Cornerstone, I likened it to the time I stumbled across the Soap Opera Awards on TV, where I marveled that the audience was freaking out about soap opera stars I'd never heard of.

"When I started Tooth & Nail," Ebel said, "I worked with an extra for that awards show." He signed up as an extra himself and was assigned to fill the seats of people who got up to accept awards. "I was with all these weird, beautiful-looking people like Ken dolls and hot girls, and I'd just sit all awkward at the table with people who'd been acting together for years. At the commercial breaks, some people wouldn't talk to me."

"I can't believe you were actually *at* the Soap Opera Awards," I told him.

"I'm just telling you," he said. "Every time I go to the grocery store, I see people I sat with at those tables on the cover of those soap magazines."

This reminded him of something. "Wanna hear my conversion story?" he asked me. I'd assumed he hadn't had one since he seemed like the ultimate evangelical insider, from his childhood in the church to the present. I was wrong. When he was twenty-seven and attending the Dove Awards—a.k.a. the Christian Grammys—in Nashville, Ebel, who'd recently broken up with a longtime girlfriend, found himself suddenly, inexplicably repulsed by the Christian music industry and slipped out to a nearby bar. Where Ebel, who'd managed to go through college as a Sigma Phi Epsilon without ever getting drunk, proceeded to get hammered on "vodka somethings," a habit he continued for the better part of what he calls his "year of darkness."

"I always tell people Christian music drove me to drink!" he joked, but it seems like he spent the time, consciously or not, working on some personal issues. When he emerged, he recommitted his life to Christ and got married. Recently, he and his wife had a son.

I asked him if he still drank, and he said only in moderation. He doesn't believe the Bible interdicts drinking, though he thinks drunkenness is wrong. "There's far more Scriptures about gluttony than about drinking," he said. "All I know is that you can probably cuss everyday and have a couple glasses of wine, and you'd be in less sin than if you were a fatty. I mean, missionaries in Europe are drinking, smoking cigarettes, sharing the Gospel; you know, they still don't die young because they're walking around, exercising, riding a bicycle. Meanwhile, big fat Christian pastors in the South are keeling over at forty-five from heart attacks."

I told Brandon he'd be terrible to smoke pot with.

"Why's that?" he asked, amused.

"It magnifies personality traits," MacKinnon said diplomatically.

"You'd talk way too much," I explained. He seemed to think that was hilarious.

Tooth & Nail's studio is run by Aaron Sprinkle, formerly of the band Poor Old Lu, a seminal Christian alternative rock group from the early to mid-'90s. Poor Old Lu didn't record for Tooth & Nail until it reunited for one album in 2002, but Sprinkle had been absorbed into the family long before that by a Poor Old Lu fan named Brandon Ebel, who installed him as his company's house producer and occasional solo artist.

As we approached the building I asked Ebel why he bought it.

"Control," he said. It's the same reason he bought the building in Magnolia. "We were downtown before, but we were spending nine thousand dollars a month on rent. I like to control where my money goes." He owns the studio because he doesn't like paying other people to lease studio time.

Inside the control room, a group called Number One Gun was waiting to hear some rough mixes that Sprinkle, a schlubby thirtysomething with sleepy eyes and a pack of Parliaments bulging from his polo shirt pocket, was nimbly assembling on a ProTools screen. Ebel led me through the various rooms of the studio, and it was clear he knew his way around it, telling me the particular advantages of its drum room, vocal isolation booth, etc.

Above the studio is a condo that Tooth & Nail also owns so out-of-town bands can stay cheaply while recording. There's a comfortable living room with a big-screen TV, ringed by a couple of dorm-style bedrooms and a totally bitchin' outdoor deck. Ebel didn't look pleased that the plants in the window boxes on the deck were dying and made a verbal note to himself to have someone look at them.

I asked him if Tooth & Nail's record deals were like some indies, where the label splits profits with the artist.

"No, it's points," he said, using industry slang for the standard major-label-style deal where a band has to recoup the costs of its recording advance before it earns a percentage royalty on sales.

"What about the cost of recording here?" I asked him.

"That comes out of their advance," he said.

That's probably a good business move for Ebel, but it's not necessarily that great for bands—essentially Tooth & Nail is advancing them money to pay Tooth & Nail for studio time, which they will pay back to Tooth & Nail via records sold by Tooth & Nail—but to be fair, it's not as if the label's groups are required to record in the house studio. And recoupable advances are a cornerstone of the music industry for a reason: it's not cheap to run a record company, and people who invest the necessary sums of money to make sure bands get heard have every right to expect a return on their investment. Still, if there were ever a segment of the music industry that one would hope could find a more equitable way to treat the people who actually create music, Christian music should be the first place to look, right?

Back in the control room, Sprinkle fed Number One Gun's rough mix through some extremely loud speakers. Ebel nodded his head appreciatively. Number One Gun play extremely competent and average alternative rock. As a critic, it's the kind of music I wouldn't pay attention to unless I absolutely had to—the only way this could be interesting to me is if it were popular, and then at least I'd have a question to build upon: What are fans getting from this?

On the way back to the office, I asked Ebel about his personal aesthetic. Tooth & Nail and its subsidiary labels put out an inordinate number of releases for a company its size: nearly a hundred in 2004 and 2005 alone. "How can you possibly keep track of them all?" I asked. He said while he now has little time for A&R duties he's delegated a lot of those tasks to staffers like Tyson Paolotti, Chad Johnson, and, recently, MacKinnon.

"What is Tooth & Nail looking for in a band?" I asked.

"I like all music," he said. "I'll go see a hardcore show, but then I'll go catch Alison Krauss or Lyle Lovett. When everyone was making fun of Creed, I bought it and said, 'Well, I can see why this is selling.' What I really wanna do is find the best bands in each genre that I like."

Ebel said that he started Tooth & Nail as a safe haven for artists with similar beliefs. "I just wanted to support a community of Christians that were being neglected. Are they being neglected now? Not nearly as much." He understands the need for calling music *Christian rock*, but he doesn't think the term really means anything.

I think that conviction comes as close to defining Ebel's aesthetic as anything—to him, Christian music comes from what he calls "a shared belief system" rather than a common set of musical influences. Why, then, shouldn't Tooth & Nail cover all the bases, putting out rock, pop, industrial, hardcore, hip-hop, electronica, singer/songwriter, emo, screamo, adult contemporary, ska, heavy metal, poppunk, or art rock records? It may not all be great music—Ebel himself says that "there's a huge lack of quality" in most Christian art—but it all has an audience. And that's just good business.

Subtly, though, Tooth & Nail's business model has changed as the label has begun selling more records. Underoath's most recent album, *They're Only Chasing Safety,* has moved more than two hundred thousand copies, for example. For all the freedom EMI affords Tooth & Nail, those are the kind of numbers that tend to make corporate parents more attentive.

"It's harder now if you're a smaller group to make it on our label," Ebel said. "We have to be more focused. We've dropped over twenty-five groups in the last couple of years. Groups that work hard, that we have a great relationship with, I'm loyal to. People who we don't get along with, or they're badmouthing us, or they don't work hard, they're gonna get canned. A few years ago maybe not."

"Does that happen a lot?" I asked.

Ebel rolled his eyes. "It's my pet peeve," he said. "It's really easy to blame your label." He said it's especially frustrating when Christian bands talk smack about Tooth & Nail not being able to get them general-market exposure. "You don't magically get on MTV," Ebel said, quickly noting that about twenty-five of his bands have been played on the video channel. "MTV has to have heard of you. And usually they hear of you because you play a show in New York with another cool band. But if you're just playing a church show in New York that your agent and manager put you on, don't blame us!"

Ebel's sympathetic to the plight of bands, especially older Christian groups, who can only marvel at, for example, Underoath's success ("Underoath are a *Christian* band?" said a friend of mine who teaches junior high in Richmond. "I see their shirts every day!"), but he also thinks those artists are trapped in a vicious economic model.

"It's the bands I call 'tweener bands' that are stuck in the Christian market," he said. "They're not really accepted in the general market; those are the ones that get real bitter." It's difficult for an older musician, he explained, to turn down gigs at churches, which often guarantee a band a couple thousand dollars. "You know, a club's gonna pay you two hundred dollars and some back end," Ebel said. "Guys who actually need to make a real living, they've got bills and stuff, they get tempted to take the [church] money even if they're not necessarily into it. I think that's a huge problem with people's integrity too, because they're like, 'Well, it's just so easy, you know?'"

What isn't easy is breaking free of the moniker "Christian rock band," something else Ebel understands quite well.

"You know a band's really trying to say they're not Christian when they go [crossing his arms and affecting a not-so-tough-guy stance], 'Dude, we're not in the fucking Christian market,'" he says, which cracks MacKinnon up.

"You're out of the community if you do that," she says, laughing. "It's a rule!"

After he gave up on killing me (the Ferrari incident occurred on the drive back to the Tooth & Nail office), I asked Ebel what kind of car he himself owned. He looked at me and grinned. "You're not gonna get that out of me," he said. A beat or two later, he told me he has three cars, and that he used to have a Porsche and a couple of BMWs.

It had been like that all day. Ebel often seems to lose himself in conversation, oblivious to the fact that he's started pounding on the table to make a point or told a reporter stuff he definitely doesn't want anyone to know. He'll talk admiringly of hang-up-free European Christians and then switch off my tape recorder to tell me about how appalled he was to see an art exhibit in New York that depicted "someone having anal relations with sheep."

He's a savvy businessman—at one point, he broke the conversation to ask me whether I was going to get Tooth & Nail act Mewithoutyou reviewed in *Spin*—whose self-diagnosed attention-deficit disorder, in combination with an inborn ability to make deals, has made him a very wealthy young man and a major player in the Christian music industry. I wouldn't be surprised if he ended up running a major label someday, before he heads off to a private island somewhere.

"I don't believe in retirement," Ebel said when I floated the idea. "In the Bible, no one retires. I'm gonna work till I frickin' keel over."

I would advise checking your seatbelt before disagreeing with him.

CHAPTER 4

The Baffled King
Composing Hallelujah

E very king must have his castle, and David Bazan is no exception. Bazan is in a curious position culturally: a beacon to
burned-out and disaffected Christian kids who just can't say good-
bye to their faith, even as they struggle with its attendant culture,
he makes his living as a respected indie rocker in the general market. But today, as far as I'm concerned, he's mostly in the curious
position of actually *living in a castle*.

To get to Bazan's fortress, you take a half-hour ferry ride from
Seattle to Bainbridge Island, then drive another thirty minutes
through the Agate Pass and up onto State Highway 3. You can't
see the large, green, wooden structure built by someone Bazan
describes as "a crazy dude who believed that every Irishman
should have a castle" from the road, which is probably just as well,
since Bazan's probably the only indie rocker I've ever met who has
to worry about crazed fans trailing him home.

I made the drive out there in my rental car with Bazan in the
passenger seat. We'd met up earlier in Winslow, near where the
ferry lets off, and he'd introduced me to his wife, Ann, and baby

daughter, Ella, at a popular bakery there. He and I then went off to a fancy diner to talk while his family shopped.

Except for his full, black beard, Bazan looks like a stereotypical sensitive-guy "emo," or emotional, rocker in his everyday uniform of black jeans, hoodie, and gas station–attendant jacket. Until recently, he recorded for one of emo's most popular labels, Jade Tree, and has as little to do with evangelical Christianity or Christian music as possible.

But, like the recovering Seattle heroin addicts he used to write songs about, Bazan can't ever fully leave his past behind. He's a singer/songwriter who just wants his baby back—and that baby's name is Jesus.

David Bazan was born in 1976 to Mexican-American parents. His father, David H. Bazan Jr., played piano and cello growing up and, after getting a degree in music from Bethany Bible College in San Diego, became a Pentecostal music pastor in various Assemblies of God churches around Arizona. Bazan described his father as a more-than-capable musician but said that it was in the role of pastor that he really thrived.

"When he was a kid," Bazan said, washing down a breakfast of eggs scrambled with walnuts and bleu cheese with a microbrew, "he latched on to the idea of being Christlike. He really liked the idea of being a servant. When he had a choice of hiring a drummer for the church services or using the really terrible drummer at the church, he would always go with the really terrible guy. So very rarely would anybody feel left out, which is sort of his legacy."

Growing up, Bazan's dad was terrified of missing the Rapture—Pentecostals, like many fundamentalist Christians, believe that when Jesus Christ returns, he will instantly take all Christians living and dead to heaven, kicking off a seven-year period of tribulation during which the Antichrist will reign before Christ returns for a final apocalyptic battle. The divine event will be so rapid, the theory goes, that

Bazan's dad avoided movie theaters just in case Jesus didn't notice he was missing.

"He was deathly afraid," Bazan said. "He came home from school on many occasions and couldn't find his mom or any of his brothers and sisters and was convinced that he'd missed the Rapture. I think this added to his idea of what was true and right."

One of the things the elder Bazan decided was true and right was that melody, when combined with lyrics, was a much more powerful force than most people thought and "could somehow subvert their reason," Bazan said. Because of this belief, young David was allowed only Christian music. The first singer he really connected with was a rock-influenced lounge singer named Carman, whose epic story-song "The Champion" became David's favorite song in third grade.

The song describes an epic boxing match between Jesus and the Devil, with God as the referee. "They're duking it out," Bazan explained, "and they'll make reference to different events in the Bible that were triumphs for one or the other, and then in the end, the Devil knocks him out.

"But then—this is so funny—God starts counting backwards from ten, and when Jesus gets to one, he basically raises from the dead."

"So God changed the rules?" I asked.

"Apparently!"

David loved this song so much that he called the local Christian radio station to request it at least four times a day. "Finally, the guy was like, 'Dude, go buy the record. I'm not playing it anymore," Bazan said. "And I was like, 'Oh yeah. Hey, Dad, can we go buy this record?'"

From Carman, David dived into as much Christian music as he could handle. Leon Patillo, Petra, his mom's Sandi Patty records—he listened to them all constantly on his Walkman. Once, he played a Petra song for his uncle, who told him, "Yeah, it sounds pretty good. But you know what, man? Sounds like the message is getting lost in the music."

David, who was obsessed with "trying to do Christianity right," started to keep certain songs by Christian artists such as Russ Taff to himself. He never brought his Steve Taylor tapes, in particular, into the family car. "I didn't want there to be any scrutiny," Bazan said. "'Cause I liked these songs a lot, and I wouldn't be able to account to any of my elders about them."

Taylor struck a chord with David because of what he describes as the "ambiguity" of his music. A song called "Sin for a Season," in particular, caused what Bazan called "dissonance" within the young fan. "There's a passage in, I think it's Proverbs, that sin is pleasurable for a season. But in the end you reap sorrow. For the time and the culture, I was surprised he was able to get away with it."

By which he means the suggestion that sin could be pleasurable at all.

When David reached eighth grade, his father relaxed the secular-music ban a bit and allowed him to have a Beatles tape that a friend recorded from his dad's albums, with the second LP of the "White Album" on one side and the first LP of the "blue" *Beatles 1967–1970* greatest hits record on the other.

"I would just listen to them on a loop constantly," Bazan said. "Finally, the last straw was I was walking around my house singing 'Yer Blues' by John Lennon: 'I'm so lonely I wanna die.'" That was the end of Bazan's Beatles jag. "My dad was just like, 'That's it. You can appreciate the Beatles and listen to them occasionally, but you can't listen to them all the time like this.'"

His strict control of young David's listening habits aside, David H. Bazan Jr. raised his kids in a relatively liberal manner, emphasizing the importance of looking out for the underdog and of being honest and building relationships with people.

Compared to, say, Episcopalians, Pentecostals practice a fairly rambunctious style of worship. "It's very untheological. It's very emotional," Bazan said. Pentecostals believe in the "second blessing," which means being filled with the Holy Spirit, as evidenced by speaking in tongues. Other manifestations of the second blessing include being "Slain in the Spirit," a worship rite in which congregants come up to the front of the church (an "altar call") and fall to the ground as the pastor pushes their foreheads.

David's father was in charge of this part of the service, but he generally declined to schedule a time for being Slain in the Spirit. Neither he nor his wife ascribed to the "prosperity theology" that swept American churches in the late '80s, teaching that personal wealth was a sign of God's favor. This was just as well since, in most Pentecostal churches, Bazan explained, the senior pastor made quite a bit more than his associates.

As a music pastor, David's father was near the bottom of the ecclesiastical pecking order when it came to salaries. ("The pastor would drive a Cadillac, and we would have a Cavalier," Bazan said.) Bazan remembers a wrenching fight when his dad, taking a job at a new church, asked for less money than his mom thought he should.

In 1991, the Bazans moved to Seattle to join a church where the pastor didn't believe in such an extreme salary disparity with his associates. By this time, David's father had lifted the ban on secular music for good, just in time for young David, who'd been listening to ever-harder Christian music, to hear Nirvana's just-released *Nevermind* on a youth-group trip. "Those first chords come in, then the drums pop in, I was just like, 'Oh my God, this is crazy,'" Bazan remembered.

Still, it wasn't until he discovered the Washington, D.C., group Fugazi that Bazan's musical world really opened up. As famous for their way of doing business—saying no to music-industry fripperies like videos, huge advance checks, and high ticket and record prices, while selling enough records to make major label executives weep—as for their self-critical lyrics and fierce instrumentation, Fugazi fitted David's slow emergence from the all-encompassing faith of his youth perfectly.

"They're sort of the general-market equivalent of what I loved about Christianity growing up," Bazan said. "There was this authenticity and this really strong ethical sense about what they were doing. You felt it in their music, you felt it in everything they were doing."

David's faith in his church had been built on sandy ground for a while by the time he discovered politically correct, dub-influenced posthardcore. When he was five years old, his fondest wish had been to emulate Enoch, whom the Book of Genesis taught had walked so closely with God that he'd gone to heaven without dying. "I remember thinking, 'Aw man, that is what I want more than anything,'" Bazan said. "Just as soon as I thought that, I remembered that wasn't possible. Like, I'm already such a fuckup."

When he was eight, David went to camp for the first time. Each night ended with a ninety-minute or longer service punctuated by a two-part altar call. The first was brief, but the second, Bazan said, was the big one: "for that second blessing, to be filled with the Holy Spirit, with the evidence of speaking in tongues."

David, who hadn't felt such a call all week, went to the front on the last night of camp. "I was praying, I was wanting to have this experience," he said. "Praying and praying and praying, everybody's just crying—it's a really bizarre scene.

"But nothing happened. I'm down there for over an hour, praying, just, 'Please, please, can I have this thing,' so pretty soon I'm looking around, and everybody else has already had it, so, finally, a youth worker comes around to me, and they can see I'm struggling, so, genuine as they could possibly be, I'm guessing, they start coaching me, saying, 'Just relax and aim to loosen your jaw, and if you think of any words to say just say them.'"

"I'm going along, thinking the whole time there would be this undeniable thing welling up in me. Like, it wouldn't be me doing anything, it would just happen."

Nothing.

"So, sincere as I could be, I started saying, 'Omnitababadada-bada,' and they're just like, 'That's it! That's great!' You know, 'You got it!'"

David left camp with a hollow feeling. He didn't attempt to speak in tongues again for two years. Then, one night in his bedroom, at a loss for anything to pray for, David remembered being taught that anyone in such a situation could use glossolalia instead.

"I decided to start praying in tongues," he said, "and I remember really distinctly—you know how on Bugs Bunny when Daffy Duck or somebody said something really stupid and they'd turn into a jackass or a sucker? I had that feeling. I felt so taken."

Bazan said he was already aware of a lot of inconsistencies in the church, but his failure to speak in tongues hadn't further distanced him from God. "I just pictured the all-seeing eye looking down on me in my bedroom going, 'Blah blah blah blah blah,'" he said. "I was just making shit up."

Years later, when Bazan went to college, he asked his Pentecostal history professor what the theological explanation of this doctrine was. "It was smoke and mirrors," he said. "The guy basically said, 'Yeah, exegetically, it's not possible to prove this, but we still believe it.'"

In high school, David, now free to explore any music he liked, joined Columbia House (he ran his selections by his dad as a courtesy). He remembers getting a Cure album and a couple of Beatles LPs, but soon found the best way of learning about music was from his classmates. Seattle in the early '90s was a magnet for groups hoping that a bit of Nirvana's major label magic would rub off on them, but the Pacific Northwest had been home for years before that to a thriving indie rock scene, one less concerned with "making it" than with "making it yourself."

David and his friends Eben Haase and Damien Jurado decided to form a hardcore punk band called the Guilty. After a couple name changes, they settled on Coolidge, which released a four-song EP recorded by Poor Old Lu's Aaron Sprinkle. Jurado eventually decided to split for a solo career that landed him on Seattle's legendary Sub Pop label, while Bazan decided to form a new group, one named after an imaginary children's book and inspired by the slowed-down indie rock of groups like Sebadoh, Bedhead, and Low.

Then, in 1997, the nascent Pedro the Lion did something Bazan is still coming to grips with: they put out a record on Tooth & Nail.

The *Whole* EP opens and closes with telling lyrics. From the first song, "Nothing." "If only the rules were/Built upon philosophy that I embraced/I'd hug your neck and kiss your face/But it's very obvious/That your ideals are not for me." From the penultimate (the EP's last song is an instrumental) "Lullaby": "You know I want to be like Jesus/But it seems so very far away/And when will I learn to obey, obey?"

It takes less than fifteen minutes to go from the kid who decided speaking in tongues was bullshit to the one who wanted to go to Heaven without dying. *Whole* is a remarkably detailed snapshot of Bazan's evolving trademark confliction. Interestingly, he chooses to express what he sees as the growing incompatibility of his two goals—being a good Christian and living by his own code—through the lens of heroin addiction.

Bazan is in character when he sings, "The chances are slight/That I won't shoot up tonight." He hasn't tried heroin. But if you wanted to understand junkies, you could have done worse than being a hipster in Seattle in the early '90s.

"A buddy's girlfriend had been a heroin addict for a long time," Bazan told me, "and then she stopped doing it for a couple of years.

And then out of nowhere she ran into an old buddy, it was a good fit, and she got tangled up in it for another year.

"It just seemed like such a tragedy, something that is always with you. You're always susceptible to falling back into the same thing," he continued. "I just felt a parallel, like, 'It's not possible for me to habituate virtue the way I want to.' It's this endless cycle of failure that I can't break out of."

He wasn't, however, being anyone else than young David Bazan when he sang "Lullaby," arguably the best song on the record, but one he now says he will never play again. The lyrics tell the story of a weary young man comforted by Christ, who tells him, "Rest in me/Little David/And dry all your tears/You can lay down your armor and have no fear."

"That song makes my skin crawl," Bazan said when I asked him about it. "It was written at a time where I was still heavily influenced by Christian culture, and there was a really manipulative tone.

"I was eighteen when I wrote that song," he said. "Still struggling to get out of Christian culture without being willing to throw everything I believed in out. And the band has basically been a document of that."

It would be a while before Bazan went cold turkey on Christian culture. First, there was the issue of what Pedro the Lion was going to be. Some of the band's other members wanted it to be a ministry, an idea with which Bazan was uncomfortable, even though as a band on Tooth & Nail in the late '90s, shows at churches were pretty much the only ones available to them. That wasn't for lack of trying on Bazan's part—he'd taken the ten-inch vinyl version of *Whole* to every club in town to no avail.

Bazan was left in the position of explaining to youth pastors why an altar call, standard for Christian bands at the time, would not be part of Pedro's performance. There was good money to be made playing churches, better than would be possible for a few years in clubs, but Bazan couldn't stomach the compromises.

"The youth pastor would call up: 'We're trying to do this thing to reach out to the young people, we're trying to do a Christian coffee-house. What it is, is—'

"Just like, 'We know what it is, man. No coffee. You're gonna have bands play and put some Christmas lights up.' Try to have the kids bring all their non-Christian friends in, basically bait-and-switch these kids into converting to Christianity."

It's probably not a surprise that by the time of Pedro the Lion's next record, the band's membership had dwindled to one. Tooth & Nail had offered to sign Pedro properly (the EP was done as sort of a dry run for both parties), but Bazan said his lawyer was appalled by Tooth & Nail's offer.

"He said, 'What is this, Columbia Records in the '50s?' Like he [Brandon Ebel] was trying to get your publishing and all this stuff." Bazan decided instead to go with Made in Mexico, a label started by a former Tooth & Nail employee, James Morelos (whom Ebel told me "now owns a hair salon in New York" while making a mincing gesture).

It's Hard to Find a Friend cemented Bazan's position in Christian circles, but its accomplished mope rock found purchase in the rocky ground of mainstream indie rock. KEXP, the University of Washington's radio station, began playing the record, and, finally, Bazan was able to book what he called a "legitimate club show" at the Tractor Tavern in Ballard. From then on, Pedro began to wean itself from church shows.

"We were at that point firmly in the Christian ghetto," he said, "and really trying claw our way out of it as best we could." The first thing noticeable about *It's Hard to Find a Friend* is how much more sophisticated Bazan's songwriting had become since the *Whole* EP. Indie rock is rife with songwriters whose pride in their lack of musical training results in, as musician and critic Stephin Merritt is fond of pointing out, most melodies in the genre consisting of no more than five notes.

Bazan's music follows the sonic template of a lot of indie music, especially the subgenre called "slowcore"—glacial tempos, dramatic chord progressions, shambling beats—but his melodies are often quite complex, especially on numbers such as "The Longer I Lay Here," a late-night lament that evinces Bazan's Beatles influence via major chords that drop to minor to announce choruses and a melody whose ascent echoes, but does not ape, the chord progression.

His lyrics, too, are a lot harder to pin down. The album opens with a quasipolitical statement, "Of Up and Coming Monarchs," in which the narrator—it's never a sure thing that Bazan's speaking for himself— bemoans the fact that Canada, once a happy place to sit out a war, is now firmly in the United States' pocket. It bears noting that this album was recorded at the height of premillennial peace, Clinton's second term, when the U.S. tended to wage war with isolated missile strikes.

"Big Trucks," at 120 beats per minute—virtually speed metal by Pedro standards—introduces another frequent theme in Bazan's work: conflict with a father, biological or otherwise. The narrator asks his dad why he let a trucker get away with nearly running the family car off the road. You're young, son, his dad replies, and you don't understand that you just have to look out for guys who are bigger than you and who just want to get home, too.

In "The Bells," Bazan regrets breaking a promise to his father and is absolved. "Secret of the Easy Yoke" finds him once again flaunting his doubt (or maybe flouting his debt): "I still have never seen you," he tells God, "And some days I don't love you at all." By song's end, he's warily eyeing salvation: "If this is only a test/I hope that I'm passing/'Cause I'm losing steam/And I still want to trust you."

Despair and cynicism are bad words in Christian culture. The critic reviewing Pedro the Lion's 2004 album, *Achilles Heel*, for a Christian website named Phantom Tollbooth praised Bazan's songwriting and called his sarcasm "infectious" before warning his readers against listening to the album too often. Such repeat auditions, he cautions, could turn a good Christian into "a cynic of the Bazan variety. While this may be valuable at times, I have to think that in the long run it would become unbearable."[1]

As you might expect, this is the kind of criticism that drives Bazan completely bananas, even though it comes from a mindset he understands—after all, U2's song "I Still Haven't Found What I'm Looking For" made him unbearably sad as a kid. To think that someone like Bono could be a Christian and still feel unsure!

"It's very difficult," he said. "We who have grown up Christian are fed propaganda from the time we are little, and you have to be really cynical to overcome that. And that's not a place that very many people want themselves to be found in."

With *It's Hard to Find a Friend,* Pedro the Lion came to the attention of Delaware's Jade Tree label, which, having had the foresight to sign an emo group called the Promise Ring, had just experienced a burst of growth. Label cofounder Tim Owen says he fell in love with *Whole. "It's Hard to Find a Friend* sealed it for me," he told me via e-mail. "And fortunately it worked out that we ended up being able to work with Dave after that album was released." For Bazan, signing with Jade Tree was the culmination of a lot of hard work. He was finally free of Christian rock. Now he began the arduous process of pissing his old milieu off completely.

With 2002's *Control,* Bazan began incorporating less than Christian language in his songs. It wasn't just lyrics such as "All the experts say you ought to start them young/That way they'll naturally love the taste of corporate cum" that sent Christian critics to the barricades. It was his ever-converging critique of evangelical Christianity and American capitalism, a product of his increasing interest in leftism—that, and the fact that one song on *Control* features a narrator who's cheating on his wife in a hotel room and compares reaching orgasm to the Rapture.

Control was the most visible example yet of the radicalization of David Bazan, who first began to reexamine his political beliefs after hearing Fugazi's pro-choice song "Reclamation."

"I was evangelized to their point of view about what was right, what was true and what transcended our own ideas of culture," Bazan said. "I mean, I grew up listening to Christian music, and, yet, when something that seemed true to me came around, I was very sympathetic to it." That sympathy later expanded to include books on liberation theology and the hard-left politics of Noam Chomsky.

And especially because of Chomsky's work, September 11 was a turning point for Bazan, intellectually.

"That was a major thing, too, as far as my faith was concerned," he said. "It started to make sense. There was an element where I was really frustrated with wealthy people in the church, their attitudes about things. In the Bible, Jesus is clear about the corrupting elements of wealth, and more than anything, the poor and the widowed were to be taken care of and not taken advantage of."

"And you saw a parallel between the failings of the church and those of the U.S.?" I asked.

"The bully, you know, somebody punched him in the nuts," he said. "I was strangely looking for that. I was looking for some retribution from somewhere. So, when it happened, there was this really morbid sense of satisfaction that came along with that event."

An openness to allegory is a product of intense religious instruction, so perhaps it's not surprising that Bazan reads September 11 this way. American evangelicals have a very cozy relationship with what's called "American exceptionalism," the idea that our country was called by God to be a shining "city on a hill."

Evangelical culture is not shy about naming the moral impediments to America's taking its rightful place in the firmament, such as legalized abortion and prayerless public schools that teach Darwin's theory of evolution. What's relatively unexamined in modern evangelicalism, though, goes the leftist critique, is the fact that, at some point, the interests of capitalism and faith merged. Prosperity theology is only the most recent, and, to some people, the most indecent, manifestation of this alliance.

Bazan said liberation theology—the idea that salvation is as important on earth as it is in heaven—"helped me to understand my faith. Not what Christianity is but what Jesus talked about—it's very much in line with these things that I'm starting to think and feel about politics. About the belief in the unfair nature of corporate America, the political process, things like that."

He says he originally structured *Control* as an album about September 11, but, in the end, he made a record about what, for Bazan, has always been the only issue: power in all its forms. The boy who wasn't allowed to listen to music unapproved by the Christian business community began lashing out at the corporate culture that he thought made Christianity powerful. And boy, did he ever begin to blow some fans' minds.

You'd be forgiven if, at this point, you were wondering why David Bazan has any Christian fans at all. Here are some user reviews of *Control* from Christianpunks.com.

> This dude isnt a christian. FOr the past 2 hours i have been searching the internet to find out if he was or was not and God has just revealed to me that he is not. The bible says that God is not the author of confusion and this dude is lukewarm at best. Hes decieving people b/c he's singing about God yet his personall beliefs are totally wrong. i really wanted to like his music, but this is a false prophet who's decieving many. (jesusadvocate)

I love Pedro's sound, but the lyrics are disgusting. i read options and rapture and then i stopped. i really hope no non-christians listen to pedro thinking it's a christian band- they will be very confused as to what christianity is all about. If you think Pedro is ok, search your heart, cheating on your wife is never ok, and s*** is reflecting what is living in his heart (ElmoLuvsEmos)

WHAT THE CRAP IS THIS CRAP! SOMEONE DELETE THIS FREAKIN ALBUM FROM THE SITE QUICK. GET THEY SHOULD DO THIS CD THE SAME WAY THEY DID TO EVANSCENCE!!! KICK IT OFF THE CHRISTIAN MARKET!! A TOOL OF SATAN (Jus10_loudtunage)

This album is amazing. Basically the plot is a tragedy by classical definition. The protagonist is eventually killed for his vices and hubris (infidelity). I do not understand why people can rate this album so low just because it of some questionable language. This album definately is for mature Christians, but Bazan takes an overwhelmingly Christian stance at the end of the album. Vocals are a little dry, but the beauty in the lyrics more than makes up for that. (last_laugh)

But here's the thing: the last review is typical of how most Christian music fans view Bazan's music. Pedro the Lion has consistently been one of the most popular acts at the Cornerstone Festival. Moreover—and this is coming from someone who's gone to a shopping mall with Pharrell Williams—I've never seen anyone mobbed the way David Bazan is whenever he steps back into the Christian world.

Onstage at Christian festivals and colleges, fans pepper him with queries both goofy and dead-serious when—as at every show—he stops between songs to ask whether anyone has "any questions."

Offstage, kids swarm him and demand to know the meaning of a certain lyric, thank him for writing a note to a sick friend, or challenge him on some point of theology. And he has time for all of them, especially the people who dismiss his work as non-Christian, because there was a point when he would have done the same thing to someone who sang lyrics such as his.

For as strongly as Bazan has come to despise the evangelical church and the business of Christianity, especially the Christian music industry, he's sympathetic, almost to a fault, when it comes to individual Christians. He's told me on a number of occasions that he considers his brief annual forays into evangelical culture a "missionary position," pun possibly not intended. I'm not totally convinced that these journeys are optional for him—like that of most recent converts, Bazan's zeal to undo what he sees as the destructive, manipulative part of his childhood seems irresistible.

I don't think it's as simple that, in a culture that knows from messiahs, Bazan's become an alternate savior. He's got a sizable cult following in the non-Christian world, too, where his songs have proved universal enough to people struggling with more than just faith. But for those kids in their rooms feeling stupid about speaking in tongues, Pedro the Lion is plangent in a way that, say, Relient K never could be. Whether it's Bazan's empathy for those who came up the same way he did or the thrill of hearing a marginally sanctioned heretic (let's not forget that the root of the word *heretic* is the Greek noun *haireses,* meaning the action of making a choice) who's somehow still allowed inside the Christian cloister, Bazan's become a leading figure in alternative Christian culture because he's a reflection of those who can't square their desire to believe with their contempt for the system in which they find fellowship.

You can take the boy out of evangelism, but you can't take evangelism out of the boy. Bazan seems to have dedicated a sizable part of his career to leading his listeners out of the desert of certainty, preaching the gospel of doubt.

David Bazan's castle is made of wood. It doesn't belong to him; he, Ann, and Ella rent the ground floor from their friend Ben, who once played in Pedro the Lion but mostly devotes his time now to fixing up the castle. It's a beautiful spot, with a creek favored by ducks, egrets, and frogs (which, Bazan told me, drive everyone nuts during mating season) running through the backyard and friendly Clydesdales sauntering over to the fence from the farm next door.

Before we got to the castle, Bazan asked me to stop at a motel in Poulsbo where Pedro's then drummer was staying and, according to Bazan, smoking a ton of pot while he worked up the nerve to ask his wife for a divorce. The drummer had come up from California and was getting ready to call his missus back home in California and break it to her. The band was scheduled to rehearse for a couple days before heading down to Texas for the South by Southwest music festival.

Pedro the Lion is essentially a two-man band at this point. Tim "TW" Walsh was a software engineer from Boston when he became intrigued by a review of *It's Hard to Find a Friend* in a fanzine. It sounded to him like Bazan was doing what Walsh hoped to do with music, so he sent a demo to Made in Mexico, which eventually agreed to put out Walsh's first album. After a long courtship during which TW Walsh (his nom de guerre) opened for Pedro, Bazan asked Walsh to join Pedro the Lion temporarily. It happened at a good time since the dot-com crash had rendered Walsh unemployed. Now, he and Bazan are Pedro the Lion's only constants. They treat their band like any full-time job, practicing and recording every weekday from nine to five (Walsh and his family have, obviously, since relocated to Washington). Any other members of the group, like this drummer, are essentially hired guns.

Bazan was skeptical of his drummer's plan to fly home, divorce his wife, drive around in the California desert all night, and hop an early flight to be ready for practice on Monday, but he dutifully stopped at an ATM to get the guy $200 (he never did return to the band). Later on, after we'd done some more interviewing around Bazan's dining room table, he and I went out for beer. He was hosting a birthday party that evening for yet another former Pedro the Lion drummer, and while Ann seemed to have preparations firmly in hand, she'd put Dave in charge of the libations.

For a state that's got a fairly effete reputation, Washington becomes geometrically more *Cops* than *Frazier* the farther you get from Seattle. In the lot of the convenience store where we stopped, guys were chugging freshly purchased beers in their trucks while moms in their late teens herded outsized broods around the aisles. (Die-hard blue-state haters will be relieved to know that the store nevertheless sold a range of truffles.)

A twelve-pack of Olympia in hand, we returned to the house, and Bazan told me that Ann had been campaigning to go back to church now that they had Ella. I asked him if he'd be able to manage that, and he said he wasn't sure. When I'd met Bazan the year before, he'd told me he could no longer consider himself a Christian because of the cultural implications of the word. You don't have to spend too long with the guy, however, to realize that his faith is a lot more solid than he lets on.

You wouldn't necessarily know it from his take on morality: that it's an outgrowth of good ol' American pragmatism. When we first talked at Cornerstone, after I'd asked him whether he was going to perform the song "Foregone Conclusions," the one in which the word *fuck* is a lyric, he told me, fittingly, a parable: "If I put a needle into my arm there are repercussions to that. I complicate my life in a way that could cause me irreparable harm. To say the word *fuck*, it's simply a word that means *screw*, or *sex*, or is just an exclamation point. So, these ideas are irrelevant to my life, the idea that that word is inappropriate."

Bazan's feelings about fidelity are likewise grounded in practicality, not a small thing for a guy who spends a good deal of time away from his family among strangers who adore him. "It's a really good idea," he said about monogamy, which he views as a contract essential to the well-being of his marriage. He and Ann met in high school and both attended the same youth group. She's as reserved as he is loquacious, and when they got married (at twenty-three), Bazan's mother sat him down and told him, "You need to give her *a lot* of space. She can't adopt your ideas about things. It's a dangerous thing because you guys might come down on very opposite sides of things once you guys are tied together."

You get a better peek at David Bazan, reluctant Christian, when he explains why he doesn't buy into the view, modish in some evangelical circles, that women are biblically ordered to be subservient to men. "The major theme of the Gospels," he said, "is, if you wanna be the greatest, you must become the least. Jesus, the greatest person in God's kingdom, will be the servant of all. And if I want to look at Jesus' example of how to be the so-called head of my household, it's self-sacrifice and service—to the point of sacrificing all my potential to serve my wife. And it doesn't have anything to do with me telling her what to do. In my reading of it, there's no implication at all of a hierarchy."

Every time I've seen Pedro the Lion play for a Christian audience, someone in the crowd asks him whether he's still a Christian. I asked him why he always says no.

"There's sort of a qualifier," he said. "I'm not equating myself with Martin Luther by any stretch—but him and people that were part of his movements just stopped calling themselves 'Catholics.' I'd rather there just be a misunderstanding—'The guy's flipped out and totally abandoned his faith'—because it's not necessary for strangers to know exactly how I feel."

When we got back to the house, I asked to use the bathroom, where I noticed that Bazan doesn't unpack his toiletries, leaving them in an ever-ready travel bag. "You must want to spend more time at home," I put to him a few minutes later. "Obviously, you think the Christian music industry is bullshit. Why don't you just publicly renounce your doubting ways, sign to Sparrow for a million dollars, and then be home more?"

"I would have to be so medicated to do that," he said. "It would ruin my marriage; it would ruin Ella's life. That's something my parents instilled in us, just being honest about stuff. I really want Ella to be able to say, 'One thing my dad wasn't was a liar.'"

Steve Taylor

Nowadays, Steve Taylor is a pillar of the Nashville Christian music community, but there was a time when he was its Marilyn Manson, Dr. Demento, and Eminem rolled up in one. Taylor first started blowing toupees back with his *I Want to Be a Clone* EP in 1982, the title track of which lampooned unthinking, "assembly line" Christianity. But the then twenty-five-year-old Taylor was just as harsh on the secular world: in "Whatever Happened to Sin?" he blasts a country where "the closets are empty, and the clinics are full."

In *The Encyclopedia of Contemporary Christian Music,* Mark Allan Powell reckons that Taylor, who soon took on racism in the church, as well as moral relativism and euthanasia, managed to maintain a prominent place in the industry because he basically attacked the church from its right flank with "critiques . . . that do not question the basic assumptions that underlie some of the foibles of American Christianity."[2] Regardless, Taylor didn't choose an easy road for himself in the only genre where, as Powell also notes, controversy "tends to *hurt* sales."[3] His antics made him a hot potato for record companies, even though he sold lots of records for the time and was one of the genre's first real superstars.

Taylor took a break from the Christian music industry in 1991, when he moved to London and formed a group called Chagall Guevara, which signed to MCA in the general market. No experiment is a failure, but Chagall's self-titled debut certainly bombed, saleswise, despite good reviews from secular publications. Taylor returned uncowed to Christian music with the excellent *Squint* in '93. Inspired by albums like the Clash's *London Calling*, Taylor's insistence on first-class recording and playing, as well as his sharp wit, set a new standard for the often middling Christian market.

He also introduced Christians to the art of the remix, from the three versions of the title track on his first full LP, *Meltdown at Madame Tussaud's*, to an album of nothing but remixes in 1985. With his recording career ceasing to hold his attention, Taylor began to produce other artists, notably Newsboys, and direct music videos.

In 1992, Taylor founded his own record company, Squint Entertainment, where he signed Chevelle, L.A. Symphony, and Burlap to Cashmere. Squint really made its bones, however, with its first signing, Sixpence None the Richer, whose single "Kiss Me" went to No. 1 in ten countries, in no small part due to Taylor's ferocious championing of the band (pestering the single's way onto the *She's All That* soundtrack, for instance).

In one of those moves that must make sense to record executives, the successful label was wrested from Taylor's control by its corporate parent, Word, in 2001, and then shuttered, its bands distributed to other Word-owned labels or dropped, its unreleased records mostly shelved. Since then, Taylor's mostly devoted himself to film and production and completed his first major motion picture, *The Second Chance*, which was released through Sony Pictures Classics in February 2006. It stars Michael W. Smith as a pastor in a comfortable, predominantly white, Nashville evangelical church, who's forced to confront racial inequity within and without the church.

I spoke to Taylor as he was waiting to get his cars inspected.

It seems like your film is addressing something of an elephant in the room when it comes to American evangelical Christianity: race.

STEVE TAYLOR: Yeah. It's certainly an insider's peek. And, you know, I've actually found that most Christians I know don't mind being criticized. They go to church every Sunday to hear a sermon, usually directed at them! They don't especially like it coming from the outside.

That was sort of how you made your mark on Christian music in the beginning.

In some regards, that's kind of my MO.

Do you think the appreciation of criticism is genuine?

As far as fellow Christians? Yeah, because the Bible is full of stories of people who God used in spite of their faults. And, as Christians, you know, we believe that we are sinners saved by grace and Christ's atoning work, so it's always an odd thing when you see a Christian maybe who works within the public eye who comes off as arrogant. And it's particularly troubling when maybe you see a talk show host or something like that who, uh . . .

Calls for the assassination of a world leader? [Televangelist Pat Robertson had urged the U.S. to "take out" Venezuelan prime minister Hugo Chavez a few days before we spoke.]

Yeah! Well, exactly. Because it's so completely at odds with the Gospel message, and I guess, to his credit, [Robertson] apologized, whereas some people wouldn't bother to apologize. You know, you could sort of excuse it from people with other points of view, but Christians, we really don't have any excuse for that kind of behavior.

Are you very politically minded?

I've always had a very strong pro-life viewpoint, but as far as politics in general go, I've kind of stayed more apolitical—just because political affiliations invariably involve a lot of compromises and a lot of alliances, and, usually, you throw your hat in the ring and stay with somebody, and they disappoint you. I certainly wouldn't consider myself a very politically engaged person outside of those areas where the Bible speaks really specifically and strongly to me. And those would be pro-life areas and also peace and justice and helping the poor. So, my political views don't usually end up sitting very well in either party.

Do you know the band Pedro the Lion?

I don't know David, but I'm real familiar with them.

He told me that one of your songs really affected him when he was a kid, "Sin for a Season." He didn't even want to play it for his parents because he was worried it might be too ambiguous.

Oh, right!

He grew up in a really strict home. You were a real turning-point artist for him, apparently.

Huh. That's a high compliment because I really like his lyrics.

Were you allowed to listen to secular music growing up?

No. In fact, I didn't have a radio till I was fifteen or sixteen.

Holy mackerel. You were a music major, right?

Yeah, in college. That's not to say we weren't musical. I would listen to Top 40. The DJ at the Top 40 station was real kind of arch and opinionated. He would play certain songs and say, 'Frankly, I hate this song, but . . ." Even though I didn't know that much, I still became a really opinionated guy! As I've told people, I didn't get fully musically engaged until [the Clash's] *London Calling.* A real turning point for me.

You said in a documentary I saw [Why Should the Devil Have All the Good Music?] *that* London Calling *really changed your life.*

I was still musically minded, but that was the thing that made me wanna get serious.

So you got saved, so to speak. And when you started making music, you were almost immediately controversial.

It would be a little disingenuous of me to say I don't know why. The songs weren't done with the intent to offend, but I had a feeling they would be controversial, just because there was no satire to speak of in Christian music at the time.

Was it commercial suicide?

There was a song on a later record called "I Blew Up the Clinic Real Good." It was probably satirical. [*It was about an ice cream man who destroys an abortion clinic to ensure future customers.*] I'm not even totally sure it was such a good idea in retrospect, but I remember I was on a tour in Australia, and some kind of Geraldo-type guy in Australia picked up on and started doing these attacks on the song. This guy would come into town, like, "This needs to be stopped!" and I ended up being on Australia's version of the *Today Show* saying it was a satirical song.

Conventional wisdom would say, "What a godsend for a tour!" And every date ended up being canceled except for the Sydney date! It was a disaster! So, yeah, that's where I realized that old saw "any publicity is good publicity" doesn't work in Christian music.

What about that early stuff—do you like it now?

Well, I don't like any of my work, particularly, because the more I've got into producing, the harder it is to pull yourself out and listen to these things with any kind of objectivity. I'm like, 'That's a stupid sound. What was I thinking?' And plus, you know, like, maybe every other song lyrically feels like, that feels pretty good, but a lot of them, they were just so much specific to their time, and now they seem either dated or melodramatic, or there's a verse that I wish I wouldn't have put in, so I really just have nothing but regrets!

Your production career seemed to mark the rehabilitation of Steve Taylor.

Well, the producing has been a strange trajectory, because I followed up. I dabbled in it a little bit, particularly with my own stuff, coproduced things, and had done one really obscure record in England right before we started Chagall Guevara.

It was right when the band—we hadn't broken up yet, but we were trying to get out of our MCA deal, which led me to producing a Newsboys album. And, you know, originally just helping them out on some lyrics turned into a full-blown production, and it was very much a pop production. And what they needed lyrically was, generally speaking, not something that I would have done with my own records. But, on the one hand, it was great fun and a great experience as more of a craftsman I suppose—

I imagine in some way it's like taking you out of the equation.

In some way it was. Because there would be songs, most of these songs were songs I would never have done for my own records. But, on the other hand, I really loved doing it. One of the difficulties of being an artist is that, no matter how hard you try, you still get boxed in by your past work. And if you totally ignore that, you do so at your own peril. I remember a string of records Neil Young did in the '80s where there was a rockabilly record, one was an electronic record—what are you this month? But, at the same time, [he was] learning how to make records and learning how to use the studio to full effect, learning to become a better musician in the process.

You've had an impact on secular music, too, particularly modern rock.

I would call it, maybe, a moderate impact, but hey, I'll go along with you!

Stick with me kid!

When I was doing the Squint label, when I felt like a band had real talent, I was just really passionate about bands that I thought were great. And, certainly, Sixpence was a band like that. And Chevelle was a band like that.

This hip-hop collective L.A. Symphony—that record never got released. We had Will from Black-Eyed Peas do four of the tracks, before, you know, Black Eyed Peas got ruined by that chick singer! And Prince Paul produced a track, but beyond all that, they were fantastic rappers; they were just, like, writing some of the best lyrics I was hearing anywhere. So, I don't miss the record business at all. And I don't really miss running a record label. But I miss that sense of, you know, when you find a really great talent, you wanna do whatever you can to get the world to hear it.

But that's almost an unproductive attitude in the music industry.

Yeah, it's not a commonly held belief. Part of the reason of having a record label where I controlled its destiny was because the frustration of making a good record, and the *Squint* record is the one record I made that I can still listen to, and having, in that case, what appears to be a relationship with Warner Bros., and the possibility of getting it heard further, and just coming up against brick walls that had nothing more than people deciding, 'Well, that's not my department." And it's really frustrating.

Did you ever feel that being a Christian ever kept you from more mainstream acceptance?

Probably nobody would have articulated that as such, but yeah, I think that's true. A lot of Christian artists use that as an excuse for not making good music, but you still are dealing with a certain amount of prejudice, mostly along the lines of the kind of old school belief that rock 'n' roll is primarily about rebellion, and how can a Christian be rebellious?

But I do think—and part of it's because, frankly, I could have held out for a few more years and waited to get signed to a mainstream label, but the early response came from a Christian label, and at that point, in the '80s, nobody knew how separate the two worlds would become in the next few years. And now, of course, we live in an age where they're less separate, actually.

Things do seem to be converging. Obviously, one of the bigger innovations has been better quality.

Right. I think also—you know, when I was touring, we were playing in theaters. I kind of had a rule not to play in churches, but even if I wanted to play in churches, there weren't that many churches that would have had us. And that's really changed, and now there's almost, like, a circuit of churches and church gymnasiums and things like that where these bands played. And so, a lot of them are frankly better than their mainstream counterparts. They can play better; they've had more road experience. In the '80s, the flavor of the year one year was signing Australian bands, and it was because all these bands were growing up playing in pubs in Australia, and they were better bands. Part of the problem in America is, if you're a young band, you can't really play in clubs because they won't let you in if you're under eighteen. So, this circuit for Christian rock bands developed [and] allowed bands to actually get good.

It almost reminds me of the punk underground when I was a kid. Do you stay in touch with that scene?

I don't at all. My answer would so completely be based on ignorance. I know there's a lot of good bands around, I'm just not listening to it. I've gotten to where I actually enjoy music again, which—

Oh, man. I am so jealous of you.

Well, that's it! When you work in it, it's almost impossible to enjoy it because you're kind of evaluating everything as you listen to it. But, like, my favorite album of the last year is the Arcade Fire. And there's a great indie record store in town where I'll just go and say, "Tell me what's good." They'll load me up.

Do you ever get besieged by crazed Christian rock fans?

I still get a lot of CDs and demos. I just went through another stack the other day because I felt bad about not listening to them. But I don't have a way for people to e-mail me.

It was hard for me to find you!

I know, I know. There's a guy in Memphis who does a fan website, and I think once in a while he'll forward me something.

What would it take for you to start doing music again?

It probably would take a long stretch of open time, and a complete failure of this movie, frankly.

Is movie-making where it's at for you now?

That was always kind of the idea. Even when I was in college, I studied music as a major and film as an undeclared minor. And I was doing some short films in college and right out of college. I figured I'd get into film sooner or later. As I got going, I kind of felt like music was kind of a younger person's game, and that film, I might actually benefit from accumulating a certain amount of years and wisdom before I jumped too seriously into that. So, you know, I still dabble in music videos and things like that. But that was kind of my long-range plan, to get into filmmaking.

So, what's your next film?

Well, the next project, I'm hoping it's just a straight comedy. I gotta start raising money for it. The script's almost done. I think it's funny. It seems funny to me and the guys writing it. When we were doing *The Second Chance*, the editor's one of the cowriters, and I kept telling him, 'You know, if this was a comedy, I'd know exactly what to do with this." So, that's, hopefully that'll be the next movie. And then, after that, I'd love to do something—outside of being as hopefully funny as it is, no spiritual themes or anything like that. But then, I'd like to do another movie after that that would be a more logical follow-up to *The Second Chance*.

You don't want to be known as a Christian filmmaker, too.

No, you know, it's weird. 'Cause if I had a chance, what would I do differently? And my original plan was to do the comedy first. But I planned another movie prior to that, and I just couldn't get the script right. In the meantime, you know, you're supposed to write about what you know, and I started writing this script with some other friends that became *The Second Chance,* and you kind of go with whatever project seems to have the juice behind it, and that was how this one was.

So, in a perfect world, I might have started with the comedy first. But I think, in retrospect, the movie I just finished, I can make mistakes, and it wouldn't be fatal. And with comedy, there's just very little room for error. If people don't laugh, you're in big, big trouble.

CHAPTER 5

Clarity

The light is different on the West Coast. I'm sure of it. Everything is . . . *clearer* somehow, and dusk falls with a romantic glow. I'm not feeling terribly romantic, though, because I'm circling a large warehouse-style building at sunset in Seattle's Ballard neighborhood, looking for a place to park. It's 5 PM on a Sunday evening, and I'm late for church.

As skateboarders jump over stuff in the parking lot, young families with better excuses than I—try getting *anywhere* on time with a baby, pal—quick-step past the corrugated aluminum walls toward ushers who seem to disappear just as I run panting up to the doors of Mars Hill Church.

Inside, the nave is exquisitely minimal, like the type of nightclub in which pro athletes party after games. The ceiling, as well as its numerous cables and rigging, is painted matte black. The walls are beige with taupe accents, and oversize parchment lamp shades hang in a huge grid over the nave, softening the lights within. There are no crosses anywhere, but there are plenty of video screens. The sanctuary is a big stage, basically, and a rock band is playing when I walk in. The music is really quite loud. The members of the six-piece group—piano player with a voice like Michelle Branch, bassist, guitarist, drummer, and two backup singers—are all dressed, as is most of the congregation, as if they were going to see Weezer. In fact, the bassist kind of looks like Rivers Cuomo.

After the band tears through a couple of ear-splitting worship numbers, Pastor Mark Driscoll ambles onstage. He, too, is dressed casually, but with a whiff of spiff; his sideburns and polite pompadour make him look like a slightly older emo dude, say, one whose serious job means he can't go out on weeknights anymore, but whose ironic greaser style and winning grin imply he can still tear it up on the weekends.

"You guys wanna see some baptisms?" he asks, grinning. Everyone claps. A barefoot young man named Andrew walks onstage wearing a bathing suit and a T-shirt. He gives his testimony—grew up in a semi-Christian home and drifted away (his pastor became an insurance salesman, which he notes was "a bit of a switch"), but he's been living in a Christian group house for a while and leading Bible studies, and he's ready to rededicate his life to Christ.

He walks over to a pool at stage right, where a camera over the pool shows two guys awaiting him.

"Love the bapto-cam," Driscoll stage-whispers.

"Do you accept Jesus Christ as your personal savior?" one of the men in the pool asks Andrew, who's now standing between them, his hands on their shoulders.

"Yes," he says.

"Then be baptized, brother."

They dunk Andrew, who emerges to applause from the fifteen hundred in attendance. There's another baptism, then Driscoll clears some business off the schedule.

"Here's our new building," he says, as a slide of another warehouse appears above him. "What a dump!" He explains that Mars Hill has outgrown even this cavernous space and will move to the new digs as soon as they can raise enough money to finish the deal and refurbish the space. There's a quarter million from some land they sold. Four million lined up from the bank. And the rest?

"Three million is going to come from you," he says, and nobody gasps, or applauds, or seems to think this is remarkable at all. In fact, Driscoll says it so matter-of-factly that it's hard for me not to feel like a small-timer.

That's because Mark Driscoll makes most pastors look maladroit at best. In the nine years since Driscoll founded Mars Hill, the congregation has swelled from twelve members to about thirty-seven hundred. There are four services every Sunday just to keep up with demand. That's pretty remarkable anywhere, not least in what Driscoll calls the "least churched city in America, except for San Francisco."

To attract people in such hostile territory, Mars Hill has consciously buffed off some of evangelicalism's sharper edges. The crowd is young—average age twenty-five—and hip. Women wear short skirts. Men have bleached hair and tattoos. There aren't any Lincoln Continentals parked outside, and no one's belt matches his shoes. Advertising executives would slide naked down a splintery board to reach these people. And the message they're nodding their well-coiffed heads to?

Dating is prostitution. You should probably get married, definitely to another Christian and, if possible, via a church-and-family supervised courtship. Arranged marriages are not such a bad idea.

"The more that we continue to drink from the toilet," Driscoll preaches, referring to modern ideas about pitching woo, which he's already traced back, in an engaging and humorous manner, to women's magazines at the turn of the twentieth century, "the sicker we become, and the thirst is not quenched. I would like to just first establish that the way everyone else does it is wrong. We can argue it biblically; we can just look at it practically. We can look at the results and say, 'Do you want an average life like the average person?' No.

Why? 'Cause it's destruction and death and heartache and disease and abortion and nightmare and folly and sadness and grief. It's not good. God's word is true and helpful. That's what I'm trying to say."

Probably only a preacher as charismatic as Mark Driscoll could successfully preach the virtues of abstinence and getting hitched to a crowd decked out in Abercrombie and Fitch. But Driscoll, who in his profile on the Mars Hill website lists "red wine and red meat" as two of his favorite things, is the kind of guy American evangelicals have increasingly come to depend on to reach a generation that has never known a world without the Internet. Driscoll told the *Seattle Times* that he learned pacing and timing from Eddie Murphy and Sam Kinison records, but the content of his preaching is even more influenced by pop culture.

When I saw him preach, Driscoll dropped references to the Hilton sisters, Hooters restaurants, and guys who play way too much Xbox without ever sounding like *Saved!*'s Pastor Skip, who never misses a chance to drop some opportunistic sizzle into his sermonizzle. In fact, Mars Hill, Driscoll told me a week later when we spoke on the phone, was named for a place in Athens where the Apostle Paul used the words of contemporary poets and musicians in an attempt to convert non-Christians.

"He went to a cool place with some culturally connected people," Driscoll told me. "He got involved in an arty conversation, and that's definitely more what our church is about."

Because of his surroundings, Driscoll said, being hip isn't a luxury. "We're in a place that's not Christian, we're talking to people who aren't Christian, and their primary concern is culture and art, creativity and music, and we have to be conversant in that language."

Mark Driscoll is thirty-five and grew up behind a strip club in the seedy environs of Sea-Tac International Airport. Raised Roman Catholic, he converted to evangelical Christianity at Washington

State University, where he studied communications. "It was one of those weird deals where God spoke to me and told me to be a pastor, so that's what I decided to do," he said. He and his high school sweetheart, Grace, whom he married when he was twenty-one, worked at a church for a year before starting the Bible study that grew into the juggernaut that is Mars Hill.

Driscoll was nonchalant as he rattled off statistics—a characteristic of his sermons as well—about Mars Hill's astonishing growth. "There are about 425,000 Protestant churches in America. Only 425 of those are 3,000 or more on a Sunday. And out of those, we're one of the forty fastest-growing."

Besides Driscoll, Mars Hill employs seven pastors and has twelve deacons and four worship bands. It runs an all-ages club, the Paradox Theater, and is starting a record label. Driscoll writes a column for the *Seattle Times,* has written a well-regarded book called *The Radical Reformission: Reaching Out without Selling Out,* and has co-founded a "church-planting" organization called Acts 29. He says he sleeps "not a ton." As you can probably imagine, Mars Hill's website is a thing of beauty.

And the church's sound system? Don't get him started. It was custom built for the room—a former hardware store, incidentally—by an audio engineer who also designs sound for Broadway and Las Vegas shows. Driscoll waxes rhapsodic about the system's Meyer cabinets, in-ear wireless monitors, and three soundboards, and he enthusiastically describes how they used a Sims analyzer to "dial-in" even coverage—as "opposed to a normal rock show where you've got all your speakers up front just blowing to the back, there's consistent sound at every inch of the room."

That's why Mars Hill's worship bands sound so loud and crystalline, which is an inspiration for the groups to step up their game a little bit. Unlike a lot of modern churches, Mars Hill doesn't pay to present the worship hits of the day—it writes its own. Hence, the new record label, Floodlight, which may also become a home for some of the musicians in the audience.

Not that Driscoll's much of a Christian rock fan. In fact, he doesn't like it at all. "We tend to be more mainstream indie rock fans" at the church, he said. "Death Cab for Cutie, Modest Mouse, Karate—that's definitely more what I'm into. I'd much rather have our bands signed to regular labels, in regular bars and clubs."

Among all this hypermodernity, Driscoll preaches a return to a biblical, "godly way of doing things," which he doesn't see as a conflict with his pop-culture-saturated lifestyle.

"In the Bible," Driscoll told me in a follow-up interview conducted, naturally, via e-mail, "we are told to be culturally relevant, love people who disagree with our Christian beliefs, and have friends and fun like Jesus did. Jesus was often invited to parties by scandalous people, was surrounded with large crowds who liked hanging with him, and was accused by stuffed shirt religious types of eating too much, drinking too much, and having the wrong kind of friends. But, Jesus never sinned. For example, he drank alcohol but did not get drunk, ate a lot but was not a glutton, and had some messed-up friends but never shagged any of the loose women who considered him a friend. In short, Jesus was essentially hip and holy for his day and wants us to be hip and holy, too, in our day."

But that should by no means be taken as an endorsement of an anything-goes view of society, especially when it comes to gender roles. Driscoll's taken a lot of criticism for his views on women's biblically inferior role to men. "If I could change one part of the Bible," he told the *Seattle Times*, "that would be the part, just so I could be left alone."[1]

On first glance, this facet of Driscoll's theology would seem to be box office poison, especially in a church with lots of hip young women. But when I saw Driscoll preach that Sunday, I saw nothing but heads nodding in agreement when he delivered this part of his homily:

I'm not telling my daughters, "Sit there till [the right man for you] comes." You ladies live your lives, but, but, *but,* expect your life to be completely interrupted when your husband comes along. . . . Different place, different family, different friends, *different.* Paul says this in First Corinthians, he says the man is not made for the woman, the woman is made for the man. Says in Genesis that the woman is supposed to be the helper for the man. So ladies, live your life—if a guy comes along that you wanna marry, you're gonna jump tracks, you're gonna roll with him, whatever he's doing, work, church, wherever he lives, that's where you're gonna be. A lot of ladies say "I don't wanna do that." *Then don't get married.* If you like the guy and where he's rollin', roll with him. If not, just keep rolling on your own."

Back in my hotel room, I looked up the passage in First Corinthians that Driscoll had mentioned. "But I want you to understand that Christ is the head of every man, and the husband is the head of his wife, and God is the head of Christ," the Apostle Paul wrote.[2] Well, that does seem pretty unambiguous, I thought. Then I read on. In the next two verses, Paul says that men can't wear hats when they pray, that women should remain veiled "to have a symbol of authority on her head,"[3] and that it's "degrading"[4] for men to have long hair.

Well, if Willie Nelson isn't getting into heaven, I thought, I don't want to be there either. I e-mailed Driscoll to ask him about this, too. "Can you just pick and choose what parts of the Bible you want to obey?" I asked. Here's what he wrote back:

Some parts of the Bible easily translate into our culture because there are cultural correlations. An example would be not getting drunk, or being nice to your enemies. But, sometimes our culture is so different than the culture that existed at the time the Bible was written that we need to pull from the Bible a timeless principle and then apply it to our culture. For example, in I Corinthians 11 women were told not to shave their heads or walk around without a head covering. In that culture only prostitutes did that. But, today nobody thinks a woman is a prostitute if she has short hair or no scarf on her head. So, the principle is that a Christian woman should not dress in such a way as to be perceived as a prostitute. If Paul were writing today he may instead say that a woman should not have her thong underwear hanging out of her low cut jeans, wear clear heels, or have a stainless steel pole in her living room if she is a Christian unless of course she is married and only wears the thong and heels to dance around the pole for her husband, in which case he's a happy Christian man and she is not sinning.

I'm not a theologian, so I can't address the validity of this argument with any sort of authority. To my amateur eyes, it raises another question: why isn't the bit about husbands being in charge of their wives a reflection of outdated mores too? I think Driscoll would say that's an easily translatable principle. But the interesting thing here isn't the argument so much as the fact that a growing number of young women and young men in Seattle find Driscoll's thoughts on these matters persuasive. He's not luring them in with skateboard videos and slang; he's touching on something that resonates with these kids.

There is a movement in evangelical Christianity that encourages women to revel in their biblical role as helpmates. Proverbs 31 Ministries is closely aligned with the Promise Keepers, a phenomenally successful ministry for men whose CEO, Bill McCartney, believes that men should take the "spiritual lead" in their marriages. A Proverbs 31 woman, according to the organization, "loves, honors and respects her husband as the leader of the home" (Proverbs 31:10–31 catalogs a wife's ideal qualities).

In an article Grace Driscoll wrote on the website for Acts 29, a church-planting network cofounded by her husband, Mark, she calls the strictures of submission a "privilege that we can either embrace from the Lord or reject in sin."[5] Or, as her husband told the *Seattle Times*, "It's pretty much take it or leave it."

The kids in Seattle were taking it. Mars Hill is a rock of certainty in an uncertain world, albeit one with a kickass sound system and a worship band so loud my ears were ringing as I walked out into the balmy March night. No pastors were at the door to greet people as they left—I suppose that's a practical impossibility with so many parishioners—and while groups of friends met up here and there, most people just headed for their cars and went home. It's almost like a Home Depot model for a church. You go in, get what you need, and leave. If a project is too big, you can ask for help, and someone on staff will show you what you need to tackle it yourself.

Heck, look at the buildings themselves, I mused, continuing the thought. They're essentially fungible—this former warehouse will do until a bigger, better one becomes available. I have no doubt that the new Mars Hill will be as artfully minimal as the next, with lots of muted colors, video screens and no cross (evangelicals tend to take the whole no-graven-images thing pretty seriously). That's the kind of thing that freaks out Catholics and "mainline" Protestants—Episcopalians, Lutherans, Presbyterians—especially.

The ceilings of old-fashioned churches suggest heaven via soaring arches or opulent paintings. The ceiling of Mars Hill says "Why are you looking at the ceiling? It's just a bunch of cables." Mars Hill's message comes from the front of the house, but it's dialed in so that it diffuses through the congregation and, like the light in the city it serves, comes through clear as a bell.

CHAPTER 6

Drinking Blood Out of Skulls, Living High in the Kingdom of Death, and a New Way to Be Christian

I decided to drive to Grand Rapids, Michigan, where I would attend Calvin College's Festival of Faith and Music. This mode of travel came down to thriftiness—my trip to Seattle had eaten up about a quarter of my budget for the book, and a flight to Grand Rapids would have left me with very little room for error in the future. So, I decided to make a few days of it and gather my thoughts in the process.

I left on the day Terri Schiavo died, and between discs of the audiobook of *The Da Vinci Code*, which I had finally remembered to buy because the Vatican had come out against it a few days earlier, I tuned in to right-wing talk radio.

The vitriol amazed me. One woman called in to say she was praying, as was most of her church, that Schiavo's autopsy would show that her husband had abused her. I thought that demonstrated how strange this debate had become—it was somehow okay to pray that Schiavo had been abused and starved to death? The host, with the brutal rabidity exclusive to small-market members of his profession, agreed wholeheartedly.

It was also three days before Pope John Paul II died, and the media's death vigil was swinging from prurient to ghoulish. It seemed like a good weekend to think about religion's place in society.

Calvin College is nestled in a lovely campus between the Wal-Mart belt on the edge of Grand Rapids and the city's revitalizing downtown, home to bars, cute shops, and apartments in former furniture factories. Grand Rapids is also the American center of Dutch Reformed Calvinism in all its incredibly confusing flavors. Besides that, it's hard not to be intrigued by a town that produced Gerald Ford, Chico DeBarge, and Andy Richter.

I'd heard about the Festival of Faith and Music from Paul Goode, a friend in Richmond who's tight with a rangy scene of Christian musicians affiliated with the Asthmatic Kitty and Sounds Familyre record labels. Both companies are owned, at least in part, by a singer/songwriter: the former by Sufjan Stevens and the latter by Daniel Smith. In the past few years, quietly, each of these men has built a bigger audience outside the Christian subculture than within it, even while singing explicitly about faith. I was keen to see them outside of a nightclub, in front of an audience that didn't view their lyrics as quaint, or as an abstraction.

Before I left for Grand Rapids, I spent a couple frustrating days trying to set up an interview with Stevens, whose most recent record, *Seven Swans,* I'd reviewed enthusiastically for the *Washington City Paper.* Through his publicist, Stevens declined. This had already happened to me a couple times with artists who'd moved out of the Christian music world to some degree, and I wasn't sure whether Stevens' flack was running interference, especially since he signed off with "Sufjan is really not Christian rock." So, I e-mailed back, asking whether Stevens had any specific concerns, saying I'd be glad to address them. I wasn't writing a book merely about Christian rock, I insisted. Christians making rock music was going to be just as much a focus.

Silence. Then a note saying he was "talking it over" with Stevens and would get back to me soon. I hadn't heard anything since.

Paul Goode had given me a DVD for Mike Kaufmann, Asthmatic Kitty's associate director, who, when we met up in the lobby of Calvin's Fine Arts building, told me that Sufjan "usually says no to everything" but that he really wanted to try to get him to talk to me. I told him not to bother because it was all getting a bit silly, really. I don't see the point of doing interviews with people who'd rather be elsewhere. Kaufmann mentioned that dinner with Stevens and a few others was a possibility, and I said that would be fine.

Kaufmann introduced me to John Ringhofer, another Asthmatic Kitty artist, and suggested that the two of us walk around together. So, we did, awkwardly at first, like people on a blind date. I'd never heard his music but guessed it would be much like Ringhofer himself, an implausibly gentle fellow who was as enthusiastic about the first Beatles record he had heard as a child as he was about the fact that I, a total stranger, had recently become a father.

Back in the Fine Arts building, Ken Heffner, Calvin's director of student activities, opened the festival with a short speech and then prayed for God to look after music and pop culture, which he called "all Your works." Then, he introduced David Dark, the festival's keynote speaker, who started his presentation with a prayer of his own "to calm my own agitatedness."

That "agitatedness" was quickly on display. With his wild, curly hair, big glasses, and tendency to jump from quotation to quotation, Dark comes off like a slightly demented high school English teacher from Tennessee. Which, as it happens, he is. David Bazan, who was due to give a presentation at the festival the next day, had told me he was a huge fan of Dark's books, especially his new one, *The Gospel According to America.*

Dark's speech was a meditation on a quote from Jack Kerouac: "And so I struggle in the dark with the enormity of my soul, trying desperately to be a great rememberer, light from darkness."

And that's pretty much all I understood. The next forty minutes were a whirlwind of allusions and quotes from Norman Mailer, Acts 2, U2's *The Joshua Tree,* Cornelius (the first Gentile convert to Christianity), Dave Eggers, Keats, Chesterton, and Bruce Cockburn. At one point, Dark posited that without what he calls "Jewish-Christian values," we'd all be "drinking blood out of skulls in the woods," but honestly, I can't tell you how he got there. I simply lacked the cultural context to decipher Dark's lecture, which reminded me of the completely inscrutable record reviews that *Spin* used to run when I first started working there in the late '90s. I was always sure that they were often works of art in their own way, but I rarely had any idea what the writers were saying.

What I could gather as Dark's central thesis, and I hope he'll forgive me if I've gotten this wrong, is that there's no harm in Christians engaging popular culture—in fact, it's "probably blasphemous" to think there's such a thing as a "secular molecule in the universe," since everything is shaped by God.

During the question-and-answer period that followed, I noticed a prevailing skepticism among the Calvin students regarding the convergence of conservative Christianity and politics in the U.S. Already this wasn't what I'd been expecting. I hadn't heard a single word about Terri Schiavo, the pope, or even *The Da Vinci Code.* I'd come completely unprepared.

We broke for workshops, and I decided to attend Ken Heffner's, called "Holy Worldliness—Culture and the Problem of Evil," figuring that I'd easily get some fire and brimstone there. Again, I was unprepared. Heffner called the concept of holy worldliness "a small, elegant oxymoron" and then began to argue persuasively for his reading of Jesus' instructions for the delicate dance of being in the world but not of it.

We are in rebellion against God, Heffner announced, and as a result we will die a horrific, "threefold" death: Creation will die, we will die, and God—in the form of Jesus—will die. Until Jesus returns, the Kingdom of God and the Kingdom of Death (which I inappropriately noted to myself would make a completely ruling name for a metal band) will do battle.

The Puritans, Heffner said, thought Europe was the Kingdom of Death. But death, he said, is all around us. The "problem of evil," he argued, is "not in certain activities," such as making art. "Popular culture," Heffner announced, "is not the problem. But the problem is in pop culture."

Drawing on Dark's keynote, Heffner said we should look for the Kingdom of God everywhere. The answer to the problem of the Kingdom of Death, he said, is to be in the world but not of it. "Has forming Christian pop culture solved the problem?" he asked. "You're less safe when you think you're safe."

Then he did something interesting. He played the Christian band MercyMe's 2001 crossover hit "I Can Only Imagine," a meditation on what heaven might be like: Will the singer dance for Jesus? Will he fall to his knees? Will he just worship Him all the livelong day?

"Please, if you're going to use pop music," Heffner said, turning off the song after the verse and chorus repeated, "use all three minutes. Okay, what's right with this song?"

"Mournfulness," one student suggested.

"It pitches the possibilities of heaven," said another.

"That's pretty good," said Heffner. "There's a kind of creativity in that. Is heaven really going to be a chronic worship service going on forever?" This brought a lot of laughs.

"Okay, so what's wrong with it?" he continued. For one, it's clichéd, he said, pointing to the piano glissando that flits throughout the song as a particular offender. But the main problem with "I Can Only Imagine," Heffner said, was that "for a song about imagination, it is so unimaginative."

Then, Heffner played "Candy," a song by folksinger Martin Sexton about a woman who "needs another lover like she needs another dose in her blood" but who's Sexton's "lost angel," someone he "just can't let go."

"Candy is a hooker," Heffner said. "She's objectified, and he's showing mercy. He's showing redemption, even if he doesn't know why. Christians should bring what they're doing into the world." Discernment, he said, was the key to enjoying so-called secular culture.

One of the students, who attended a smaller Christian college than Calvin, said he was frustrated by his college's restrictive booking policy for musicians—everyone who appeared at the school had to be especially safe. "This makes me feel great," he said about the conference, "but what happens when I get back to school with my green notebook?" indicating where he'd been jotting down Heffner's words.

"Come on, this brother needs help here," Heffner said after no one spoke. He advised the student to start small, booking artists such as Derek Webb, the former singer of CCM favorites Caedmon's Call, whose solo work is considerably more nuanced, spiritually, than that of his former band.

I enjoyed the seminar, but I left the room wondering whether I'd just driven seven hundred fifty miles to hear Christian kids get the okay to listen to Eminem.

The issue of "the world" is one with particular resonance in Christianity, which has a rich tradition of duality, beginning with the paradox that Jesus was fully human and fully divine. To accept Jesus as savior is to put "the world" aside—not just literally but also figuratively. The world is out there, full of sin and temptation, but it's also your sinful nature, the part of you that looks at porn and ignores homeless people and cheats on taxes. Both must be guarded against. The First Letter of John urges Christians "not to love the world or the things in the world" because "the world and its desire are passing away, but those who do the will of God live forever."[1]

But then there's the "Great Commission," the mandate in Matthew 28:19 to "make disciples of all nations." Which is kind of difficult to do if you're holed up in your compound in Idaho growing your own food until the Rapture comes.

Debate over how to navigate this antinomy has consumed theologians for a long time. In *Mine Eyes Have Seen the Glory*, Randall Ballmer relates the story of how a British theologian named John Nelson Darby captured the imagination of nineteenth-century American evangelicals battered by German "higher criticism," which cast doubt on the very origin of most Scripture, and Darwin's theory of natural selection, which, if it were true, meant a literal reading of the Bible is impossible.

Darby formulated a theory called "dispensational premillennialism." This approach is based on his belief that the Bible divides history into seven periods marked by covenants between man and God. Darby figured that, based on clues in the Bible, we are now in the penultimate period before Jesus will return and take believers with him to heaven in a Rapture. Following a seven-year "tribulation," they will reign with Christ for a thousand years before the final battle between God and Satan preceding Judgment Day.

This imminent sense of doom, besides eventually creating a massive market for the *Left Behind* books, was taken by American followers of Darby to mean that, while it's still important to try to bring people to Christ, it's just as important for Christians to make sure they themselves are ready. Hence, the idea of a personal relationship with Christ being crucial to salvation—after all, anyone whose house is built on sand will be looking at some serious tribulation time after the Rapture. Society has problems, sure, but there's only so much you can do when time is running out, and, anyway, God will judge society soon enough.

Ballmer says this idea "relieved evangelicals of the obligation to labor for the amelioration of social ills" and that they "increasingly stood in judgment of culture and awaited its destruction, which would follow their translation into heaven."[2] In other words, all is not lost for unbelievers, but their salvation, much like their socioeconomic status, is their own responsibility.

This way of thinking lends itself to political conservatism, but it's had an economic implication as well, as Christians have built an alternate culture to sustain themselves while they wait out the last days. Christian plumbers service pipes installed by Christian contractors in housing developments built by and for Christians who attend Christian concerts, read Christian books, and watch Christian television with Christian friends.

This is entirely understandable behavior. How many people have friends who don't work in the same field, attend the same social events, have the same hobbies, support the same sports teams, or enjoy the same arts as themselves? But in shutting out so much of the world outside, Christians have opened themselves to the criticism that they have no frame of reference for judging the quality of Christian art.

In his book *Addicted to Mediocrity: 20th Century Christians and the Arts,* Franky Schaeffer says it would be absurd to live in a shoddily constructed house just because the guy who built it was a Christian. Reflexively hiring someone because they're Christian is as simpleminded as the slogans on most Christian bumper stickers, which he says, "are notoriously bad for patching roofs."[3]

Schaeffer's conclusion is remarkably similar to that of David Dark and most of the folks at the conference. "Either God is the Creator

of the whole man, the whole universe," he writes, "or he is the creator of none of it. . . . When our Christianity is allowed to become
merely spiritual and inward without the . . . outward expressions of
God's presence in the world, our faith is no longer meaningful in all
areas of life."[4]

In the past few years, a few "emergent" Christian churches have
developed, taking eagerness to engage the world as a central
premise. Shawn Young, who teaches at Greenwood College, a Christian school that offers a degree in CCM, characterizes the emergent
approach to art as "looking for the fingerprints of God."

"What I tell my students," he said when we spoke a few months
after the Festival of Faith and Music, "is if, indeed, all artistry is a
product of God, if we don't have creative ability outside of ourselves other than the Creator gives us, wouldn't that include Marilyn Manson?"

Michael Kaufmann is one of my favorite kind of weird people—the
ones who look completely normal. Kaufmann dresses so square he
could pass for a Mormon missionary—rail-skinny with short, dark
hair, wearing a button-down shirt and tie. A native of San Diego,
Kaufmann is the son of a pastor named Richard P. Kaufmann and a
veteran of a band called Soul-Junk, which formed after Glen
"Galaxy" Galloway became a Christian and split from the '90s indie
rock group Truman's Water.

Kaufmann is twenty-nine and recently moved to Indianapolis,
where he's "planting" a church, a term that refers to the idea in evangelical culture that new churches require care, feeding, tending,
maybe even pruning.

"I'm not sure U2 is the right way to connect to anyone under
twenty-five," Kaufmann said, referring to Dark's keynote, which
leaned heavily on the speaker's teenage obsession with *The Joshua
Tree,* causing a lot of laughter in the room. "I'm gonna play some

music that hopefully will clean out all the U2 talk." Paul Goode's illustrations—so *that's* what was on the DVD I brought to the conference!—appeared projected behind him.

The wild feedback skronk of Rhode Island bass-and-drums noise act Lightning Bolt blasted through the classroom's speakers. If I'd been any closer, the music would have trimmed my ear hair (like my own unironic love of U2, apparently, undeniable evidence of the aging process).

After Soul-Junk packed it in, Kaufmann moved to New York City in 1999, where his dad had moved to be a pastor at the thirty-five-hundred-member Redeemer Presbyterian Church. The twenty-four-year-old read the *Village Voice* listings "religiously" and tried to experience as much "weird stuff" as he could. But bohemia called, and Kaufmann soon moved to Olympia, Washington, where he and his friend Wayne Feldman developed a theory of music consumption called "progressive economics," which posited, for example, that a CD should sell for whatever the consumer made in an hour.

He and Feldman also made music, and they decided to experiment with long-form shows. One lasted thirty hours. Perhaps not coincidentally, Kaufmann soon left town and moved back to New York, where he took a job at the New York Public Library as a film librarian. In New York, he organized an event called Christ-a-Go-Go, which combined his vision of the worship music at his dad's church being "run through a Kaos pad"—an effects pedal that can turn anything into aural soup with the flick of a touchpad—with projections and light shows. "Experimental worship" didn't catch on, I'm guessing because you could probably get much the same effect by taking ketamine at Sound Factory and being as solipsistic as you wanted.

After Kaufmann's head-clearing exercises, he mapped out an idea he's been working on: "horizontal aesthetics." While culture clings to "vertical" issues like high- and lowbrow art, he argues, aesthetics can be mapped on a plane where NASCAR is equal to baseball and macramé. And like U2 (sorry) "Looking for the baby Jesus under the trash," Kaufmann, too, subscribed to the festival's dominant theme— God is in every part of culture.

So why doesn't the evangelical church get this? he wondered rhetorically. "The church creates a subculture and refuses to compete," he said. "But the church wants desperately to fit in. The church," he paused, "is a teenager."

"This is all music that communicates to me," Kaufmann said, playing snippets of glitch-hop, followed by something that sounded like bossa nova that had melted in the sun, some Tuvan throat singing, and some gamelan music.

"Do you think Christians are ready for music like this?" asked one kid.

"I personally don't care," Kaufmann said. "I'm more concerned with convincing people like myself to accept CCM." His biggest fear with Asthmatic Kitty (he met the Brooklyn-based Sufjan Stevens during his second stay in New York) is that the label is fostering an alternate Christian subculture. "Christians' place is where God places them," Kaufmann said. Postmodernity is over in non-Christian society— Christians worried about relativism are "five years behind" culture at large, Kaufmann said.

"Don't be afraid of culture and all its strange weirdness," Kaufmann said. "We don't claim enough boldness. It's okay to engage evil—we have a pretty good hand."

I used the dinner break to hook up with David Bazan and Tim Walsh, who had just gotten into town but didn't have a way of getting around Grand Rapids. In the interest of full-service journalism, I drove over to the Days Inn where they were staying and brought them back to the conference, where they went off to dinner with Heffner, Dark, and some of the other festival *machers*. Me? I went to Wendy's and thought about what I'd seen so far.

It was too easy, I decided, to look down on Christians struggling with whether to engage the world outside. If you were raised, as David Bazan was for example, in a Christian culture where you had to twist yourself in intellectual knots trying to figure out a way to enjoy non-church-sanctioned music that nonetheless spoke to you, it's a radical idea to allow yourself to look for God in the work of, say, Lil' Flip. (In fact, Dark's previous book is called *Everyday Apocalypse: The Sacred Revealed in Radiohead, The Simpsons and Other Pop Culture Icons.*)

Surely there must be limits to this approach. Is the divine revealed in John Waters films? Okay, bad joke. But what about in porn? In music explicitly hostile to religion? And are kids who've grown up experiencing every innovation in music, every film, every television show through the filter of evangelical Christianity, with its insistence on absolute truth, really going to have the tools to be as discerning as Ken Heffner wants them to become?

I went back to Calvin with time to kill. Everyone I knew was at dinner, and the call to join Mike Kaufmann, Sufjan Stevens, and John Ringhofer never came, which was just as well since I suspected vegetarianism among that group would be rampant (I'd earlier decided to see how many hamburgers I could eat over a weekend and still control my feet). Strolling around the Fine Arts building, I looked at a display honoring the school's College Band, which tours Eastern Europe every three years and seems to visit German restaurants whenever possible.

Back downstairs, I checked out the college's impressively eclectic schedule of upcoming concerts, which featured no Christian artists other than those playing this festival: Gavin DeGraw, Iron and Wine, indie hip-hoppers Gift of Gab and Lateef, Patty Griffin—Ken Heffner walked it like he talked it.

And then Ken Heffner walked up to me. "David Bazan told me about you," he said, mentioning that he'd enjoyed reading some of my stuff in *Spin* and was very curious about this book. We made plans to meet up for a drink later. Then I found Bazan and Walsh, and we went into the auditorium for the first night's concert—Brother Danielson and Sufjan Stevens.

Daniel "Brother Danielson" Smith is a pretty interesting figure in indie music. His father, Lenny Smith, wrote a classic modern hymn called "Our God Reigns" and used to encourage his kids to hold worship services in their living room using toy instruments. Dan Smith went to Rutgers, where he put together a group with his siblings as a performance art piece for his senior thesis art show.

The Danielson Famile performed in white medical outfits and sounded kind of like a back-alley gene splice of the Pixies, the Chiffons, and the Shaggs. Smith's manic falsetto vocals, which one uncharitable soul describes as a "Mickey Mouse voice," anchors songs that lurch unpredictably between primitivism and pop, like the children of Captain Beefheart's Magic Band imitating their parents using Fisher-Price instruments.

If it's a marvel that Danielson records were ever issued at all, it's a minor miracle that the group's 1997 debut was on Tooth & Nail. Odder still, to date, Danielson is the only Tooth & Nail artist ever featured in *Spin*; the group's overt wackiness won it fans among the same New York City folks—mostly centered around the free-form radio station WFMU—who a decade earlier made a cult hero out of folk naïf Daniel Johnson.

Brother Danielson is Smith's solo project, and in live performances, Smith performs inside a fake hollow tree—he sings and holds his guitar through holes in the "trunk," keeping time by stomping on an amplified board. Within seconds, he had the audience wrapped around his little twig. There's something so immediate about Smith's sincerity, even when couched in such over-the-top whimsy, that he manages to communicate as well with jaded hipsters as he does with painfully sincere Christian youths.

Between sing-alongs that evening, Smith experimented with holding the audience rapt, pausing strategically in songs to experience the ultimate compliment for a rock performer—an absolutely silent audience. After a while (six seconds or so), Smith's voice gets a bit grating, but it was an impressive performance by any standard.

I wanted to hate Sufjan Stevens' show because of how things had gone with my interview attempt. But from the moment he and his band appeared in long-sleeved, white T-shirts with feathers for epaulets, brothers and sisters, I got a vision. It's a rare form of ESP that favors me once or twice a year if I'm lucky—I just knew this show was going to rule.

That feeling had nothing to do with Stevens himself, who looks like an even more droopy-faced version of Mark "The Rat" Ratner from *Fast Times at Ridgemont High,* or his perky, coed bandmates (though, to be fair, Stevens could have made Elliott Smith look carefree in comparison), or the sly symbolism of his recent album's title, *Seven Swans* (fun fact—the "seven swans a-swimming" in the Christmas carol "The Twelve Days of Christmas" represented each of the seven gifts of faith in Catholic catechism). No, there was just something kind of magical about Stevens' show from the start.

Ken Heffner had told me outside that Stevens had shown up at the first Festival of Faith and Music a few years ago without any instruments, talked his way onto the bill, and stunk up the room with an inept, timid performance.

Well, things have changed. I'm a bit of a geek, so I was particularly blown away by Stevens' guitar playing, especially parts that I thought were two guitars on record. But it was the tasteful fullness of his band's arrangements, or maybe his strong vocals, or his *desafinado* banjo playing . . . oh hell, I don't know; it was just awesome.

After the concert, I experienced what it was like to walk around a Christian campus with a Christian celebrity. From the moment we stepped out of the auditorium's side door, David Bazan was set upon by his public. Walsh and I stepped aside and watched Bazan's head slowly disappear into the widening circle of fandom.

"This could be a while," Walsh said. "Maybe we should go wait in your car."

A half-hour later, Bazan broke free of the scrum, and the three of us left for the Grand Rapids Brewing Company, where a bunch of folks from the conference were meeting.

It was most convivial. Calvin is a dry campus, so there was an infectious sort of counselors-away-from-the-campers atmosphere among the folks at the bar—Jeff Rioux from Messiah College, who had recently earned a place in Christian college lore as the guy who managed to book Bob Dylan; Josh Jackson, the editor of *Paste* magazine, who took great pains to make sure I wouldn't characterize his fine publication as a Christian music magazine, which it most assuredly is not; Heffner; some other workshop leaders and folks from the college; and Steve Stockman, a Northern Irish minister and author who wrote a good book on U2's spiritual journey based on interviews with the band and their lyrics.

When the subject of Tooth & Nail's Brandon Ebel came up, Bazan said, "I love that guy, man."

I interrupted him, saying I noticed that whenever he used that phrase, it usually preceded an insult.

"It's not an insult," Bazan said. "It's just that what he represents as a professional is truly evil."

"Oh yeah, no insult at all," said Jackson.

Rioux told us about how he takes great pains to teach his kids that they have no possessions, that everything, including their toys, belongs to God. "I'm cool with that," Bazan said.

The next morning, Bazan, Walsh and I decided to blow off the worship service and go to soothe our microbrew headaches at IHOP

instead. Heffner had urged conferees not to skip anything, but, man
. . . pancakes. I felt a little sheepish when I walked into the auditorium later. I could swear Heffner was giving me the stinkeye—
ridiculous, right? He probably didn't notice, but I couldn't help
feeling like I'd disappointed him.

He opened the morning by saying how great the worship service
was, especially since it featured music from Leonard Cohen, Patti
Larkin, and Rage Against the Machine. Damn, I thought, that did
sound interesting. But then again . . . pancakes.

Here are some of my notes from David Dark's second speech.
Perhaps you can make some sense of them.

Who among us is truthful?
Fred Friendly created pain in the mind of listeners that could only
    be relieved by [can't read]
William Stringfellow big influence on DD
Spin—rarely self-applied criticism
Objectionable subject matter—does it exist?
A friend asked him whether *Bury My Heart at Wounded Knee* was
    biased
It was an unsanctioned news source
Spiritual v. reality, reading bible makes him more reality based
Principality of Power, a thought system that has gotten cold
    thought
Natives were a special interest
Frank Brady books? JCT? This present darkness political world
Principalities of Power become their own realities
Own copyright on thoughtfulness
Objectionable unseemly challenges
P. sets up to own reality studio
"We are more than equipped to cast the first stone when we think
    we are without spin"

It's probably blasphemous to believe that secular humans exist
Talks of Christian music as reflective of the personal private rela-
   tionship with God
The personal private relationship with God
This world is just a waiting room
We write what we can says FOC [Flannery O'Connor?]
Thinks bible not written by humans
"Is he swell?"
"Who can say?" ⟵ a confession

I'm pretty sure it was another significant speech. Maybe I was trying too hard to take notes to follow it. We broke, and I headed to
David Bazan's workshop.

"I'm certainly most comfortable with people sitting at my feet,"
Bazan joked as fifty or so students tried to squeeze into the small
classroom he'd been assigned to. His workshop, called "Discovering
the Red Pill and the Creative Process," only briefly touched on *The
Matrix*, to which its title referred, although Bazan mentioned he
considered it a "decent Word picture." (Interestingly, there is a number of fan websites devoted to the idea that *The Matrix* is an allegory
for the life of Christ.)

In case you haven't seen *The Matrix*, there's a pivotal scene in
which the protagonist, Neo, is offered a choice between two pills—a
red one that will reveal the truth about the world, and a blue one that
will allow him to go back to a life of blissful ignorance. Neo—who is
called "The One" by many characters in the movie who start to see
him as a prophesied savior—of course, chooses the red, and then we
have a movie.

For Bazan, the red pill is deciding to adopt "a posture of discovery" as regards one's own faith. "To be Christlike," he argued, "we
must relinquish power."

Now, the prospect of sitting through yet another workshop where a speaker essentially gave kids the go-ahead to question authority was beginning to wear, but it was fascinating to see Bazan among so many others who shared his background, especially when he quoted a Bible verse from memory and asked, "Was that First Timothy?" "Second!" shouted everyone in the room except Walsh and me.

Characteristically, Bazan picked arguments that would have caused maximum confusion in his younger self. "Darwin has had as big an impact on the evangelical church," he said, "maybe even more so than Jesus. Darwinism has set the tone and focus of the evangelical church in a way that's ludicrous." By insisting that the Bible is an authoritative text on science, history, and the cosmos, Bazan said, the evangelical church has forced Christians to cultivate a faith that will "flounder" if the Bible's authority is challenged successfully.

"It is important," he said, "that we cultivate a faith that is not the house of cards that the evangelical church endorses." Absolute truth, he added, is impossible since humans cannot escape their point of view. He also posited that it's hotly debated among biblical scholars whether King David existed at all.

That seemed to set things off. "If any part of the Bible isn't true," asked one attendee, "how can we trust that anything in it is true?"

"When presented with contrary evidence," Bazan answered, "you can be threatened by it, or you can say my faith is not threatened by literal truth."

Was Bazan really the only one here who'd considered the possibility that the Bible wasn't literally, consistently true? More important, what was all this focus on absolute truth? Then, I remembered: without such a thing, there is no faith. For me, absolute truth is a series of inevitabilities: *If* I don't save up enough money, I will *probably* have a miserable senescence because I will *definitely* have to work until I die, which is the one item in this sentence that is *nonnegotiable*. But I didn't grow up Christian. David Bazan did, and I think he knew exactly what he was doing with this workshop: he wasn't just presenting these kids with the symbolic red and blue pills; he was making them think about the possibility that such a choice exists. And by that, he was hoping to strengthen their faith in a slightly perverse way that would drive their youth pastors completely coconuts.

In answer to another student's question, Bazan described his daily inner struggle as "the drunken monk battling the bitter man flipping the bird." This workshop evinced a remarkable balancing act between the two.

During the lunch break, I went over to the student union, where Dan Smith, Sufjan Stevens, and John Ringhofer were scheduled to have a panel discussion, moderated by Mike Kaufmann. I hoped this would be as good as an interview with Stevens, and it was: he talked enthusiastically about his musical awakening when he attended a Christian college in nearby Holland, Michigan. His first tape was a Pearl Jam album, and—irritatingly, because I've never had much luck with the instrument despite hacking away at it for twenty years—he didn't start playing guitar till his sophomore year of college.

There isn't an Asthmatic Kitty sound, but these artists do share an aesthetic. It has less to do with detuned banjos (although those are prevalent with this crowd) than it does with making music that sounds handmade, as well as a tendency to guide the audience's experience. It's a conflation of punk rock do-it-yourself-ness and appeals to authority that seems to be ringing more than a few bells with the kids at this conference. "I don't think of myself as an artist," Stevens said. "I think of myself as a craftsman."

My wife called me to tell me that the pope—I suspect to the immense relief of CNN's producers, who were completely running out of cogent guests—had died while I was in Bazan's workshop. I grabbed a candy bar and went to Steve Stockman's workshop.

I'll bet Steve Stockman is murder on record-store clerks. When I worked in such a capacity, I regarded customers like him with a mixture of awe and annoyance. British people call them "anoraks": they know everything about a certain group, producer, or record label— and they'll gleefully tell you about it, or hector you if you can't find something they're sure is in print, because they'd read about it in *Goldmine* or some other periodical exclusively read by unemployable virgins. Now, Stockman is neither of those things—he's not only a dean of residence at Queen's University in Belfast and a BBC radio host but a father of two—but he's got the gleam of unconditional fandom in his eye, which I can still spot from one hundred yards.

Unlike many of his sociological brethren, though, Stockman's put that fandom to good use. Despite having only met Bono briefly, he's written the aforementioned *Walk On: The Spiritual Journey of U2*, a careful reading of their interviews and lyrics that's not only a fascinating chronicle of the band's evolving take on Christianity but also makes a quite convincing case that what many fans consider the band's "dark period" (the decade between *The Joshua Tree* and *All That You Can't Leave Behind,* basically) is actually among the group's most interesting eras, artistically as well as spiritually. "I have no idea what they think of the book," he said to an attendee of his workshop who asked the obvious question. "I'm presuming since I haven't been in court at this point that maybe that's good news."

Stockman's been doing a Christian rock show called *Rhythms of Redemption* on BBC Ulster radio since 1996. Now he's working on a book about social justice and faith for an American audience called *Crumbs from Your Table* (another U2 title, natch). By way of introducing the need for it, Stockman talked about his first appearances on Christian radio stations to promote the U2 book. He was stunned to discover that, in between ads for "Christian mortgages" and Christian singles dating services, most of the stations could play U2 songs covered by other artists, but not played by U2 themselves, because the band's spirituality wasn't explicit, mostly because its members drink, smoke, and swear.

When Stockman brought the absurdity of this policy up with one show's host, the host asked him whether it was indeed possible for a Christian to embrace such conduct. "As far as I'm aware, drink is mentioned in the Gospels three times," Stockman replied—none of them having to do with prohibition. Social justice, on the other hand, is something Jesus talks about a lot.

"How many people are wearing a white plastic wristband at this time?" Stockman asked the workshop attendees, holding up his wrist. No one raised a hand—it was months before the One Campaign made a marginally effective push in the U.S. with the Live 8 concerts and those wristbands, which urged the world to MAKE POVERTY HISTORY. "If I were in the U.K., doing this seminar, every one of you would have this wristband on. No questions."

Stockman talked about his visits to South Africa and his devotion to Fair Trade products, all focused through the lens of Bono's activism. "Thirteen percent of evangelical Christians in America are interested in a pandemic that's wiping out the countries of Southern Africa," Stockman said. "That's why Bono's raging. He says, 'History will judge us.' But God will judge us harder."

"You guys are the last to grasp this," he said, making a compelling case that it's the duty of Christians to buy fairly traded projects and to campaign to rescind Third World debt and halt the spread of AIDS. "This is what it means to follow Jesus," he said.

I had dinner with Stockman in the faculty dining area, where we talked about the differences and similarities between the American and British evangelical churches. He told me that Belfast's Protestants are quite similar to American Christians politically, though with a much lesser emphasis on achieving their social goals through legislation. We were sitting with a self-described "Americana" singer/song-writer affiliated with the college who talked about how much he disliked George W. Bush, a common theme at this very surprising conference—weren't Calvinists supposed to be conservative? (In fact, six weeks later, three hundred faculty members signed a letter protesting Bush's policies when he spoke at the college's commencement.) I mentioned the talk radio show I'd heard on the way up, where a caller had said she was praying Terri Schiavo's autopsy would reveal she'd been abused, and suddenly the guy's attitude turned.

"Well, with Terri's husband there *are* a lot of unanswered questions," the singer said.

Half-Handed Cloud opened the evening's concert, Ringhofer performing zany songs on piano that required him to set off wind-up toys and take bites of an apple in between lines, and Stevens and Kauffman to fire the odd toy rocket over his head. Surprisingly, even with the gimmicks, his Beach Boys–esque music revealed a touching, childlike wonder at faith that seemed completely uncontrived. David Dark's wife, Sarah Masen, played next, followed by Bill Mallonee and Pierce Pettis, but it was a long night for me. While I appreciate Americana—folk singing mixed with alt-country—from a remove, up close I find it monotonous. Americana trades heavily in notions of authenticity, but as with microbrews, I find it nearly impossible to tell one Americana singer from the next.

Bazan closed the evening with an impromptu solo performance arranged by Heffner. I sat with Walsh, who'd never seen Bazan play some of the band's more recent songs without him. Bazan also premiered a new song, an open letter to a journalist who gave him a bad review, suggesting that if the hack ever wanted to do anything real with his life, he should start a band himself.

It was a fascinating show, especially when during the standard question-and-answer part of the set, an audience member asked Bazan if he knew any hymns. He played an eighteenth-century one called "Come Thou Fount" that quickly had the whole room (I didn't know the words, alas) singing along, effectively making it the festival's closing song.

After the show, Walsh and I waited in the lobby for Bazan, who had been cornered by a concert attendee. When we walked to the car, I asked him what that had been all about. "He was offended by my music," Bazan said. "He thought that it was characterized by despair."

If someone offended me, I said, I'd just leave. I sure as hell wouldn't talk to them about it.

"You're not Christian," said Walsh.

We were on our way to have celebratory drinks with the festival's organizers and artists at a bar downtown, but the weight of that statement lay on me from the moment I arrived. I liked these people, enjoyed their company, and they'd made me feel completely welcome. But it bothered me that I wasn't a Christian and would never be one. They embraced me like they hope to embrace culture, but I'm still not sure how hard either of us can hug them back.

I left early since I had to get up at 6 AM to drive back to Virginia.

John DeLorean introduced Jay Swartzendruber to the broader world of Christian music. Well, okay, the automaker—then under indictment for allegedly trafficking cocaine—was on the cover of the first issue of *CCM* magazine read by Swartzendruber when he was sixteen. Like most of the magazine's readers, young Jay wasn't too interested in CCM's experiment with being a Christian lifestyle magazine—he wanted to read about music. "I flipped to the back-issues section and saw that Steve Taylor had just been on the cover," he says. "I figured if they were cool enough to put Steve Taylor on the cover, they were cool enough for me."

Swartzendruber, thirty-eight, not only ended up working for Steve Taylor, but he now edits *CCM,* the *other* bible of the Christian music industry. Under Swartzendruber's leadership, the twenty-seven-year-old magazine—whose name was once as synonymous with big-haired easy-listening artists as it is with the genre of Christian contemporary music—has actually managed to become hip without alienating longtime readers who *like* big-haired, easy-listening artists.

With a zippy design, columns by Christian music stars like Paul Coleman and Michael Card, and smart, funny writing by people like Chris Well and Margaret Becker, *CCM* is a beacon of quality in a music scene where good intentions often trump execution. True, the magazine's record reviews seem to work on a grading scale of A+ to B–, and its chronicling of scenester marriages and births can get a bit fluffy, but, on the whole, the magazine makes the Christian music scene look attractive, inclusive, even fashionable.

That's a tribute to Swartzendruber's deep love of Christian music, which isn't blind, by the way. He's critical of what he calls "music as a tool" and the "dadgum inferior" Christian music of the '70s and '80s. Swartzendruber's also leveraged his considerable Rolodex to encourage Christian artists to work for social justice. The aWAKE project, a nonprofit he founded with Charlie Peacock and Taylor, among others, is closely aligned with DATA, an organization founded by Bono that encourages fair trade and debt relief for Third World countries. In 2005, Swartzendruber was asked to be a delegate at the ONE Campaign's conference during the G8 Summit.

Did you listen to Christian music exclusively growing up?

JAY SWARTZENDRUBER: Not until I was about fourteen or fifteen. I listened to Christian pop radio. I was one of these sad, pathetic kids who thought Men at Work was the real deal and the Police were the flash in the pan. But there was a phase from fifteen to nineteen when I listened to pretty much all Christian music.

Did you throw out your old secular records?

I threw out a lot of them. I didn't feel like if it was quote-unquote secular it was bad—I felt like if it was depressing, it probably wasn't a good thing to put into my head. That kind of thinking changed later as I got older, but that's where I was in my mid-to-late teens.

Because when you're older, you're depressed all the time?

[*Laughs*] Exactly.

How did a Men at Work fan get into Christian music in the first place?

My parents listened to some form of Christian music throughout pretty much my entire childhood, whether it was hymns or chorales, Andraé Crouch, or Evie, who was kind of the Amy Grant of the '70s. I don't know if I just associated that music with older people, but when I would hear Christian radio, it would seem easy listening–esque, for lack of a better term.

It wasn't till I happened upon a Christian radio show one night in late '83 that I was like, "Wow!" It opened up a whole new world for me of bands I'd never heard of. I had no idea that Christian artists rocked hard.

Whose show was it?

It was a show [on Atlanta radio station WVFJ] called *StarFlight*. They introduced me to music like Steve Taylor, the Seventy Sevens, Resurrection Band, Daniel Amos—pretty much anything progressive back then that the adult contemporary station wasn't playing.

So, you're listening to Christian radio. Gradually, your old records are gathering dust. What happens next?

Well, I'm mowing yards to make money. That was about the same time I came across *CCM*. And I think it was in *CCM* that I came across a store called Long's Christian Music, where you can order through the mail. The ad was like, if it's out, and it's by Christians, we have it. Send for a free catalog. So I did. And it was amazing, they had everything under the sun. The first cassette I got was by Steve Taylor. Then, I got some other artists. And it wasn't until I moved to California a year later that I really felt—like it was really at the edge of my fingertips. Like, "Wow! Bands tour here!" When I lived in Alabama, the first time I saw Steve Taylor in concert, I had to drive to Birmingham, which was, like, two hours away.

Did you have friends who were into Christian music, or was it you on your own?

Oddly, it was me on my own in Alabama—not oddly, it was probably pretty normal.

But you weren't part of a community.

No, there was no sense of youth group—oh this is Christian music, let's go do this. When I got to California, I started tapping into that a little bit more. And then, once I was at Bible college, I was like, "Wow, I've never known so many people into"—for lack of a better term—"cool Christian music!"

So how did you end up in the music business in Nashville?

I was just Joe Superfan. I was really drawn to the more eccentric, alternative-type Christian artists, which would include everything from, like, Steve Taylor and Charlie Peacock to U2—U2 would consider that description a nightmare. Some of these artists would see me repeatedly at some of their shows.

In the middle of my graduate study work in Illinois, Charlie Peacock came to do a performance, and I went. He was like, "What are you doing out here? I'm used to seeing you on the West Coast." I told him, and on the fly, he said, "What are you doing this summer? I'm looking for an intern." I was like, *"What?"*

So, I came down to do an internship in the summer of '91, loved Nashville, and decided to move down. I worked for a year in the Yellow Pages proofing ads. By day, I would look for a job in the business. I got an internship with a small indie called R.E.X. They were primarily a metal label. They had Believer and Living Sacrifice, these really hard bands. And, literally, my first day there, the A&R guy said, "Hey, what do you think of this band? It's kind of different." They had kind of an Edge guitar intro to it, and then a female vocal. I was like, "That's pretty cool, actually. What are they called?" He said, "That's a band called Sixpence None the Richer."

So I became their publicist. They did a minitour with 10,000 Maniacs, which was *unheard* of back then by a Christian artist. Completely unheard of. And now, it's, like, you couldn't even get press on that if it happened. But back then, it was shocking.

Charlie Peacock asked me and another friend of mine if we'd like to help him start a record label called re:think. So in late '95, I left R.E.X. to do that. R.E.X. closed its doors four months later. And I had no idea that was gonna happen. I was very fortunate in that respect.

re:think put out a record by Sarah Masen, who's a pretty high-profile independent artist now—

I saw her in Michigan. She's David Dark's wife, right?

Yes! Exactly. And they're dear, dear friends. And, long story short, re:think had a vision for the general market as well and spent a lot of money in the mainstream to the point where Charlie was kind of cleaning out his own pockets and decided, if he was gonna be a good steward of his family's finances, he had to stop. So, he sold re:think to Sparrow.

And right as he was selling it to Sparrow, he signed Switchfoot to re:think. And so, I never did their official PR because, when re:think went in-house to Sparrow, they didn't bring me as a publicist.

That was their concept album, right?

The Legend of Chin, yeah. From there, I did independent stuff for a year, and then Steve Taylor offered me a job—same kind of thing, he was starting a record label, "I'd like you to come aboard, help me start Squint." And, oddly enough, that reunited me with Sixpence. So as fate would have it, I got to do PR for every Sixpence record except the last one. Which was cool. We, of course, brought in a big-gun mainstream publicist when things got crazy. So I worked at Squint with Chevelle, L.A. Symphony, Burlap to Cashmere.

Oh, I didn't realize Chevelle were on Squint.

It was kind of funny. [Steve Taylor and I] discovered them open-ing for the Insiderz, a ska band that was supporting a praise-and-worship record. They were, like, "You've gotta come see this opening band; they're great! They're these three home-schooled kids, but they're great!" So we went down and saw 'em; we were *blown away.*

That's interesting; Chevelle really play down their Christian rock roots.

That's quite an understatement [laughs]. I think their record scanned about fifty thousand copies for us. Squint had been in exis-tence for four years at that point, then *it* got caught up in label politics, and the entire system it was part of was being sold to Time Warner. And they put us in freeze and wouldn't let us put out the L.A. Sym-phony record and literally had us in limbo for probably over a year.

They eventually closed our doors, sent all of our staff home. And, a week later, I ended up landing a job at Gotee records, working with Toby Mac—he owns Gotee—Grits, Relient K. . . . So, I did that for two years, and then—out of the blue! not looking for it!—*CCM's* publisher called me in and said, "We get your e-mails, we see your press releases, and—there was kind of a blog-esque thing I would do before blogs were even known as blogs, I wouldn't post it on the Net, I would send it out, where I would write an informal update about Gotee artists and other artists.

I started doing it at Squint, and Steve Taylor and the owners at Gotee were very cool about floating other records 'cause they were like, "Hey, you know what? If you're floating anything under the sun: (1) people are more likely to read your e-mails; and (2) it's good for everybody if the albums you're supporting do well." So they were like, "We've seen your writing, we like your tone and style, we like the way you know the industry. We'd like you to come edit *CCM* magazine."

That's incredible. So you had no editorial experience?

Only press releases, artist bios, and whatnot. It's really bizarre, actually! So bizarre that they even said, you know, as you come in, it would probably be best if we didn't start you out as editor. You need to be managing editor and prove yourself. I thought, "That makes sense to me." So I came in as managing editor, and there was no editor!

Tell me a little bit about CCM. What have been some of the challenges and rewards?

Here's this flagship publication for this favorite hobby of mine that I get to influence both its direction and its contents and get to expose our readers to the kind of things that excited me as a teenager and a twentysomething. And even as an industry person in my thirties, I still love reading *CCM*. So that's been so much of the fun. I even feel like there's an education element to it, where it's not just affirming a believer's faith through the music but expanding how they view their faith and these artists—frankly, *CCM*'s quite different than it was in the late '70s and early '80s.

The hair is smaller. . . .

Exactly! That's pretty funny. My experiences of the breadth and width of Christians in the arts—it's kind of fun to see this kind of stuff communicated to readers who've only come onboard our magazine within the past five years.

As far as the challenges—you know, it's interesting, coming from a PR and marketing background, it's amazing how many rabid Christian music fans out there don't know about *CCM*. And when they find out about it, they're like, "Wow! I had no idea."

There's still that element of the challenge of getting the word out there that, Hey, this thing exists, you know? There is an official magazine of Christian music, and we're it.

One thing we're doing to gain ground is we are partnering with artists to get inserts in CDs. To where a fan buys an artist's CD, opens it up, there's an insert that says *CCM* magazine and has a cover image of the artist on the cover.

Now, does that mean if the next Steven Curtis Chapman record blows, you have to be nice?

[*Laughs*] I'm an idealist, man. I come from an idealist background. People like Charlie Peacock and Steve Taylor have been my bosses, Joey Elwood and Toby Mac, people that encourage integrity. Our advertising people don't tell us how to write reviews. Only twice have I gotten e-mails from the advertising side saying, "Please cover this artist, they bought an ad." And I wrote back saying, "Please don't do this."

How'd you get involved with DATA?

In mid-2000, I took a trip with Steve Taylor and Dave Palmer at Squint. We went to Capitol Hill for a to-do in honor of the author of *Roaring Lambs,* a guy named Bob Briner. While we were out there, we befriended the chief of staff for [Pennsylvania Republican] Senator [Rick] Santorum, a guy named Mark Rogers. He mentioned in passing, "Oh yeah, we had Bono here for a time like this," and I was like, "*What?*"

So skip ahead to early 2002, and I'm at my desk at Gotee records, minding my own business, and I get this e-mail from Mark that said, "Jay: How would you like to host a meeting between Bono and Christian artists in Nashville?"

After I picked myself off the floor, I said, "Hey, sounds great, lemme know what I need to do." Hit "send" totally in disbelief. And completely keeping it quiet. Because I've been in the Nashville Christian music scene long enough to know that Bono's beyond icon status. So hush-hush was a given. He responds and says, "Great.

Email me a proposal, I'm meeting with Bono tomorrow morning, I'll give it to him."

So I did what many people do in panic mode: I turned to my mentor. I went over to Charlie Peacock's, and we banged out a proposal together and had it off to Mark by 10 PM that night. And Bono wanted to know more. So Charlie and I brought in Steve Taylor and five other people to brainstorm with us. And from there, it just grew.

In December Bono came, and we met at Charlie Peacock's house with about twenty artists—members of D.C. Talk, Sixpence None the Richer, Amy Grant, Michael W. Smith, CeCe Winans, Out of Eden, Third Day, Switchfoot. It was very intense. But five minutes into his conversation, you forgot you were listening to Bono. He was so riveting.

From that, a lot of Christian artists really got involved, like, I felt the burning calling myself. I had to respond to this. And so my wife and I and a couple friends, including Charlie and Steve Taylor, started a nonprofit organization called the aWAKE project, and it's very much a grassroots thing. And the past three years, we've been working with artists to raise awareness. You know, a lot of people don't know this, but Christian artists were first to be on board with the One Campaign. When Bono announced it in Philadelphia, he had one artist at his side: Michael W. Smith. And Jars of Clay was also down there. Right away, we started getting the word out. It wasn't even a big national thing for another year.

So . . . dude, you know Bono.

I wish I did, man, I wish I did. I rode with him in the van over to [Charlie Peacock's house], and he was like, tell me about this meeting, so I had a great chance to talk to him for about twenty minutes, just about Christian music.

Did he know anything about it?

He said, "I know nothing about Christian music." So we're talking a little bit, and then, out of the blue, he goes, "Will Larry Norman be there?"

What's your work for One, aWAKE, and DATA like?

My main role has been as conduit between DATA, the artists, and some of the senators on Capitol Hill when it comes to the topic of Africa. So what I do is, they will send me updates, and then I have this database with more than a hundred VIPs in the Christian music business, from artists to label execs to management to radio people, just people who wanted to be in the loop on this topic. And so they'll send me updates, and I'll send them out to this list. Sometimes it's very artist geared, and sometimes it's more general; sometimes it's like, "Hey, your fans need to know to call now."

And then I'll come across an interesting article on Africa, on poverty, on the church, and I'll forward it to the list. In June [2005], DATA contacted me and asked me if I'd like to go to Scotland for the G8 summit as a One delegate. It sounded like, "Wow, it's so impressive," but DATA had invited like thirty grassroots delegates. Some of them were college students, just people who'd been very active in one way or another. In the end, there were more than one hundred of us.

It's a long way from being Joe Superfan.

Well, this connects to my history in a very deep and long way. It connects with both a hobby—the music I've loved for more than twenty years now—and my faith, which defines me.

CHAPTER 7

Salt and Light, Inc.

Do you ever get the feeling you're not wanted? Here's what I wrote on my application for press credentials for Gospel Music Association (GMA) Week, the Christian music industry's annual conference in Nashville:

> I'm writing a general-market book about Christian rock, to be published next year by Da Capo Press. I'm a senior contributing writer at *Spin* and a frequent contributor to the *Washington Post*. I'm also a friend of Doug Van Pelt from *HM*. I'm attaching an article I wrote for the *Post* this summer.

Two weeks later, I got this response:

> Hello,
>
> We have processed your media credential applications and they have been denied. If you would like to attend GMA Week, we will need you to register by going to www.gospelmusic.org, or by calling (XXX) XXX-XXXX.

Dang. Registering for this thing on my own was gonna run me about $500. Plus, I needed to get a ticket for the GMA Music

Awards, another $60 for the cheap seats. On top of a hotel room and car rental, plus meals, it hardly mattered that I was getting my flight to Nashville via frequent-flyer miles.

I was just about to join the Gospel Music Association to get a discounted rate on registration when Doug Van Pelt himself e-mailed me to see whether I was coming to GMA Week. I told him my sad story. The next day, I received an e-mail saying that my credentials had been approved—they'd been denied, the GMA told him, because I was not clear about who I was or what I was doing. Apparently they didn't know that I was friends with the Tony Soprano of Christian rock.

My hotel was more or less situated on an off-ramp of I-65, affording me easy access to downtown with the trade-off that, when I lay on the bed, southbound traffic looked and sounded as if it were hurtling toward my window at seventy miles per hour. On the plus side, it had a fridge.

That first evening in Tennessee I met up with Van Pelt, his wife, Charlotta, and Heather Reynolds, *HM*'s director of advertising sales, for a movie screening in nearby Franklin. The movie was called *Madison,* a boat-racing story that was finally hitting theaters after languishing in MGM's vaults for four years. Hint: the delay wasn't because it was too good to share with the public. To be kind, it would probably be an okay TV movie of the week, but I'm guessing the reason MGM was debuting it at GMA Week was more practical than the men introducing it let on—it's not that *Madison* is "true family entertainment," it's that it stars Jim Caviezel, who played Jesus in *The Passion of the Christ,* which evangelicals, flexing economic muscle that Hollywood definitely noticed, had recently made one of the top-grossing movies of all time.

The next morning, GMA Week started in earnest with an early-morning worship service in the Renaissance Nashville Hotel's humongous ballroom, which fairly percolated with Christian music industry professionals shaking off long flights and clapping old friends on the backs. Over the sound system, we were introduced to Louie Giglio, an Atlanta ministry entrepreneur who founded the wildly successful Passion movement, an organization that puts on large-scale gatherings on college campuses and also runs sixsteps-records, a worship label with some of the biggest names in that scene—Matt Redman, Chris Tomlin, and David Crowder.

Worship music is Christian music, and it's rock music, but, confusingly, it's not quite the same thing as Christian rock. Most good-size evangelical churches have their own worship bands, which lead the congregation in a sort of amplified folk mass. Worship music has "hits," songs that appear on compilations like *Worship Jamz* and are licensed to individual churches through Christian Copyright Licensing International, a company that also keeps track of the most-performed songs in churches and pays songwriter royalties, much like ASCAP and BMI.

As I mentioned in chapter 1, if you've seen that TV commercial for Time-Life's *Worship Together Collection*, you've heard worship music. Much—not all, but enough to tar the whole genre—of it sounds like Christian pop scrubbed of any remaining hint of menace. It's usually an updated form of folk-rock, anchored by drum loops and crystalline acoustic guitars, reminiscent of artists like Counting Crows or Hootie & the Blowfish, but with earth-shattering choruses that make those artists look like amateurs.

The perky Giglio tried to rouse the crowd from its early-morning haze. "When I say 'Good morning,' you worship back!" he instructed after getting a lackluster initial response. People began to take their seats. I hung out in the back near a few people who also had press passes.

As Giglio spoke, musicians filtered in behind him and picked up their instruments. Finally, Giglio introduced Chris Tomlin, a squat fellow in a baseball cap who'd been strumming his acoustic guitar softly through Giglio's short prayer about how we were here "to do the business of the kingdom." Multicolored lights swirled as Tomlin gingerly entered into the chorus of "Adeste Fideles"—"Oh come, let us adore him," he sang, almost as a meditation. Then, the drummer pounded in, the electric guitarist with tousled hair and a NEW YORK T-shirt started soloing loudly, and folks in the audience started lifting their hands in the air.

This gesture is probably the characteristic of evangelical services that looks the most unusual to outsiders. Some call it a "hug from God," and as the music that morning lifted in intensity, more and more hands popped up till the ballroom looked like a psychedelic classroom in which *a lot* of students had questions.

On either side of the stage, screens projected the words to songs over images of waterfalls, crashing waves, and sunsets. "Forever God is faithful," the crowd sang. "Forever God is strong." After a particularly blistering solo from the guy in the NEW YORK shirt, the band went into a bass-and-drums breakdown, and the worshippers started clapping double-time, singing, "His love endures forever." The lights were choreographed in time with the music—high production values and high moral values go hand in hand.

After the last towering chorus of Tomlin's worship hit "Indescribable," the band faded back, and Tomlin softly sang "How Great Thou Art." The entire room—even the other press folks, in fact, everyone except me and the convention center guys furiously trying to add more chairs—sang along, in a touching reminder of the GMA's Southern gospel roots. Giglio walked out again as Tomlin strummed softly, the music portion of the service sliding seamlessly into the sermon. "How true, how true," Giglio said.

His homily was about keeping the Sabbath holy, admittedly difficult for a conference that starts on Sunday morning. It isn't necessary to emulate the fast-food chain Chick-fil-A, which famously stays closed Sundays, he said, though he admired how that company is

"God-centered" and "isn't afraid to put money in the bank." Giglio talked about creation and resting on the seventh day, and he shouted, "It is about a love affair with the King; it is not about merchandising the Kingdom!" to a roar from people paid to do just that. We need to remove ourselves from the story, Giglio said. It's not history; it's His Story. Then, he mentioned another Jim Caviezel bomb, *Bobby Jones*. If Caviezel ever ran for office, I mused, this convention would be a good place to kick things off.

During Giglio's benediction, a gangly, wild-haired guy in thick-framed glasses and a jumpsuit took a seat on the stage and began tuning his guitar. "This is a big week for us," David Crowder said once Giglio left. "Our new record comes out Tuesday."

I was intrigued by Crowder's look, but I was worshipped out and decided to check out the exhibition hall instead.

There was no way, I pledged, that I was going home without an iPod Shuffle. Every booth seemed to be offering a drawing for one. Mind Spin Research, a Christian-oriented radio research firm, the Maker's Diet, Gospel for Asia, iTickets.com, Seekers—a Christian coffeehouse with franchise opportunities—production companies, Compact Disc manufacturers. . . .

I ran into Tooth & Nail's Brandon Ebel in the Renaissance's wildly overpriced coffee shop near the pressroom, where I rested once I'd run out of places to enter for iPod Shuffles. He was waiting for some retailers from a bookstore chain. He told me he came to GMA mostly to meet and greet, with artist managers, store buyers, industry folk. He also had another mission.

"The studio business is real bad right now," he said.

"So you're buying up assets?" I asked.

He shook his head. The problem with the music industry, he said, was that it pays too much for everything. What he was hoping to do was negotiate discounts—offer studios guaranteed business, say, six months' worth, in exchange for a steep discount on rates. "It's like Costco!" he exclaimed, before adding, "Don't put that in your book."

Then I went down to the lobby to meet Anthony Barr-Jeffrey. Barr-Jeffrey and I had exchanged e-mails for a week or two before the conference. He's a writer for *CCM* and had generously agreed to show me around.

"What are these, the street-cleaner awards?" he stage-whispered to me when we took our seats at the sparsely attended Radio and Retail ECHO awards. Barr-Jeffrey lives in Seattle, where he's finishing a doctorate in clinical psychology at Seattle Pacific University, though what he really specializes in is sniffing out free food. While some of the bigger up-and-comers in Christian music—Building 459, Day of Fire—played for oblivious, schmoozing programmers, Barr-Jeffrey schooled me on the finer points of label hospitality rooms, breakfast meetings, and which publicists are most likely to take you out to lunch. "Have you tried the white barbecue sauce they have in Nashville?" Barr-Jeffrey asked while Matt West strummed his heart out for inattentive radio nabobs. "I have a new theory that food is a place setting for condiments." I liked him immediately.

We walked up to Union Station, an old train station that's been converted to a luxury hotel, for a press event Barr-Jeffrey had heard would feature lunch. It was the introduction of *The Word Becomes Flesh*, an audiobook version of the Bible read by some fairly serious names in Christian culture—Rebecca St. James, Amy Grant, Beverly LaHaye (wife of Tim, author of the *Left Behind* books), Sandi Patty—sales of which were to benefit Mercy Ministries, a charity that helps young women who are pregnant, have drug or alcohol problems, or, according to the ministry's website, are lesbians.

The Bible comes in a snappy, pastel-striped CD case, I guess to emphasize that it's meant for women. Denise Jones, a singer in the multiplatinum CCM group Point of Grace, spoke about how this Bible makes it easier for women doing "mom stuff" to get their Scripture on.

"For most moms, we spend so much time in the car," she said. "I'm just so excited about what God is gonna do through this Word."

A stout guy in an argyle polo shirt in front of me kept making a weird hissing noise. At first, I thought he was trying to ask a question, but as the stories of life-changing miracles were related, he started raising his right hand, wiping away tears, muttering. I realized he was saying, "Yes, Jesus. Yes." Some of the women on the CDs—St. James, singer Tammy Trent, author Donna VanLiere—sat on stools taking turns reading a chapter of Paul's Letter to the Philippians. As they got going, tinny *Chariots of Fire*–style music filled the room. I looked around the room, trying to figure what jerk forgot to turn off his cell phone, before I realized it was background music being piped in for effect. It's on the CDs, too.

Barr-Jeffrey split for a label dinner, so I walked down Broadway past the Gaylord Entertainment Center where crews were preparing for the next evening's Country Music Television awards show, stinky honky-tonks where no-hopers in cowboy hats pounded out covers for tourists, and Hatch Show Print, a poster shop sacred to country music fans. My main musical choice for the evening was another worship service, this time led by CCM superstar Michael W. Smith, but I had a little time before that to eat and catch a showcase called Adrenaline Circus that promised actor Stephen Baldwin as an emcee.

Baldwin, a recent Christian convert, was harder to avoid at GMA Week than free iPod Shuffles. A triptych of video screens in the Renaissance's lobby showed excerpts from *Livin' It*, the evangelical skateboarding video he'd produced for Luis Palau Ministries. A banner with a larger-than-life image of him (sporting that congenital Baldwin facial expression that suggests that at any moment, he might decide to kill you) loomed over the exhibition hall. And seemingly every time I passed a secular news crew, he was doing a stand-up interview.

Evangelicals have an odd relationship with celebrity. Christians often complain that the mainstream media ignores Christian music, film, and art, and the very existence of their subculture presumes a need to set up an alternate universe with its own celebrities. The world outside this subculture is often portrayed as treacherous and best left alone. Salem Communications, which owns ninety-five radio stations in the U.S. (and also owns Salem Publishing, home to *CCM* magazine), has had tremendous success with a contemporary Christian music radio format called "The Fish" whose tagline is "Safe for the whole family."

Which makes it all the odder that Christians completely freak out when the outside world takes notice of one of its products. There may be a good deal of carping when a Christian band makes a run at the mainstream, but if one has any measure of success, it is feted like Napoleon returning from Egypt. A non-Christian pop fan may vaguely remember a single called "Just between You and Me" that peaked at No. 29 in 1996. Well, D.C. Talk, the band that recorded that song, is one of the best-selling Christian artists of *all time*—due in no small part to the perception, at least, that the band brought its message to the general market.

Likewise, when a celebrity converts to Christianity, all sense of perspective seems to go out the window. Take Gary Cherone, for example. The former singer for Extreme, which had a huge hit with the power ballad "More Than Words" in 1991, languished in funk-metal purgatory, then joined and essentially killed off Van Halen on the worst album of the band's career, 1998's *Van Halen III*. I defy you to find one Christian rock fan unaware of Cherone's new, explicitly religious direction. Or Alice Cooper's, or Brian Welch's. Christian music has internalized its slight presence in mainstream press to such a degree that it weights general-market fame, no matter how faded or C-list, much higher than it does its own artists who sell many more records than, say, Lou Gramm from Foreigner—now touring on the Christian circuit himself.

Not that Stephen Baldwin's career is undistinguished (hey, we're not talking about his brother Daniel). He was excellent in 1995's *The*

Usual Suspects and, depending on your taste, 1998's *Half-Baked* (in which he played MacGayver Smoker). Still, for the past few years, he's specialized in straight-to-video police, sci-fi, and action films like *The Snake King* and *Six: The Mark Unleashed.* I always cheer for comebacks (especially when I suspect the actor might attack me), and let's just say Baldwin . . . is due.

Still, Baldwin hadn't shown up yet at the Adrenaline Circus concert, and after a few minutes of watching an Evanescence knockoff, I left for another worship service.

The Ryman Auditorium is a lot smaller than its place in country music history. Walking in for the first time, I thought about my dad, who grew up listening to the Grand Ole Opry, broadcast from the Ryman's stage each week. It must have seemed like the biggest place in the world to him. In fact, the auditorium seats only about twenty-four hundred people in pews that betray its beginnings as the Union Gospel Tabernacle.

There are definitely two crowds at GMA, divided not by age or politics but by dress. The first group has embraced mainstream youth culture and looks like a bunch of typical record-biz dorks in black clothes a few years too young for them, with earrings, tousled haircuts, and tasteful tattoos. These are the folks who "work" Christian alternative music.

The mainstream Christian music industry people are spiritual heirs to the honyockers in leisure suits and bad toupees who turned a few small-fry companies that distributed vinyl LPs of sermons into an industry that's grown to a substantial slice of the entertainment business as a whole. That's not to say these folks are unfashionable— far from it. Most are dressed in high-end business casual—polo shirts and khakis for the men, skirts and cardigans for the women.

I threw in my lot with the J. Crew set, and as ever more of them squeezed into the Ryman's upper level, elbow room in my pew quickly disappeared. Jim Chaffee, then chairman of the Gospel

Music Association's board of directors, kicked things off by introducing Dr. Wess Stafford, president and CEO of Compassion International, who wrote a book called *Too Small to Ignore: Why Children Are the Next Big Thing*. The foreword was written by the evening's star, Michael W. Smith, who jumped out from behind the gold velvet curtain and mugged with Stafford for a second, delighting the crowd before disappearing again.

"I can't wait to get to heaven, guys," Stafford said, urging the assembled to "make worship a lifestyle"—to work for social justice among prostitutes, widows, kids with AIDS. "We are the church; we need to *be* the church," Stafford said to much head-nodding and murmured agreement.

Except for the media, with its tut-tutting about declining journalistic standards, loss of public trust, and elitism, there's no group in America so willing to listen to critiques from within as the evangelical church. I happen to think that in both cases, it's because such criticism confirms their suspicions that everyone besides themselves is getting it wrong.

The curtains parted, revealing Smith at a grand piano, backed by a band and a fifty-strong chorus of CCM luminaries, some of whom I recognized from the *Word Becomes Flesh* event a few hours earlier.

Quentin Crisp once said, "A lifetime of listening to disco music is a high price to pay for one's sexual preference." I'm not saved and don't think I ever will be, but if such a miracle were to take place, I can't imagine anything worse than being forced to pay for my salvation by listening to worship music for the rest of my days.

Worship music is the logical conclusion of Christian adult contemporary music—not just unappealing but unbearable to anyone not already in the fold. Every song follows the same parameters. It opens gently, with tinkling arpeggios or synthesized harp glissandos that portend the imminence of something celestial in glacial 4/4 time. In the second verse, the band—invariably excellent players—soft-pedals in, gaining in volume to the bridge. And then the chorus. Heavens, the choruses. They could put U2 out of business for good, they're so huge. Another verse. A middle eight. Then, a breakdown when the audience takes over singing. Another massive chorus. *Fin.*

This isn't music to appreciate; it's music to experience. People at a worship service close their eyes and, as ecstasy spreads across their faces, begin to rock rhythmically, arms out, mouthing the lyrics. It's more than a little sexual and a tad uncomfortable if you're sitting next to an attractive person who's been overcome by the Spirit.

Worship tunes tend to evince an adolescent theology, one that just can't get over how darn *cool* it is that Jesus sacrificed himself for the world. "Our God is an awesome God." "O Lord, you are glorious." "How can it be/That you, a king, would die for me?" Moreover, it's self-centered in a way that reflects evangelicalism's near-obsession with having a personal relationship with Christ. It's *me* Jesus died for. *I* just gotta praise the Lord.

Not for nothing is "Amazing Grace," which marvels at the author's salvation, one of the few traditional hymns to be regularly included in modern worship services. Absent is any hint of community found in hymns such as "The Church Is One Foundation"—the Jesus of worship music is a mentor, a buddy, a friend whose message is easily distilled to a simple command: praise me. Not "feed the poor, clothe the naked, visit the prisoner." Simply thank Him for His gift to *you* (and make sure to display copyright information at the bottom of the screen so royalties can be disbursed).

All of which I could bear, or at least imagine defending, if all the songs didn't sound the same. Now, I don't want to be a total bully here. Obviously, worship music means a lot to many people, and there are worship songs that stand up on their own, as music—I left Nashville humming one called "Blessed Be Your Name" for weeks—but they're in the minority. As is any hint of evangelizing—this is music by the saved only, for the saved only, an art form where the images projected on giant screens are more fruitful sources of meditation and reflection than the lyrics superimposed on them.

After an hour, I could barely feel my head, and it was uncomfortable to forever be, the only person in the room not singing along. I slipped out of the Ryman into the warm April night and caught ten minutes of a mediocre folk-rock band at the Rhythm Kitchen fronted by a doughy young man with a wedding ring on his finger. I headed back to my room on the Interstate, thoroughly depressed, and composed a mainstream Christian song of my own.

With every drop of sweat
From every open pore
As every T-shirt stains, Jesus, I just love you more
Caught up in the lies
I take time to adore
The ruler of my life, Jesus, I just love you more

Even more depressing, the gas station next to my motel didn't sell beer, and I really, really needed to drink this day away.

Anthony Barr-Jeffrey, on contrast, had a great night. He bounded up to me the next day in the Renaissance Nashville's lobby, agog over a Phil Keaggy show he'd seen while I morosely parodied Christian folk-rock. Moreover, he'd made two major discoveries, a guitar-pop band called Downhere and the raunchy rockabilly of the Elms. We made plans to meet up later, and then he went out to have lunch with a label rep.

I decided to attend a press conference with Jeremy Camp but was stopped at the door by a publicist.

"Am I in the right place for the press conference?" I asked.

"You would know if you were supposed to be here," she said with a bit of snoot, and refused to let me in. I'm always amazed at how effective some publicists are at keeping press away from their clients. To be sure, that's an important function of their job sometimes— they have to act as a filter after all—but a press conference seems like an odd time to exercise that particular muscle.

After sitting in on a couple of boring panels instead, I went to a workshop called "whyhiphop?" People wearing shirts with that slogan had been everywhere that weekend. Plus, the food there was really good—crab cakes *and* chicken fingers in the buffet line. Naturally, I ran into Anthony, and we sat together.

The whyhiphop? campaign was a collective effort between a Christian hip-hop record label and ministry called the Cross Movement, some pastors, and several DJs and rappers from a crew called Holy Hip-Hop, all of whom were campaigning for the greater acceptance of hip-hop by the Christian community. The moderator, Deuce, after opening with a prayer that noted how good the food in the buffet line was, led with a rhetorical question: "Why should GMA, which is doing fine without Christian hip-hop, go out of their way just because we like it? We have to build a stronger case. It can't just be because, 'Yo, I led someone to the Lord this way.'"

Nevertheless, the second question from the room was a request from an elderly white gentleman who wanted to hear conversion stories—had hip-hop saved anyone recently? Personal testimonies are the secret currency of evangelicalism. Everyone has one, even kids who grew up in Christian homes. In his book *Mine Eyes Have Seen the Glory,* Columbia University religion professor Randall Ballmer (who grew up evangelical) describes a visit to a summer camp in the Adirondacks where he watched children—many of whose parents had long been saved—recommit their lives to Jesus during an altar call, even though few of them had done much in the past year to repent.

"For a child in a fundamentalist household," he writes, "a second-generation evangelical who already adheres to most of the standards of 'godly' behavior, it is difficult to grasp the significance of any such conversion, since it demands no alteration of behavior. Instead of assurance, very often they feel anger and resentment because their conversions failed to deliver the religious euphoria and freedom from doubt implied in their parents' promises."[1]

Deuce got it wrong: most likely, hip-hop's *only* hope for penetrating mainstream Christian culture is numbers. And the numbers that count are: (1) record sales (and Christian hip-hop is simply not there yet); and (2) souls brought to Jesus via dramatic conversions. Plus, there are still some organizational issues to address. The Christian hip-hop community's rifts mirror divisions in the larger Christian culture. Holy Hip-Hop has a set of guidelines, for example, that forbids battle-rapping, songs or contests where MCs call one another out and try to prove superior skill on the mic, because "Christians should not battle Christians." This prohibition does not sit well with Tunnel Rats, a coalition of Christian battle rappers from L.A., none of whom are aligned with whyhiphop? for this very reason.

Then, there's the elephant in the room, illustrated neatly by another attendee, a DJ from Alaska whose hip-hop show on a Christian radio station invariably draws irate calls from listeners wondering why he's playing "that black music."

Evangelicalism has as complicated a history of race relations as any institution that has developed in the American South. From its beginnings in the Great Awakening and the Scotch-Irish churches of the Piedmont, evangelical Christianity has always had a race problem. Segregated services in the eighteenth century, the often church-centered "citizens councils" crucial to the Southern tactic of "massive resistance" to desegregation in the '60s, Bob Jones University's antimiscegenation rules—the roots of racism in the American church are deep.

To their immense credit, white evangelicals—notably Ralph Reed, former leader of the Christian Coalition, and Bill McCartney, founder of the Promise Keepers—began a concerted campaign to banish racism from the church in the early '90s, and to a great extent, they've been successful. Now racism is viewed as much a personal failing, much like alcoholism, drug use, or any number of other moral shortcomings. That's been incredibly important in opening up the evangelical church, though the characteristic insistence on focusing on individual rather than societal racism has led to problems such as this panel was addressing, allowing Christians to express disappointment at the moral blind spots of others while doing absolutely nothing further. "I've done my part," this attitude reasons. "I've changed myself. It's up to others to do the same."

And the thing is, there already is Christian hip-hop. It's just that the most popular rapper in Christian music is a forty-year-old white guy.

No one is more cognizant of the bizarreness of this situation than Toby Mac himself, who's dedicated much of his career to combating racism. With his fellow bandmates in D.C. Talk, which has officially been on hiatus for several years, he founded the E.R.A.C.E. foundation back in 1997. Mac's label, Gotee, is home to some of Christian hip-hop's most prominent artists, Grits, L.A. Symphony, 4th Avenue Jones, and DeepSpace5 among them. His most recent album, *Welcome to Diverse City,* is a terribly eclectic affair, mixing pop punk, reggae, heavy metal, hip-hop, and even funk, courtesy Parliament/Funkadelic's Bootsy Collins.

Still for all Mac's work, the Christian music industry is overwhelmingly oriented to pop and rock. "The non-urban-to-urban ratio of music in our industry is *way* out of proportion," Mac told *Christianity Today*'s Andree Farias in 2004. "If you take the *Billboard* charts in the mainstream . . . they're serving middle America. Christian music, I think, should be serving middle America." Still, he sees progress. "Things are looking up. . . . From a Gotee perspective, if I sign a hip-hop group, I find myself competing with two or three other labels, whereas before, I'd be the only one sniffing."[2]

Mac's labelmates Grits have a less generous take on the situation. In another *Christianity Today* interview with Farias, the group's Cof said, "Deep down . . . we know it's a black-and-white issue. That's why the CCM world and the gospel world are two separate entities. It can be ridiculous. We pray to the same God, read from the same Bible, and quote the same Scriptures. But to get them together, people are like, 'We can't do that.'"

"We've been told our stuff is too urban," said the group's Bone. "[T]hat's basically telling us, 'You're too black.' . . . That's why, for us, sometimes we'd rather be in a more mainstream environment. They're more diverse, and at times play more Christian songs than so-called Christian radio. . . . There are even moments where we feel as though we're the Affirmative Action of Christian music: 'Well, let's put Grits up there just because we have to.'"[3]

There was little action of any type at RCKTWN that evening. The club, owned by Michael W. Smith, is a stationary youth-culture cruise ship, with a skate park, coffeehouse, and music venue that features both Christian and general-market bands (I was there the year before to see A.F.I., Thursday, and Coheed & Cambria). On this evening, it was hosting a sparsely attended showcase for Christian R&B artists that was dwarfed by the club's cavernous confines. I appreciated the professional way one singer, seventeen-year-old J3, tried to get the two sides of the room to engage in a clapping competition, no small feat when you're playing to thirty people.

There was no such problem at the Tooth & Nail/BEC showcase at the Nashville Hilton, which was heaving with kids and radio programmers, all of whom Doug Van Pelt—whom I'd run into on the way—seemed to know. I watched high-energy three-song sets by Falling Up and Hawk Nelson, a group of well-scrubbed Canadian lads who played their Christian-radio hit "Letter to the President" (with a chorus equating same-sex marriage with murder, date rape, and car theft) and closed saying, "Thank you! Eat your carrots! And smoking is a very bad idea!"

Van Pelt was strangely insistent that we leave before KJ-52, a white rapper who's done for Christian adult contemporary music what Jay-Z did for *Annie*, refitting Rebecca St. James and Jeremy Camp songs as hip-hop numbers. We ended up in a small ballroom at the Renaissance, where we failed to win iPod Photos at a funk-metal showcase called NY Underground.

Back in my hotel room, I wondered what the hell I was doing here. I hadn't seen any particularly interesting music, I couldn't win an iPod Shuffle to save my life, and the industry stuff was utterly closed to me—I was asked to leave a couple panel discussions that I tried to sit in on, in fact. I'd put in ten interview requests before I'd left and hadn't heard back from anybody. I was sick of good-looking, clean-cut kids who made music that took all its cues from a world they wanted no part of, I was sick of artists who profited from the low expectations of their audience, I was sick of white rappers, and I was really sick of fat front men with minibeards.

Christian culture's strong preference that young people marry rather than date has not just resulted in a divorce rate higher than the national average,[4] it's produced a bumper crop of chunky singers. It's a sad fact that once men are freed from the fear that each woman they meet may be their last chance at happiness, they tend to scarf that third hot dog without reflection. The net effect of this is a business filled with stocky musicians whose ring fingers flash in the stage lights as they play.

I believe this, as much as anything else, is holding back Christian rock from greater commercial acceptance. Rock stars aren't supposed to look like normal people. That's why we pay them so much money. We want rock stars to be everything we're not—impossibly skinny, stupid rich, unshowered, smelly and miserable. If we wanted to see happy, pudgy dudes with Van Dyke beards and spiky haircuts onstage, we'd pay more attention to the roadies.

The next night, I was determined to hang out with Anthony Barr-Jeffrey since he'd once again had an evening filled with musical epiphanies, including a "Christian crunk" show by an artist named Mr. Del that he characterized as "ridiculously fun." I was not having fun—I was just feeling ridiculous—and I hoped an evening with Anthony might pull me out of my funk, which was growing ever more spiteful.

We met at the B.B. King's club on Second Avenue to see the Dying of Thirst tour, featuring a bunch of underground Christian rappers. It was running on hip-hop time—meaning an hour after the doors opened the artists hadn't even sound-checked, so we walked backed up Commerce Street to the Renaissance, where we caught a little bit of Toby Mac's E.R.A.C.E. show—the Mac wasn't on yet, but we caught a few minutes of Tommy Sims, who cowrote Eric Clapton's "Change the World," which ought to keep him in pillbox hats for a while.

Back at B.B.'s, Macho, a rapper affiliated with L.A.'s Tunnel Rats crew, was making the most of an unenviable situation—getting a small crowd fired up, basically to benefit the artists who come on after him. Dressed in a Boston Celtics jersey and matching hat, he meticulously rapped about how he knows he'll never get played on the radio because you have to mention thugs and girls "to get that radio love." At another point in the show, he noted that his album is on sale in the back but said he didn't "like to promote his own records."

In hip-hop, this is basically suicidal behavior. Macho doesn't swear, look down on women, or rhyme about drugs or material goods. He's everything people say they wish rap was, and maybe forty-five people came out to hear him. Toward the end of his show, he brought on Dax Reynosa, the founder of the Tunnel Rats, who couldn't quite get his flow on. Dax blamed the crowd for not being close enough. By the time Dax got through his rap, after three false starts, Macho's CD of backing tracks had finished, so Macho gamely beat-boxed while his boss spieled.

Barr-Jeffrey introduced me to Reynosa after the show. A short, squat guy with long curly hair that shot out like vapor trails, Dax exuded hostility. "What kind of book are you trying to write?" he asked me, contemptuously. "You want to write fiction, or you want to write the truth?"

"Well, Dax, I'm a journalist, so it's nonfic—"

"So what kind of book do you want to write? Do you want to write the truth?"

I realized that this wasn't going anywhere.

"Okay Dax," I said resignedly, "I want to write the truth."

"If you want to write the truth, I'll talk to you." Then he told me I could set up something with his "assistant," directing me to Macho, and walked away.

"He's pretty frustrated with journalists," Barr-Jeffrey told me apologetically. "He's been doing this for a long time."

A group called Glue played next, and they were really good—two nerdy white guys from the Midwest whose bearded, balding MC, Adeem, used his Christianity as a lens, not a subject itself. "Who are we fighting? We're fighting ourselves!" he shouted in a rap that called out the war in Iraq and internecine doctrinal disputes within the church with equal anger.

I had an enjoyable chat with Macho—he's a youth counselor in L.A. and had just started running Tunnel Rats' record label. I never did get around to setting something up with Dax.

After Glue, Barr-Jeffrey and I headed up to the Rhythm Kitchen to see Grits, but the place was so crowded I couldn't move. The headliners weren't scheduled to go on for another couple of hours, and the Christian comedian onstage was explaining the difference between black and white women when it came to punctuality. Bedtime, I decided. I needed to rest up for the Gospel Music Awards the next night. Glue and Macho had poked some holes in my bad mood, and I wanted to go back to my room and enjoy the beams of light shining through.

I'd come to Nashville to understand the Christian music industry, but I'd had no more luck doing that than scoring an iPod Shuffle. The mainstream Christian industry—the big-business part of it, on display everywhere—lay tantalizingly out of reach. I was hoping that the next night's GMA awards were going to help remedy that. Mostly, I had found a lot of smaller scenes—hip-hop, alt-rock, country—at odds with one another. There was no doubt that a lot of money was around Christian music, but it was a lot less cohesive, and a lot less evangelical, than I'd expected.

The day before, Anthony had brought me to meet Josh Niemyjski, Jon Madison, and Jae Choi, who run a Christian hip-hop indie label called Illect. Niemyjski told me that GMA was a "dark week" for him, but they all really needed to be there to try to nail down distribution. As I left, Choi asked me if I was a Christian, and when I said no, he handed me a tract.

I was on the plane home before I realized that I'd been working on this project for six months, and it was the first time anyone had tried to evangelize me.

CHAPTER 8

If We Are the Body

"**D**ude! I'm at the Gospel Music Awards!"

He was in his late teens or early twenties, wearing long red shorts and a black T-shirt, sitting on a concrete bench outside the Grand Ole Opry House.

"Yeah, Skillet wanted to get a bunch of people to rush the stage when they play," he said, sounding amused in a jaded, adolescent voice that implied he did this sort of thing every few days, "so I signed up on their website."

"If you're with the Skillet group, follow me, please," said a carefully coiffed woman with a clipboard and a voice that was all business (and no Nashville). She led Phone Dude and fifty or so other kids in jeans and T-shirts to a roped-off pen away from the theater entrance. Most of the remaining women were wearing diaphanous cocktail dresses and were accompanied by men in cowboy semiformal—jeans, boots, shirts with bolo ties.

The Doves, now in their thirty-sixth year and properly known as the Gospel Music Association Music Awards (or GMAs), are the Christian music industry's Grammys. In years past, the Doves operated like most other awards shows, presenting the awards that— let's face it—most people don't care about in a preshow ceremony and saving the main show for the glamorous categories, e.g., Artist of the Year, Song of the Year, etc.

This night was going to be different. In an admirably democratic move, the Gospel Music Association decided to present all forty-four awards during the main ceremony, which would be televised two months later on independent TV stations through a syndication service.

I'd already purchased a ticket for the GMAs after my press credentials were initially denied, and since the press pass I'd subsequently received allowed me only to watch the show on TV in a windowless press room, I decided to go ahead and use my ticket, which had cost $60.

As it turned out, if my seat had been any further from the stage, I'd have been back dodging traffic in my hotel room. Luckily, the Opry building, which succeeded the Ryman Auditorium as the home of the venerable country music broadcast in 1974, is a beautiful facility with no bad sightlines. From my vertiginous perch on the balcony, I could see the stage and video screens perfectly, plus all the swells up front and the mid-level industry folks behind them. Even better, I was among hardcore Christian music fans, most of whom clutched pens and programs they were using as score sheets, so I wouldn't particularly stand out by taking notes.

That program, incidentally, included a note from President Bush, who commended the nominees and the GMA for their "dedication to sharing the good news through music. Your work reminds us of God's love and boundless mercy and inspires others to serve a cause greater than self," he wrote. There ain't no flies on George, I marveled, remembering how closely the Republican message for the 2004 presidential election mirrored the political concerns of so many evangelical Christians.

During that election season, in fact, Toby Mac and Michael Tait from D.C. Talk published a book called *Under God* that attempted to prove definitively that America was founded by Christians who would probably be evangelicals today. From a historical standpoint, it's a breathtaking piece of revisionism—for example, the book holds Thomas Jefferson and Benjamin Franklin as particular examples of Christian values, and doesn't mention that Jefferson *rewrote the Bible* to exclude all mention of the supernatural and had children with one of his slaves, or that Franklin gleefully expressed his own moral values with women other than his wife on both sides of the Atlantic.

Under God echoes an interesting characteristic of evangelicalism—an egalitarian view of authority that derives from Martin Luther's assertion in the Ninety-Five Theses that he didn't need the Roman Catholic Church's help and would interpret the Bible for himself. The result, according to Randall Ballmer, is a "theological free-for-all, as various individuals or groups insist that their reading of the Bible is the only possible interpretation."[1]

But why limit this self-appointed expertise to theology? Late last year, the all-male Christian rock band Relient K published a book called *The Complex Infrastructure of the Female Mind*, a guide to understanding women. I found this especially intriguing since Relient K's most recent album includes such lady-positive lyrics as "The way a girl can turn a head/Well she is such a threat."

The GMA's chaplain, Bishop Kenneth H. Dupree—a former musician who was briefly married to Natalie Cole—opened the ceremonies with a prayer that "this will be so much more than a show," before Denver and the Mile High Orchestra, a Christian swing group in red zoot suits, warmed up the crowd. The group's energetic front man, Denver Bierman, is an unusual combination of lounge lizard and preacher, "warning" the audience that the next number is "a little groovy" one moment and delivering a hepcat patter about the Trinity the next.

The first hosts out were Israel Houghton and Darlene Zschech. Houghton is a Christian R&B singer; Zschech, with Rebecca St. James and the Newsboys' Pete Furler, is a member of the Australian mafia that's slowly infiltrating the genre—she wrote "Shout to the Lord," one of the biggest worship songs ever, and has an active ministry on two continents. "Any Australians in the audience?" she shouted. "We can't dance, but we can jump!" (Presumably a reference to the then imminent entry of Aussie Andrew Bogut to the NBA.)

Singer Natalie Grant strutted out in a spangly jacket and a shirt that said SEEK JUSTICE and played a rock song that ended with a burst of Sonic Youth–style noise. Then it was time for the first award: Special Event Album of the Year, for which a prerecorded voice read the name of every single artist on every one of the compilation albums nominated in excruciating detail. *The Passion of the Christ: Songs* won. Accepting the award, one of the members of Third Day thanked God that appearing on the album gave the band "the opportunity to perform on the *Jay Leno* show."

Mark Hall, the singer and songwriter for Casting Crowns, won the award for Songwriter of the Year next. Casting Crowns is a Georgia group that took the Christian music world by storm in only two short years, with a self-titled album whose lyrics challenge churches not to be so insular that they put off newcomers. "I'm just an old youth pastor," said a po-faced Hall, sharing credit with his band, their producer, Stephen Curtis Chapman, and of course, God.

The awards began to whizz by. The Crabb Family, a Southern gospel group of siblings (two of whom are identical twins) from Kentucky, were steamrolling all comers in every category they were nominated in. After a while, the members of the band stopped coming up altogether and sent their father and songwriter, Gerald Crabb, up to accept a few of their awards instead.

The word *gospel* as a description of music is problematic. Most music fans think of gospel as black music, but especially in the South, there's a rich tradition of, for lack of a better description, white gospel music. The Crabbs are heirs to an understudied tradition of music that incorporates country, blues, bluegrass, boogie-woogie, and old-time elements, from David "Dad" Carter's Chuck Wagon Gang in the '30s to Bill and Gloria Gaither today. It's almost entirely confined to the Appalachian region of the country, though R.E.M. gave the genre a high-profile boost in its song "Voice of Harold," in which Michael Stipe sings the liner notes to a Revelaires album (fronted by the sublimely named J. Elmo Fagg) out of order.

When the Crabbs performed a bit later, it was apparent how a group of youngsters had come to dominate the dusty world of Southern gospel—their performance, backed by a choir of CCM all-stars standing in wheeled-in pews, was intense. Adam Crabb, the group's young singer and harmonica player, whipped himself and the crowd into earthly and heavenly ecstasy, shouting, "Can't nobody do me like Jesus!" and "He's my man!" I wondered if his white belt was a tip to past gospel performers because his tight, tapered jeans sure weren't.

The Crabbs weren't the only artists demolishing the competition—Switchfoot and their singer, Jonathan Foreman, whose most recent album had come out long enough ago to qualify for the GMA awards the previous year, were nominated in eight categories, many of which they were winning handily. In a remarkable display of competing pathologies, the Christian music industry was trying to lay a definitive claim to a group so terrified of being seen as Christian artists that its members hadn't shown up.

Singer Jeremy Camp, who'd won Doves for Male Vocalist and New Artist of the Year in 2004, addressed the association's generous eligibility rules when he won Rock Recorded Song of the Year for the title track of his 2003 album *Stay*. "It's weird, that song is really old, but whatever," Camp said, bemusedly.

"Get your TiVos ready, it's gonna be a classic!" shouted a man in a long, red fur coat, thigh-high boots, jeans, a wig, and mirrored sunglasses. His name is Tonex (pronounced Ton-ay), and he was not exaggerating. Halfway through his performance, Tonex twirled, kneeled, removed his wig, and dropped his coat to reveal a gigantic, diamond-studded cross bouncing against a shirt that said JESUS LOVES MY TATOOS as he ran through the crowd. Up by me in the cheap seats, Tonex's stylistic bridge between OutKast, the Bee Gees, and Liberace was met mostly by folded arms and harrumphs, but it was easily one of the most compelling shows I saw all week.

Warning that they might cause "stylistic whiplash," an offstage voice introduced the next presenters, Rick & Bubba, self-proclaimed "sexiest fat men alive" and a pair of Alabamian DJs whose syndicated show brings "Christian values" to morning drive times across the South. "Tonight we're the *saintliest* fat men alive!" they shouted. Rick Burgess announced he was soon to be "officially white trash" now that his fifth child was due, and Bubba, for some reason, announced the death of Santa Claus.

When CCM singer Rebecca St. James and gospel singer Smokie Norful came out, they sang "This Little Light of Mine," St. James exhibiting an odd vocal honk between stanzas. The next awards were a blur of an absent Switchfoot and a baffled Jeremy Camp piling on honors for moldering albums.

The Traditional Gospel Album of the Year category revealed the distance the Christian music industry has to go if it's serious about effacing race differences within its community. Among white audience members, response to the announcement of this category was tepid at best, as it was during J Moss's smoking contemporary gospel performance later in the show, which nearly took my head off. I looked around me and saw that every, and I mean every, white person in the balcony was seated, while most of the black audience members were standing during Moss's performance.

A de facto segregation of awards categories exists. The only African American to win Male Vocalist of the Year is Larnelle Harris, who won the last of three such awards in 1988. Women have fared a little better: CeCe Winans broke the color barrier for Female Vocalist of the Year in 1996 and 1997, and Latina vocalist Jaci Velasquez took home the honor twice, in 1999 and 2000. DC Talk, which is two-thirds white, represents the only racial diversity in the Artist of the Year category. There have been three Best New Artists who weren't white (Velasquez, '97; Take6, '89; BeBe and CeCe Winans, '88).

While the Traditional and Contemporary Gospel categories are entirely black, the Rap/Hip-Hop Album of the Year category, something you'd think might lean heavily African-American, has been won by white or mostly white groups all but three times since the award was inaugurated in 1991. So, it wasn't too great a shock when Toby Mac won that category this year with his *Welcome to Diverse City,* a title that reflects Mac's sincere hope for a more inclusive Christian music world but which is ironic at best.

An all-star worship-music band, including Chris Tomlin and David Crowder, backed English worship leader Matt Redman on his worship hit "Blessed Be Your Name," which is so catchy it rocketed through my head weeks afterward. (Hey, I'm not made of stone!)

In an entirely nonworshipful moment, I noticed something odd about presenter and Female Vocalist of the Year nominee Joy Williams that I couldn't put my finger on immediately. Then, I realized what it was: She has big breasts. She may be the only female performer in Christian music so afflicted. In a 2004 *Rolling Stone* profile, Jessica Simpson said she was shunned by the Christian music industry when she developed her famous curves because her label head was concerned that her bodaciousness would inspire lust. Williams is almost always photographed from the neck up or hunched forward with her shoulders forward so her arms obscure her figure.

There are two notable ways in which the Christian music industry is different from the general market. The first is that controversy has a negative effect on album sales. The second is that sex does not sell. The merest hint of sexuality, so central to the mythology of rock 'n' roll, will derail an artist's career. Sandi Patty won Female Vocalist of the Year eleven times from 1982 to 1992, but her career nearly ended after her revelation in 1995 that she'd had an affair. Patty's been more or less rehabilitated (she appeared at this night's show as a presenter), though her album sales have never recovered. Michael English, who won six Doves in 1994 alone, remains shunned by his former community, however. After he announced that he'd had an affair with another Christian singer, Marabeth Jordan of First Call, he was dropped by his record company (most Christian record labels insist on such "morality clauses," which can void artists' contracts if invoked). Even now, the bestselling 2005 CD compilation *Wow #1s: 31 of the Greatest Christian Music Hits Ever* includes a cover version of English's biggest hit, "In Christ Alone," rather than risk the wrath of Christian music buyers by featuring the original.

And Amy Grant inspired calls for boycotts when she told *Rolling Stone* that she enjoyed sunbathing nude. But Grant had never been shy about her sexuality; her voice exudes sensuousness, and she'd always been upfront in her interviews about her determination that Christian women could be sexy. Which is why, when she divorced her first husband, Christian artist Gary Chapman, and quickly married country star Vince Gill, it wasn't that great a scandal. One gets the sense most Christian fans assumed Chapman wasn't up to the job.

This isn't mere prudishness (though that's certainly part of it)—this tendency goes to the heart of evangelical Christianity's gnostic struggles with the concept of being in the world but not of it. Case in point: Sixpence None the Richer's worldwide 1999 hit "Kiss Me"—a snapshot of simple, ardent, presumably monogamous love—which went to No. 1 in ten different countries. The band members were card-carrying Christians who recorded for a Christian-owned and -distributed record label (Steve Taylor's Squint). You'd expect a Switchfoot-sized display of glomming on to the band's success from the GMA, but that's in fact exactly the opposite of what happened—"Kiss Me" was disqualified from the Doves after the

GMA hurriedly composed some rules as to what constituted a "Christian" recording. The tortuous definition it came up with is a masterpiece of inadequacy:

> [M]usic in any style whose lyric is substantially based upon histori-cally orthodox Christian truth contained in or derived from the Holy Bible; and/or an expression of worship of God or praise for his works; and/or testimony of relationship with God through Christ; and/or obviously prompted and informed by a Christian worldview.

Not only does this definition put people in the music industry in the curious position of deciding whether a particular set of lyrics is "informed by a Christian worldview," or not, it more or less reduces music to the words sung over it. Instrumental music wouldn't seem to qualify at all. The GMA tried to fix this in subsequent iterations, most recently settling on:

> For purposes of GMA Music Award eligibility, the lyrics of all en-tries in the Album and Song categories will be: based upon the his-torically orthodox Christian faith contained in or derived from the Holy Bible; or apparently prompted and informed by a Christian worldview.

Note the "apparently." I get the feeling the GMA is hoping an-other "Kiss Me" doesn't come down the pike anytime soon.

After intermission, during a commercial break, with the stage dark as hands scurried around behind her, Rebecca St. James had an idea that single-handedly revived my faith in the Christian music industry. "Shall we sing a hymn?" she asked. A capella, she led the entire room in Rich Mullins' "Awesome God," its minor pentatonic melody filling even the space between the rafters where I was sitting.

Gospel Music Week had been rough for me—I'd only seen, or maybe only let myself see, the Christian music industry's flaws, which are legion, but not the whole story. Because, despite its infuriating contradictions, the CCM world is a community constructed around the honest and deep beliefs of its participants. I guess I just wish the music mainstream CCM produces was better.

After Skillet played, with their fans rushing the stage as promised to see a loud, flash-pot-illuminated version of the band's modern rock single "Savior" that was so powerful even my neighbors in the rafters unclenched their arms, and Casting Crowns won so many awards that they let their drummer speak (he thanked the group's soundman and his wife, in that order), and Steve Taylor and Michael W. Smith goofed around as presenters, Third Day won Rock/Contemporary Album of the Year. Mac Powell, the band's singer, exhorted everyone in the room to stand up and join him in a prayer for the Christian music industry. "If there's anything in the industry that's not of you," he beseeched God, "we pray you take it out." Sitting while others stood, I suggested the folks on either side of me hold hands with each other instead, then nervously scanned the ceiling for lightning bolts.

Switchfoot won Artist of the Year. Toby Mac, who presented the award, prefaced it by saying, "We have to acknowledge that they're out there in the world." The absent band got a standing ovation.

Casting Crowns closed the show with a rendition of their hit "If We Are the Body," which takes evangelical churches to task for deciding whom to minister to and whom to exclude. "Jesus paid far too high a price," singer Mark Hall intoned on the bridge, "For us to pick and choose who should come."

Bill Hearn

Bill Hearn is the ultimate Christian music insider. His father, Billy Ray Hearn, founded two of the earliest rock-oriented Christian labels, Myrrh and Sparrow, which Bill took over in 1995. Now Bill Hearn is the president and CEO of the EMI Christian Music Group, which was created when he sold Sparrow and its subsidiary labels to the British corporation EMI the same year. Hearn also presided over a key development in Christian music: the adoption of SoundScan, reporting technology for retail sales, which showed that a lot more Christian music was being sold than the secular music industry wanted to admit. Since then, Christian music sales have increased a mind-blowing 80 percent, and the EMI Christian Music Group accounts for 40 percent of the resulting $700 million business. Not bad for a guy who once got freaked out by a picture of a Mexican buffet.

Bill, you grew up around a lot of those early Jesus Music artists, didn't you?

Oh, absolutely. Keith Green, 2nd Chapter of Acts. Barry McGuire, the Talbot Brothers. My mom was kind of their second mom. It was back in the old days when artists and labels had real strong personal relationships. Now we have managers and agents that keep us from the artists!

But they would go out on the road and tour, and they'd come back in, and we'd all get together for dinner, and they'd tell us about all of the exciting things that were happening on the road. How many people were being saved, and how many people were responding to the music, and it was just really exciting. It was one big family. So, yeah, I grew up around the creative community, even though I wasn't a musician myself.

Did you listen to non-Christian music as well growing up?

I did. I was a big fan. A few years after my dad started Myrrh, ABC bought [Myrrh's corporate parent] Word, or they started to distribute Word. So my dad went to a sales conference. That year, they handed out a bunch of records there—he just gave 'em to me. It was the first time I got turned on to ZZ Top. I was in Texas, and Southern rock was really big then. I was a big Marshall Tucker Band fan and Charlie Daniels and that type of music.

He brought home this record called *Tres Hombres.* I opened it up and said, "Man, this is strange. It's got this big Mexican buffet inside the album cover." And I remember I didn't listen to the record for, like, three months because I didn't understand the packaging. I finally put it on, and I've been a big ZZ Top fan ever since.

Now I have a very diverse taste. I like just about anything. I just love great songs. I'm still a song person; I love pop music. Whoever's writing great songs, that's the music I like.

One of the common themes I've noticed among people I've interviewed for this book is that a lot of Christian artists weren't allowed to listen to secular music growing up.

I gotta tell you, I did grow up in a Southern Baptist environment, but I guess I was fortunate. I heard stories about legalistic families who just—you can't watch TV, you can't listen to music—but I just never grew up with that experience. My dad was always progressive.

That's why he had big youth groups and big youth choirs, and that's how he came up with the idea that there's a need for this kind of contemporary music. He was one of the first ministers of music to ever bring a rhythm section into a church. Live drums, electric guitar, you know, most people would have thrown him out on his ear back in those days.

He exposed me to all kinds of music, and our artist roster at Myrrh and the early days of Sparrow was predominantly Pentecostal. And my dad has always called himself a "Bapticostal," 'cause he grew up Baptist, but most of his friends, most of his artists, were Pentecostals.

EMI is an enormous company. How comfortable do you feel within such a gigantic corporate framework?

When we sold the company, we just said, look, the only thing we ask you guys—and they made this commitment—is that you never ask us to do anything that compromises our vision or our convictions. And they've never done that.

So, we came to work the next day, and we sat around, and we said, "The only thing we're gonna have to fear in this relationship is our own humanness." Are we gonna try to be too much like the world? Are we gonna focus too much on how much money we can make and how many records we can sell at the expense of what our vision is? And every day, I try to come work and say, Let's focus on the vision.

You guys actually increased market share.

We're one of the most profitable companies in the EMI system around the world. And they highly respect us for that, and we've been able to show them that we can operate a business successfully, and we can operate it with integrity and with Christian principles, but at the same time succeed. Which a lot of people don't think is possible.

So at the big meetings, are you ever like, "In your face!" to the people at Astralwerks [EMI's hip electronic music label]?

[Laughs] Hey, I love Errol [Kolosine, Astralwerks' general manager]! Errol's a great guy. You would be surprised. I talk more about spirituality with Errol than with anybody in the EMI system. He's very curious about what we do and what we believe. We've had great conversations because he's a true music guy in that he's into everything. And he has a couple bands that are Christians. He's got this band the Golden Republic; they're a faith-based band. He's always telling me, "They're really good people—they don't lie." And I'm like, "Yeah! There's a reason for that."

Now that Christian music is centered around Nashville, it seems like the lines between country and Christian music are blurring. I'm thinking of Tim McGraw's recent hit "Drugs or Jesus" or Randy Travis signing to Word.

My view on that would be that country music is just becoming more pop. Christian music is the only music that's categorized by the lyrical content as opposed to the musical side. Okay, so, we've always been in the pop media, the popular music business. And that's why we're so diverse—we have everything from emo to hardcore to inspirational to every kind of pop music there is, hip-hop, whatever. And that's because we're really just trying to impact culture through whatever the current sounds are in modern culture. And I think country has kind of moved more toward the center. There is no real market for country Christian music, though.

Oh really?

No. Because—and maybe you're right as far as the lines are blurred, but I think your average country fan is kind of a God-fearing American. Why do I need country Christian when all country is Christian? It's stories and songs, that's kind of my general view on it.

They'd just as soon buy a country record as buy a country Christian record.

You mentioned emo and hardcore. Are you able to keep up with all the flavors of Christian music?

Well, we have it all here! We have five labels. We have a gospel label, we have Sparrow and Forefront, and we're an equity stakeholder in Tooth & Nail as well as Gotee, and they focus on the hardcore thing. I have to rely on our label heads and our A&R guys to stay very current and relevant. And they keep me young by sending me music and making sure I'm up to speed on things.

So have you seen Demon Hunter?

[*Laughs*] I must admit, I've never seen Demon Hunter. However, I have been to a lot of Tooth & Nail bands' shows.

Does Christian music translate overseas?

Nah. We're predominately a North American company. Our music doesn't travel well unless we cross it over here in America. So pretty much we don't get a lot of attention internationally unless we make something happen here. We broke Stacie Orrico through our partnership with Virgin and ended up selling over a million and a half units outside of the core. But that was purely based on it being a pop hit.

Now, Stacie's an absolutely committed and dedicated Christian, and she used that platform, especially in Japan, to be very, very positive and influence kids. She appeared in a magazine over there, a pretty risqué magazine, and they asked her to do some things that she refused to do. And she also was able to communicate her message to kids through that magazine.

Does it ever feel like a rejection when an artist tries to pursue general-market success?

The only time I ever get disappointed is when a band builds a career in this market, and then the minute they have some success, they immediately try to deny any history over here. And my problem with that is, you know, just be who you are, and if you make great music, it'll be successful. You don't have to reject where you came from. I don't mind you going out there and not talking about it. But to actually reject it and say, like, that never happened and, boy, I would never be affiliated with that, it's almost like apologizing. I've told a lot of people in print that I'll never apologize for what we do. We are trying to reach people who want entertainment that's basically for their lifestyle.

Now, I wanna make better music, like everybody else. But the minute I do, I'm not gonna try to apologize. I came from here. I think Switchfoot does a really good job. They're careful about what they will do and won't do, but they never deny their faith. They never deny that they're affiliated with Sparrow, that that's where they came from, and they're proud of their affiliation, and they're glad that we're still part of their team and selling their records.

Some artists say, "Not only do I not want to be affiliated with you anymore, I don't want you to sell my records in bookstores anymore." We've had those discussions with different artists. That disappoints me.

One of the concerns that I've heard voiced by Christian musicians is that if you sign to a mainstream Christian label, you'll have people coming down to the studio asking you to change lyrics, rearrange songs. Is that valid?

You mean if you're signed to a Christian label? You mean water down your lyrics?

I don't necessarily mean water down; I think maybe pump up the "Jesuses-per-minute" factor.

[*Laughs*] I'll tell you, I think there's a lot more myth than reality to that. Our A&R people are challenged to help our artists to craft and make the best music possible. Yes, there have been times when we've said, "Are we trying to get Christian radio? Is this an important part of marketing this record? If it is, we need to give Christian radio something they want. Something they'll play." That doesn't necessarily mean Jesuses-per-minute.

It may be musical. It may be melody. It may be production. It may be the mix. But we don't have conversations like, "There's just not enough content," because, first of all, I'm hoping we're not gonna sign an artist that doesn't have some meat in their lyrics. I don't care how many *Jesus*es there are as long as it's poetic and it's creative.

Now, I'm not saying that an A&R guy's never gone in and said, "Hey, if we said this instead of that, radio might play it." I will tell you it's not a strategy of ours, and it's certainly not a mandate that our A&R guys have. I just wouldn't do that. If it's a bad song, make it better, but you're certainly not gonna make a bad song better if you throw a couple of *Jesus*es in the chorus.

Do you think Christian music's better than it used to be?

By far. We're making better music every year. And you'd be surprised how many mainstream producers, mixers, and engineers wanna work with us now. 'Cause they really respect the music that we're doing. You know what else? They respect working with us. We treat them decently. We pay them. We deal with integrity, and we do what we say. We've attracted a lot of people from the outside world to work with us. It's also helping us do our job better.

Are there always gonna be two worlds of music?

I hope not. We're working very hard strategically to make the two one—not to become like the world but to view the world as one market.

How do you do that?

You just have to be intentional about the fact that if you make real quality and culturally relevant music, you should look at it as being able to appeal to everybody, and you have to market it to everybody. Let's don't look at radio and say, "Well, we're a Christian company, so we only send our music to Christian radio." We should be working all radio formats that make sense for that music. And we should be building relationships internationally and overcoming the stigma, whatever preconceived notions people have about our music. In other words, instead of sticking our heads in the sand and saying, "We'll never sell any records in Southeast Asia, so let's don't go there," you have to go and build relationships and know that it's a long-term process. You can't go expecting a short-term success or short-term results.

CHAPTER 9

Black and White in a
Gray World

They were everywhere at Cornerstone—T-shirts that said ABORTION IS MEAN, or I SURVIVED or FORMER EMBRYO. There was one I kept trying to read on the teens wearing them without looking like a creep.

> YOU WILL NOT SILENCE MY MESSAGE
> YOU WILL NOT MOCK MY GOD
> YOU WILL STOP KILLING MY GENERATION

On the front of these shirts was the logo of a group called Rock for Life—a subsidiary of a pro-life organization called the American Life League (ALL)—whose insignia was a fetus playing guitar. Now *that's* something you don't see every day, I thought.

In a piece I wrote about the festival for the *Washington Post*, I mentioned that the shirts were selling well. A few days later, a blog post appeared on Rock for Life's site. It read, in part:

> Check out the Washington Post's coverage of Cornerstone Festival, "Hallelujah Palooza." Cornerstone is the latest festival we

attended. It's not the most glorious review of a Christian festival, but it does include a paragraph about Rock for Life. In it you can sense the disdain for the number of our shirts visible throughout the festival, along with the message we convey on them.

I failed to discern any scorn in my piece, but Rock for Life, obviously, disagreed.

Coincidentally, after I'd stewed about this for a couple days, Jon Dolan, one of my editors at *Spin,* called me and asked me if I knew of any youth-oriented, conservative Christian political groups that I could profile for the magazine's election issue. "I have just the one," I told him.

By the end of my first interview with Rock for Life director Erik Whittington, I wasn't sure whether to bring up the blog post because . . . well, I liked him. He knows baseball. He has kids. We have stuff in common. It's just that on Saturdays, I tend to mow my lawn, maybe grill out, and—far too often—pass out drunk in my hammock. He, on the other hand, stands outside women's health clinics holding a sign that says ABORTION KILLS CHILDREN.

I decided to go for broke. "I have a bone to pick with you," I said.

"Uh-oh," he replied.

"I wrote that article on the Cornerstone Festival in the *Post,* and I don't appreciate you saying that I was disdainful of your group."

He told me he'd take another look at the article. A few days later, he e-mailed me back:

I reread your article in the Post. Being in ALL's media relations department the last 2 1/2 years I've had some interesting experiences with certain newspapers. If a Christian publication would have written the same thing I wouldn't have reacted the same way. I guess I let some past issues cloud my thinking a bit. I can see things more clearly now. Hope that makes sense??

I appreciated his change of heart, but he never did share it with Rock for Life's readers. Though, to be fair, *Spin* didn't run my piece on Rock for Life.

"No diapers today?" David Bereit asked Matt Wilson as we stood in the parking lot of the American Life League's headquarters in Stafford, Virginia. At seventeen, Matt is unofficially famous around ALL for wearing nothing but a diaper and a pacifier to a demonstration earlier this year (today, he was sticking with shorts and a T-shirt). It was 5:30 am, and I was tagging along as Whittington, Bereit (director of ALL's anti–Planned Parenthood organization, STOPP), and Matt drove up to Washington, D.C.

They were going to counterdemonstrate at a Planned Parenthood rally in front of the Supreme Court. It was two weeks after hurricane Katrina ravaged New Orleans, and the Senate was belatedly beginning confirmation hearings on the nomination of John Roberts to be chief justice of the United States. The nomination was all but a done deal, but Rock for Life didn't want Planned Parenthood to be the only group in front of the cameras.

We took Bereit's Camry (Whittington's Geo was too small) and hurtled up the HOV lanes on I-95 in the dark, worship music throbbing softly through the car's audio system. Bereit moved to Stafford this year, having spearheaded pro-life activities in College Station, Texas, since 2001. He grew up Presbyterian but became alienated when the Presbyterian Church cosponsored what he called the "March for Death"—the 2004 Planned Parenthood–organized March for Women's Lives.

Bereit's national profile had greatly increased since he began campaigning against Planned Parenthood full-time in 2001. He'd been on *Politically Incorrect* and become a sought-after speaker for pro-life groups. Anyway, things were getting weird back home. "All of a sudden we had major problems with the police," he said. "Come to find out a police sergeant had asked to be in charge of clinic security. Unbeknownst to us, she was involved in a lesbian relationship with the head of Planned Parenthood."

Cops, the guys told me, are pretty unpredictable and make up a lot of laws on the spot. The night before, a few young pro-lifers, including Rock for Life's Phil Eddy, employed the pro-life tactic of "sidewalk chalking"—which some might call "writing on the sidewalk"—but were popped for it by some cops at Union Station who took exception to this particular First Amendment expression. One of the pro-lifers, a young woman, was handcuffed for a while as the cops figured out what to do—nothing, as it turned out. They released her with no citation.

There was some discussion as to what the cops would have done had the kids been chalking pro-choice messages instead. "We can put as vulgar a message as we want and say it's from Planned Parenthood," Matt chortled.

Whittington told me about his wife Tina's first pro-life rally. He'd taken her to Atlanta, where she met his grandfather, who was poorly. There, he'd asked her to marry him. Lilith Fair, a tour that featured mostly women artists, was making a stop nearby, so the newly betrothed couple went to protest the festival's pro-choice message. "She had always wondered what I did [for a living]," he said. "She just turned into a fireball," he said, describing how they badgered the festival goers. "She was having so much fun!"

The guys told me some battle stories—the time they filled up a parking lot near a Planned Parenthood fund-raiser with a bunch of cars with pro-life stickers, for instance, and got someone with a professional video camera to pretend he was covering the event. All the people "trying to sneak in and support abortion without anyone knowing," Whittington said, "were thinking they were gonna be on the evening news!"

This was my second trip to Stafford. A month earlier, I drove up on a day that was hot even for August, hot even for Virginia. "Look for the RV in the parking lot," Whittington had told me when giving directions, and I had to admit, it made an excellent landmark—twenty-nine feet long with PRO-LIFE painted in two-foot letters across the hood and slogans gaily festooning the rest of its massive expanse: STOP KILLING MY GENERATION; ROCK FOR LIFE: MAKING THE WOMB A SAFER PLACE TO LIVE; the cartoon fetus playing guitar in the womb.

The RV contrasted starkly with ALL's office, a nondescript, low-slung '60s building that once housed the Stafford sheriff's department. Suburbia was descending quickly on this once-sleepy country town as Washingtonians driven farther and farther away by the overheated real-estate market forty miles north were buying up new houses as fast as developers could plonk them down on old farmland. The traffic on the short piece of two-lane road between the Stafford exit on I-95 and ALL's parking lot was only going to get worse.

You don't just march into the American Life League; you buzz and state your business, and then, if you seem legit, someone leads you into a narrow room with one chair and a couple of flashing alarm panels, where you wait for a while until you get buzzed into the real office by someone sitting behind glass. It's hardly the type of security system that would stop a Bradley Fighting Vehicle, but it's probably very effective when it comes to keeping out protesters.

The American pro-life movement as we know it coalesced in the early '70s in response to two Supreme Court Decisions, *Roe v. Wade* and *Doe v. Bolton,* which were decided on the same day, January 22, 1973. *Roe* was filed on behalf of Norma McCorvey, an unmarried Texas woman who wished to terminate her pregnancy (she used the name "Jane Roe" to protect her identity). After months of wrangling, a 7–2 majority of Supreme Court justices decided that Texas's antiabortion law was "unconstitutionally vague" and that abortion during the first trimester of pregnancy, as well as the very decision to have an abortion, was part of a Constitutionally implied "right to privacy." *Doe*, in turn, struck down most of the severe requirements of a Georgia law restricting abortion as unconstitutional.

These decisions essentially legalized surgical abortion in the United States, and groups opposed to the practice, many of them Christians, both Protestants and Catholics, slowly mobilized. It would be years before they congealed into a coherent political force—that would take a few conservative visionaries, such as evangelists Pat Robertson and Jerry Falwell, as well as political activists like Ralph Reed and Grover Norquist, who saw "pro-lifers" as a building block of a lasting political coalition.

Meanwhile, pro-choice groups rallied, too. The Planned Parenthood Federation of America (known commonly as Planned Parenthood) runs clinics all over the United States that specialize in women's health. Most provide abortions. Along with groups such as NARAL Pro-Choice America and the Religious Coalition for Reproductive Choice, Planned Parenthood has striven to make the pro-choice position as politically powerful as its opposite, supporting political action committees and endorsing pro-choice candidates for national office.

The American Life League was founded in 1979 by Judie Brown, a Catholic antiabortion activist who left the National Right to Life Committee because she opposed any exceptions to laws banning abortion—in the event of rape or incest, for example—and thought the NRLC was watering down its stance. Since then, ALL has taken a simple, no-compromises position: no abortion, by any method, under any circumstances. ALL also opposes in vitro fertilization (which requires fertilization of multiple eggs, most of which are discarded), stem cell research (conducted using fertilized embryos), assisted suicide, and contraception.

ALL's uncompromising doctrine does not lend itself well to the flexible world of politics, and the group has been nearly as critical of Republican politicians as of Democrats. "The Bush administration continues to prove that the value they place on innocent human life is exactly 'zero,'" screamed a 2002 ALL press release after the president limited stem cell research to existing stem cell lines.

You have to learn the lingo. People aren't pro-choice, they're "pro-abortion." It's not an abortion clinic, it's an "abortion mill." Abortion isn't legal, it's "decriminalized."

Erik Whittington's appearance doesn't exactly square with this intransigent language. He looks like a music-industry veteran—rail-skinny, with carefully trimmed, short, dark hair that's just starting to show a few flecks of gray and dark spots on his ear lobes where his piercings have closed up. He's a soft-spoken and friendly thirty-five-year-old father of three. He follows the Chicago Cubs and the Chicago Bears and fully recognizes that it is thus his lot in life to suffer.

Whittington's job is to make Christian teens care about abortion. Many Christian kids grow up going to churches where legal abortion is disparaged, but that rarely translates into action. He and the other Rock for Life employees travel to Christian music festivals all summer long, giving away pamphlets and selling T-shirts, silicone wristbands, stickers, and CD compilations of pro-life bands that Whittington oversees. Rock for Life's booth always has videos and a three-ring binder of gruesome photos of aborted fetuses that they show kids who aren't sure whether they're pro-life. Usually, they have a handwritten sign stuck on a wall that says, IF YOU'RE PRO-CHOICE, TELL US WHY!

At some festivals, Rock for Life sponsors a stage for pro-life bands and speakers. At Cornerstone, I saw four middle-aged women who'd had abortions detail the damage they said the procedure had done to their health, their relationships, their spirituality. And then there are the T-shirts.

The last Tuesday in April is Pro-Life T-Shirt Day. Each year, Rock for Life encourages public school students to wear some of its most

provocative shirts to school. Almost without fail, at least one principal asks a kid to change his or her shirt, or sends him or her home.
Rock for Life immediately publicizes the incident and, with the help
of the Thomas More Law Center, threatens to sue the school system.

"The controversy about a school official who opposes the shirt
just causes more education," Whittington said when I asked him
about it.

"So are you trying to provoke schools into banning your shirts?" I
asked.

"Mostly what we're trying to do is provoke discussion," he said. "If
you wore a short that says ABORTION IS HOMICIDE or ABORTION
KILLS KIDS, then that provokes discussion. And if this girl is, you
know, 'Well that's really lame, I'm gonna tell the principal,' and the
principal says, 'That's really lame that you offended her,' it provokes
a lot of discussion, and that's what we really want, because the bottom line is that abortion does kill children."

Whittington believes that any honest dialog about abortion will
bring people around to Rock for Life's way of thinking. He also believes that most objections to Rock for Life's shirts are functions of
school officials' subservience to unions that are in the pocket of
pro-choice organizations. "Principals and teachers get upset, because, you know, the teachers' unions endorsed the March for
Women's Lives, which was a pro-abortion march. So we know that
in the public school system, it's just infiltrated, people that are
abortion advocates."

I told him I thought that was a bit of a stretch.

"We know from the Gallup Poll a couple years ago that 72 percent
of kids age thirteen to seventeen believe abortion is immoral. The
opposition comes from adults. So we have abortion advocates teaching pro-life kids, and we need to balance that out."

Rock for Life doesn't use only extreme slogans. One of the
group's most successful T-shirts says simply, I SURVIVED. "That pro-

vokes someone coming up to you and saying, 'What does that mean?' 'I survived the abortion holocaust,'" Whittington says. "That shirt isn't gonna cause any controversy in a school, obviously. But that would cause a lot more one-on-one conversation."

Another softer slogan Rock for Life uses simply reads, 1/3—the number of U.S. pregnancies Whittington says have ended in abortion since *Roe*. That figure relies on what Whittington admits is imprecise math. He starts with figures from the Alan Guttmacher Institute and the Centers for Disease Control. The most recent state that 24 percent of all U.S. pregnancies end in abortion.

Whittington says that because there are no standards for reporting abortions, those numbers are likely low. In any event, he says, those figures also don't count what he calls "chemical abortions."

"What's that?" I asked.

"You know, the number of babies aborted via birth control pills or the patch, IUDs, Depo, Norplant, the morning-after pill, Plan B, emergency contraception."

"Okay," I said, "but I thought that those, for the most part, prevent pregnancy. Are you saying that preventing pregnancy is abortion?"

"Define pregnancy," he said.

"An egg gets fertilized?" I ventured.

Boy, I walked right into that one. The definition of pregnancy, Whittington believes, changed in the 1960s. "Planned Parenthood was behind all this. They got the American Medical Association to [say] pregnancy doesn't start until your child implants his- or herself on the uterus."

So, when a blastocyst doesn't implant in the womb, that's abortion? Even for conservatives, that's conservative. "It's definitely one-third of our generation," Whittington said. "That's the concept."

As we exited Bereit's car at Union Station, I saw a lot of pro-life messages—PRO-LIFE, ABORTION KILLS BABIES, WOMEN DESERVE

BETTER—written in chalk on the parking deck walls, on the concrete stairs leading into the train station, on the sidewalk near the Supreme Court. Whittington was pleased.

At the Supreme Court building, a few pro-lifers stood already holding signs: CRUSADE FOR THE DEFENSE OF OUR CATHOLIC CHURCH, JUSTICE FOR ALL: BORN AND PREBORN. Whittington and Matt took up spots holding signs they took from a big Kinko's bag the others had brought. Matt got ABORTION IS HOMICIDE. Whittington took PLANNED PARENTHOOD STEALS SOULS. Bereit, dressed in a crisp white dress shirt, tucked into pleated gray slacks and accessorized with a purple tie and glasses, schmoozed with the volunteers there and said hello to the camera crews. There were one woman and five guys. I asked Whittington if it bothered him that they didn't have more ladies out there. "We just get who we can get," he said, but added that he wished more women had shown up. "Though it's not like guys can't have an opinion on this. I mean, we're supposed to take care of kids."

At 7:30 AM, some Planned Parenthood supporters arrived and took up spots between the pro-lifers. Whittington joked collegially with a pro-choice woman who stood next to him. "I asked her if she wanted a sign," he said after she joined the larger group gathering on the sidewalk. "She offered me a shirt. I told her I'd take a small."

There are rules for protesting in front of the Supreme Court, and Whittington has them down cold. You can't stand, sit, or leave any of your stuff on the steps. Prayer, he said, is considered a form of demonstration in D.C., so you can't drop to your knees. Rock for Life's Phil Eddy, twenty-two, completely beat from the previous night's sidewalk chalking, grumbled about how it's his country. "You just started paying taxes, Phil," Whittington kidded him.

A passer-by shouted, "Good work," at the Rock for Lifers. A steady supply of Planned Parenthood supporters in matching pink T-shirts began streaming up First Street. "When are the strollers coming by?" an older pro-life woman in a green T-shirt that said, ROBERTS YES! barked into her cell phone.

Both groups' numbers grew. In the end, there were more Planned Parenthood supporters than pro-lifers—though that's relative. At full strength, the pro-choice rally had about thirty participants, mostly young women eighteen to thirty-five years old. Camera crews begin to swirl around Planned Parenthood's spokeswoman, Stephenie Foster.

As if a switch had been thrown, everyone took his or her game up a notch. Camera crews converged on the clustering Planned Parenthood supporters, who were hoisting signs that said SAVE ROE! Whittington nodded at Bereit and quickly distributed signs that mimicked the typeface and color scheme of Planned Parenthood's and said, ROE HAS BEEN SAVED! SHE'S NOW PRO-LIFE. Bereit jostled his way into the scrum of pro-choice folks, lifting his sign up for the cameras. Whittington and some of the other Rock for Lifers stood at the back, raising their signs up highest of all.

Rock for Life's new signs were Bereit's idea—he'd seen the SAVE ROE! signs on Planned Parenthood's website and gotten the idea to rub it in that Norma McCorvey, the "Roe" in *Roe v. Wade*, was now a pro-life activist.

Foster, surrounded by some activists, unrolled an eight-foot-long petition with one hundred thousand signatures asking senators to question Roberts about his views on choice. The group, she told the cameras, would be presenting a copy of the petition to every senator on the judiciary committee. Bereit got behind her with his sign.

There is an advantage to having mostly men at a women's issue rally—guys are taller and can get their signs up higher, for the most part. Some of the male pro-choice and pro-life demonstrators began trying to block one another's signs, a somewhat childish competition that the women mostly sat out.

When the cameras packed up, the parallel rallies began to lose steam. Cell phones appeared, a sure sign that the heat of battle had passed. A few pro-choicers left, but most moved over to the south side of the court stairs, where they formed a semicircle and began chanting.

At this moment, the stroller brigade arrived, too late for TV but still in time to have some fun. Four heavily middle-aged women whose heavy makeup couldn't have contrasted more with the well-scrubbed look of the pro-choice gals unfolded six empty strollers and began pushing them in an oval in front of the Planned Parenthood supporters.

The Reverend Patrick Mahoney, a veteran of Operation Rescue who now heads a group called the Christian Defense Coalition, arrived with the stroller women, carrying a sign that said, HONOR GOD—HONOR THE CONSTITUTION. "Shame!" he shouted at the pro-choicers. "Where are your numbers? Your website said there would be hundreds! The Bible gives a pretty good representation of people who are opposed to Roberts!"

I chatted with Phil Eddy, who, I couldn't help noticing, wasn't holding a sign and was, in fact, standing on the media side of the demonstration. I asked him about the imbalance between men and women on each side (at this point, a second young woman had joined the pro-lifers carrying signs). Does it bother you, I asked, that Rock for Life has so few women here?

"It depends on the event," he said, "but yeah. If you're having an Affirmative Action rally, you don't want it to be all white people. I think men can still have an opinion on it. Otherwise, it's like saying only Iraqis or Afghanis can protest the war," which Eddy passionately opposes.

"Right-wing Christians don't have it right," he said. Eddy is consistent in his opposition to the death penalty, war, and eating meat—he's against killing, period. "Pro-life is the only thing keeping me in the mainstream," he said. Eddy moved down to Stafford this summer, having been offered a position at Rock for Life after interning for a few summers. He likes being here because he's close to the Norfolk, Virginia, headquarters of the animal-rights group People for the Ethical Treatment of Animals—many PETA activists, he says, are also pro-life.

Eddy cast his first-ever presidential vote for Ralph Nader in 2004. "I lean definitely more toward direct democracy," he says. He's a fan of anarchist demonstrations and has a tape of the 1999 World Trade Organization protest in Seattle that he calls "riot porn." A vegan, he finds it tough to travel but says he can usually find his favorite food, artichoke hearts, in most grocery stores.

"Phil, if you're not doing anything . . ." Whittington said tartly as he approached us and handed Eddy the bag of signs to hold before heading back to his station.

Eddy was pro-choice until he argued the pro-life position as a high school English assignment. "It was kind of a sudden change," he said about his moment of clarity. I asked Eddy if he's a Christian. "Most people would say no," he said, saying he's really only comfortable with the Christians he meets at the Cornerstone Festival.

"Hey! Hey! Ho! Ho! John Roberts has got to go!" the pro-choicers chanted. Mahoney, who by this time had set up a portable PA system with a microphone, continued to taunt them. "Where are your numbers?" he shouted. "Your Internet said there would be thousands! Where are they?"

I was getting hungry. I asked Whittington how long we were gonna be out here. "Planned Parenthood is supposed to be here till 9:30," he said.

"So, you'll be here till when?" I asked.

"Nine thirty-five," he said, winking.

Mahoney got louder. "Our people are down in Louisiana, helping out in soup kitchens!" he shouted. "Your people aren't helping the hurricane victims! Planned Parenthood is a racist organization! Did you know that Margaret Sanger was a racist? Where are your hoods? Where are all your people?"

As the pro-choicers wrapped up, Mahoney continued to needle them. "Where are you going? The armory is that way! [The D.C. Armory was housing some of the people displaced by Hurricane Katrina.] The armory is that way to help the poor and the needy!" He asked the pro-lifers, by now the only demonstrators remaining, to pause for a prayer that he led, asking God to bless the pro-choice protestors "who don't know what they're supporting, oh God."

Phil pulled a carrot out of his backpack and munched it while Whittington and Matt went around gathering the signs, which they put back in the Kinko's bag. As they did so, I noticed four young women putting red tape over their mouths and standing silently at the base of the steps, behind where the Planned Parenthood rally had been. I went over and asked a young man cutting a few more pieces of red tape what he was doing.

"We're a group called Bound for Life," he said. "We write LIFE on tape, put it over our mouths, and pray silently to end abortion." I took a picture of them and went to lunch.

Erik Whittington was conceived out of wedlock, a fact I pointed out to him is somewhat telling.

"Yeah!" he said, laughing. His grandparents forced his mother and father to get married, but the union didn't last, and Erik grew up in Kankakee, Illinois, with his mother and stepfather. It was not a Christian upbringing, and by the time the family moved to Portland, Oregon, Erik, a budding musician, had only a few goals in life: "just have fun, not worry about the future, have a good time."

He said he was "pro-abortion" at the time. I asked him whether that means he consciously considered himself "pro-abortion."

"Well, at the time, I really wouldn't call myself anything. But I know just from living my lifestyle, you know, sexual immorality, there was always a threat of pregnancy. So, I was for abortion, because that was a threat. I never had an abortion experience, but I would have had one if a girl had had a pregnancy test that was positive. I mean, it was preconceived—you will have an abortion."

I expressed some surprise at this. Would he really have been so matter-of-fact about it? For a lot of people, that's a difficult decision.

"Being a musician," he explained, an unwanted pregnancy "would have interrupted my life."

One October day, when he was in his early twenties, Whittington was driving around Portland and happened on a "life chain," which is when pro-lifers stand holding signs in a long line to mark Respect Life Month. "This was at the tail end of the whole Operation Rescue stuff, where all you saw on TV was, oh, they're doing a blockade, someone got arrested, someone got shot," Whittington said. "So my view at the time was that pro-lifers are, you know, crazy. But seeing peaceful people holding these signs, people were smiling, there were kids, there were older people—I didn't see anything crazy."

Life chains are painstakingly organized by a group called Please Let Me Live. Participants can only have signs with one of seven approved messages. The one PLML particularly stresses is ABORTION KILLS CHILDREN, which is the one that got to Erik Whittington. "I felt like, 'Wow, I can't believe that I believe something else.' I can't believe that I would have aborted a baby if I got someone pregnant. I don't wanna say that I cried, but I did a bit."

This epiphany caused Whittington to reexamine his solipsistic existence. "I really just looked at everything. I started meeting Christians that were musicians, Christians that were artists, Christians that were homeless, Christians that were gutter punks, just different people. I was meeting cool people, people who were just like me."

Eventually, as Whittington puts it, he "caved."

"I accepted the fact that there is a God and a creator, your basic Christian concept. And I decided to follow it and see what happens."

Whittington joined a few bands—Sometimes Sunday (an early Tooth & Nail artist), Tragedy Ann, and Twin Sister. When he wasn't playing shows, he'd set up a table in clubs with pro-life literature. This was not easy for him. "I was introverted," he said. "You have to be a go-getter to be pro-life." If he wasn't motivated, he did a good impression. Whittington used to buy as many used copies of pro-life books such as Randy Alcorn's *Pro-Life Answers to Pro-Choice Questions* as he could afford, then resold them at shows. He bought bumper stickers and other paraphernalia from pro-life suppliers like Victory Won and Heritage House and "groups I wish not to mention because I wouldn't use their stuff again, just too controversial," he said. He also got literature from the American Life League.

God, Whittington said, was still not answering his prayers, though—what he really wanted was to be a Christian rock star. The answers he was getting, he said, were different. "I was still trying to find what I was supposed to do. I would pray about it and want the answer to be a band, or music, or whatever, and I would get this mailing from a pro-life group. And then, I'd pray some more the next day, and then I'd hear a radio program that had some pro-life guy on it. And then the next day, I'd look up and see a bumper sticker on a car. It finally got to the point where I was like, this is totally ridiculous."

"Those weren't coincidences?" I asked.

"It was clear as day to me," he said.

At a March for Life in Washington, D.C., Whittington met Bryan Kemper, who was distributing the same sort of literature at rock shows in California and calling it Rock for Life. They decided to combine forces. They started putting on shows, releasing compilation CDs, attending festivals. They'd been, in Whittington's words, "courting" the American Life League for a while, hitting the organization up for donations and free literature.

"They called us up and said, 'You know, we're looking to expand what we're doing with young people, and we'd really like to take on Rock for Life as one of our projects,'" he said. He and Kemper moved to Virginia. (Kemper has since left Rock for Life under circumstances Whittington won't discuss except to say the two had a falling out; Kemper now directs a similar group called Stand True.)

"That was a pretty savvy move," I said of ALL's youth injection. "The only pro-life people I ever saw growing up were elderly Catholic women."

"I think up until then," he said, "the general consensus with a lot of pro-life groups was, [abortion] is gonna end shortly. But I think people got to a point where they were like, 'Okay, this is a cancer in society and it's spread—it's just gonna take a generation or even longer.'"

"Attempting to affect a generational change seems like a pretty big job for an introvert," I suggested.

"It's interesting how if you become passionate about something, it'll change your whole everything," Whittington said. "I would say I still am introverted in some ways. I don't think it's a black-and-white thing; I think you can be a little bit of both."

That may be the one area of his life where Whittington sees shades of gray. The American Life League's informal mantra, he told me, is, "It's the baby, stupid." In fact, I saw a handwritten poster that just said that on one ALL executive's office. ALL's dedication to the sanctity of human life is ample, even if its public-relations strategy can verge on self-parody. Browsing through a collection of the group's press releases, I found announcement after announcement of boycotts: Boycott the 2005 Academy Awards because Chris Rock made jokes about abortion. Boycott the rock band Kiss because it sells branded condoms. Boycott Samuel Adams beer because it advertised on the infamous radio show where shock jocks Opie and

Anthony allegedly encouraged a couple to have sex in St. Patrick's Cathedral.

Rock for Life is no less strident on its own website, where it keeps detailed lists of pro-life and "pro-abortion" bands and encourages disappointed fans of, say, Jurassic 5 ("Axis of Justice Benefit CD, America Coming Together benefit"), Le Tigre ("often seen giving Gloria Steinem the mic"), and Pearl Jam (too many sins to mention) to send their CDs back to the artists.

On the other hand, Rock for Life lists plenty of artists that pro-life kids can enjoy without having to keep a postage meter in their bedrooms. Without exception, they're Christian acts. I asked Whittington if, as a former musician, he was ever able to listen to music without thinking about the artist's view of abortion.

"I can listen to a good musician regardless of what their political stance is," he said. "The difficult part is going to the store and financially supporting someone like that. We're not advocating for a specific boycott right now. I would say that what we're asking people to do is to watch their money."

I asked how he determined whether a band was pro-life or pro-choice. Mostly, it's by association. A lot of bands on the "pro-abortion" list, for example, are there because of their association with PunkVoter.com, which tried to organize punk bands into a coherent political force before the 2004 presidential election.

"I think the general person just sees it as an anti-Bush organization, and they don't see the abortion tie-in," Whittington said. "But if you just look at the Web site, that's one of the things they advocate for. And I understand that, I understand that there's hidden agendas."

I said that I thought if you asked most artists why they were associated with PunkVoter, they'd tell you it was because they wanted to help defeat George W. Bush in the last election.

"Well, I would say it's important that they know that abortion isn't [PunkVoter's] top issue. But it is one of their top four. So certain information I think we owe it to a music fan to inform them about musicians and organizations that they're supporting."

"But being realistic here," I said, "and you talked about the need to be realistic about ending abortion, the bands you suggest your readers shouldn't support are among the most popular in the country. Chris Rock hosted the Academy Awards. Kiss and Samuel Adams are doing fine."

"I think the main point, the whole Chris Rock thing, [is] to inform people that he made these comments," he said (referring to a Rock standup bit where he says he thinks "abortion is a beautiful thing" and that abortion rallies are good places to meet women—"Cause you know they're fuckin'!"). "I don't think that was necessarily a boycott of Chris Rock but more of an educational tool," he said.

When I first talked to Whittington in 2004, he told me that registering pro-life young people to vote was a priority of Rock for Life. In a press release, the group said it hoped to sign up half a million kids. In the end, Rock for Life ended up handing off most of the registration tasks to groups that had organized specifically to register Christians, like Americans of Faith. In any event, politics is dangerous ground for a nonprofit—Rock for Life endangers its tax-free status if it does anything that can be interpreted as campaigning for a particular party or candidate.

Whittington appeared to come pretty close to the line a couple of times during the run-up to the election. "How many of you watched John Kerry's acceptance speech at the Democratic Convention last night?" began a July 2004 post on his blog on the Rock for Life site. "I did and I almost puked. Kerry is for the destruction of living human embryos [because of his support for stem cell research]." During the pro-Kerry Vote for Change tour that summer, the *Duluth News Tribune* reported him as saying, "Voting for Kerry isn't going to bring change in this country. I'm saying let's vote for change, elect a

Republican president who will choose judges that can help abolish *Roe v. Wade*."

Whittington insists that he was misquoted in the latter instance and would never endorse a particular party. "The bottom line is, we're gonna be hard on anyone. We've been pretty hard on Bush. Really, what has he done? We've had other presidents that have said they were pro-life; at least they did something, said more than 'We need to bring about a culture that respects life.' That's nice, but use the bully pulpit."

"Cynics," I said, "might argue that banning abortion would be the worst thing that could ever happen to the Republican party since it would demotivate millions of single-issue voters."

"I don't think that should be a politician's main concern, to be honest with you," he said. "It should always be to do the right thing. If you look back in history, presidents who make unpopular decisions, later on they're viewed as 'That was the greatest thing they did.' If you relate that to abortion, sure, maybe it would be unpopular, but in the future people would say, 'It was unpopular and his party went into shambles and they don't exist any longer—so what? It was the right thing.'"

If you're a pro-life Christian kid, and Rock for Life isn't for you, you have a few options. Stand True, Survivors of the Abortion Holocaust, American Collegians for Life, Pro-Life America, Crossroads . . . and that's not to mention local church groups. If you're pro-choice and Christian, you don't have as rich an array of religious-centered groups.

Amy Hetrick is the program manager for Spiritual Youth for Reproductive Freedom, a program of the Religious Coalition for Reproductive Choice in Washington, D.C. RCRC is an ecumenical program, which means it reaches beyond Christianity to incorporate Jewish, Unitarian Universalist, even Hindu perspectives on reproductive issues.

Hetrick grew up Lutheran in Georgia but eventually became disenchanted with her church. "There was a real disconnect between my faith values and my social-justice values," she said when we spoke on the phone. She left the Lutheran Church in college and later joined the Unitarian Universalist Church, which she says reunited her concerns. After getting a master's in public policy from George Washington University, she found the job at the RCRC via a listing on idealist.org.

Spiritual Youth for Reproductive Freedom organizes students on college campuses, trains them in educational advocacy, and plans counterdemonstrations called "Peaceful Presence" when pro-life groups stage events. "Basically they just stand there with our signs that say, PRO-FAITH, PRO-FAMILY, PRO-CHOICE," she said. SYRF activists organize clergy panels and try to ensure access to contraception on campuses—even if the school doesn't allow it. "They make it available through other ways," Hetrick said, "through student distribution, trips into town, things like that."

That's the standard pro-choice approach, but Hetrick said the difference is that SYRF activists are able to articulate how they came to their pro-choice stance in language religious folks can understand. "In all their messaging," she said, "they talk about their faith background, from what they understand their moral views to be on these issues. So, it's an alternative to the secular pro-choice movement, and it's certainly an alternative to the religious antichoice movement."

As John Kerry will assert, communicating a pro-choice Christian message is no mean feat. I asked Hetrick about the relative simplicity of the pro-life message: abortion kills. "Our message is not that easy," she said. "It's not that clear, it's not that black-and-white." And that's why I'd hate to have Amy Hetrick's job—explaining to a kid who's just seen a binder full of bloody photos why that might not be the whole picture. "We have to go into a long conversation about the nuances of the issue, the theology," she said. "And it's hard to convey, even though the meaning behind it is no less sound and grounded in theology than theirs."

The SYRF website tackles some of the theology Hetrick's talking about—the Book of Exodus, for instance, places a higher value on the life of a woman killed in a fight than on any fetus she might be carrying, for instance. But SYRF's real message is that there's no one answer that works for everyone.

"We're not trying to impose a view," Hetrick said. "We're there to be a forum for [young adults] to struggle. And be there with them in that struggle. And one of the most powerful quotes that I've come across in this work is that of Bishop Melvin Talbert, former bishop of the United Methodist Church. And he said, 'To be for choice is to be willing to enter into the pain and struggle of life in the real world, and in the face of that reality, to choose. And it's in this context that we are challenged to face the ambiguity and the complexity of con-flicting views and judgments. Our faith compels us to respect others' values, life circumstances, and decisions.'"

After the morning demonstration at the Supreme Court, there was some confusion about what was happening next. I followed Whit-tington, Eddy, and Matt Wilson to the office of Faith and Action in the Nation's Capital—an evangelical nonprofit run by twin broth-ers Paul and Rob Schenck, both pastors—where they picked up the signs they'd stashed there while we were having lunch at Union Station.

Then they wandered somewhat purposelessly around the Senate office buildings, looking for a place to rally. "It's bad when anarchists are better organized," Eddy grumbled. Other activists—pro-life and pro-choice—passed us, but no one really seemed to know where to go. We heard some chanting a block over and walked over to the front of the Russell Senate Office Building, where twenty-two people from Feminist Majority, Americans United for Church, and the National Organization for Women had a permit for a rally. Whittington led the coalescing Rock for Life troops—ten strong—across Delaware Avenue to a small park, where he asked a cop whether it would be okay to counterdemonstrate. "As long as you stay on the green," he said, pointing to the grass on either side of the sidewalk, "you're fine."

Again, Eddy didn't join them. I asked him what he thinks the future of Rock for Life is. He told me that they're looking at ways to reach out beyond the Christian community. He's got pro-life friends who are Democrats, who are gays and lesbians, who are Greens. "A lot of people think you can't be cool and pro-life," he said. "It's like they think you can't be straight-edge [spurn drinking and drugs] and have fun at a party."

The Senate police had set up plastic cordons to control access to the hearings, but as the *Washington Post* reported the next day, only 170 people had shown up for tickets by 10:30 AM. Anyone who wanted to go in could.

As a result, reporters stuck covering the event shuttled between the two demonstrations, desperately hoping for something worth writing about or broadcasting. "Anyone here got a problem with what they're saying over there?" one blow-dried guy with a booming voice asked the Rock for Life crew as the pro-choicers chanted "2-4-6-8! Separate the church and state!" and "Pro life! That's a lie! You don't care if women die!" Bereit gave at least five interviews.

There are always freelancers. Planned Parenthood, which had taken great pains to have participants in the earlier rally, had shunted some out-of-uniform women with handmade signs over to the side when the cameras were on. Here, a portly fellow with a walkman and a fanny pack on his waist alternated between three crude, hand-painted signs with slogans on both sides.

I asked him to show me the signs. They said

IMPEACH RUTH NASTY GINSBURG

IMPEACH ALL DEMOCRATS

ROBERTS GOOD SCHUMER BAD

BUILD MORE NUKES

GOD BLESS ENOLA GAY

FREE CUBA NUKE CASTRO

The last three, he told me, were from an anti-nuclear-weapons demonstration he'd attended earlier. Rock for Life made no room for him on its patch of grass; he stood on the corner waving at passing traffic.

Mahoney came by, and I asked him how he thought the morning demonstration went. "Planned Parenthood's turnout was pretty tragic," he said. I pointed out that the pro-choicers had three times the people on his side. "They said they'd have thousands," he replied. I proposed that they were keeping their powder dry until the next nominee was nominated—after all, a conservative replacing a conservative doesn't change the ideological balance of the court. "Double their numbers," he said. "Say they had 60, 90, 120 people. In the late '80s, there would have been ten times as many people out here," he said.

I asked him if he ever missed those days. He said he did in some ways, but not really. "I applaud people who get out here, no matter what they believe," he said. "The rule of thumb in activism, though, is that when you're winning, you keep your mouth shut."

"You were pretty loud this morning," I said.

"We would lack integrity if we didn't bring down some people," he replied.

After the second demonstration broke up, Bereit, Whittington, and a couple of the kids who'd been up the night before decided to be out there over the next couple of days. "We got so much media," said one guy with a beard. Bereit agreed.

On the drive back to Stafford, Bereit asked me whether I preferred professionally printed signs or handmade ones. I told him that when I saw handmade signs, I generally assumed the person was a bit unbalanced.

"I'm leaning that way myself," he said. "That guy with the handmade signs on the corner convinced me."

In March 2005, Andrew Sullivan, a prominent conservative thinker, wrote a column in *Time* praising, of all people, Hillary Clinton. "Hey, if you live long enough . . ." he said. Sullivan was encouraged by a recent speech Clinton had made that proposed a "third way" in the abortion debate: keep the procedure legal, but admit that it's a tragedy. "We can all recognize that abortion in many ways represents a sad, even tragic choice to many, many women," Clinton said. "The fact is that the best way to reduce the number of abortions is to reduce the number of unwanted pregnancies in the first place."

After I got back from Stafford the first time, I e-mailed Erik Whittington a link to Sullivan's piece and asked him what he thought about it. Here's what he wrote back:

> Hey Andrew! No i didn't see it, but have read many similar writings, especially after the latest election, which I am sure is an attempt at a shift in the Democratic Party to reach out to Pro-life America. By the way, most Americans believe abortion is immoral, its just many of those believe we should keep it legal. Oxymoron? Dichotomy?
>
> If abortion is always a moral tragedy, even the writer admits it is a taking of a human life, then why keep it legal? If there is nothing wrong with abortion, then why try to limit it? The contradictions are astounding. Promote contraception to limit abortion? All forms of chemical contraception can cause abortion. Just those numbers aren't detectable. If everyone sexually active was on

forms of chemical contraception, the reported abortion numbers (which are surgical & RU-486) may go down, but abortion would still remain, just at an earlier stage before implantation, which aren't reported. So the abortion rate won't go down, just the age of killing is earlier.

This is possibly a hidden agenda to promote contraception, (and by the way not abstinence/chastity, which is the only proven method to work against getting pregnant) and to get elected. This reeks of politics.

Bottom line, like any other serious attack on the dignity of human life, whether it is slavery, the holocaust against the Jews or the war on children in the womb (abortion) there is no middle ground. Human life should never be enslaved or killed. Those promulgating these pro-death positions will be defeated and ultimately all human life will be protected & respected. There is nothing greater to fight for.

That's my take on it. Hope this answers your question!

Erik

Like all humans, Erik Whittington is the sum of his contradictions. He doesn't believe in shouting at women entering abortion clinics because it's "counterproductive." And yet, he'll show stunning insensitivity when it comes to women who've gone through abortions and aren't repentant and who say that Rock for Life's shirts offend them.

"My argument is this," he said. "There's lots of things that will trigger a woman that has had an abortion to be depressed or respond negatively. And those things are: the flushing of a toilet, hearing a vacuum cleaner, seeing a baby, seeing a pregnant woman, even being told that abortion is wrong in any way, shape, or form. So if a stranger's ever in the house, are we supposed to ask them, 'Hey are you postabortive? Because I need to flush the toilet.' I mean, how sensitive are we supposed to be to everyone around us?"

Likewise, while he takes the long view in the fight against legal abortion and is grooming a new generation of pro-life kids to take his place, he won't consider an incremental approach to removing abortion from common practice. It's all or nothing for Erik Whittington.

And, of course, he mostly works at getting kids culturally predisposed to being pro-life to step up their political involvement—for the moment, anyway, Rock for Life isn't about reaching out to people who aren't evangelical Christians or strict Catholics. I asked him what he'd learned from pro-choice people who'd taken up his offer to chat with him at festivals.

"There are people that are adamantly pro-abortion that won't respond to that sign," he said, "but will do things like leave notes on our table." He showed me a Rock for Life flyer on which someone had written, "This is not Christ's way," and another (in the same handwriting) that said, "Christians shouldn't hate."

"Why do you keep this stuff?" I asked him.

"Well, I'm trying to reach this person as well," he said. "So, having it sit here on my desk keeps me thinking about what can I do to be more effective for that person."

"Do you ever look at something like this," I asked him, "and say, 'Gee, do I come across as if I hate people?'"

"I do ask myself that question," he said, "because I don't want to come across hating. But I think, generally, my perception is that their perception on what hate and love is [is] different—because we're out there trying to educate, and stop the killing.

"So, I don't—you know, what are they trying to do? They're advocating, most likely, for abortion, which is killing. So, if that's their version of love, then obviously we have a problem with what is love."

"What if they're taking issue with the way you're expressing that?" I asked.

"Well, yeah, we'll definitely take that into consideration," he said. "I know generally what most people that are supportive of us respond to. And those are generally those shirts that have the blatant statements on them."

"You still haven't told me why you think pro-choice people disagree with you," I said.

"I just think they're misinformed. I just don't think they understand the consequences of their beliefs. And they're for a lofty goal, you know, rights for women, but it's so detrimental to women; it's obviously detrimental to the babies they're carrying."

"They're just like any other person," he continued. "We all have sins, we all need redeemed. We're all humans that ultimately need God, I guess. We're all human, and we all need help and assistance, and I think that women that are pregnant and scared need someone to hold their hand, they need financial assistance, they need spiritual assistance.

"I think a lot of women just need someone to tell them that everything's gonna be okay, that I'll help you out, I'll love you, I'll be with you through this whole thing, thick or thin. But if they don't have that, I can see it seeming like an easy choice to make at the time. It's just like, after my own experience, you just need someone, one person who has the guts to say 'this is the truth' or 'this is wrong.'

"True love would be being blunt, and being honest," he continued. "No, you can't get an abortion because you're carrying a baby. You can't kill your child. Sure, it's the easy thing to do, sure it's only $300 today, but that pales in comparison to what you'll experience for the rest of your life. If I really cared about you, I wouldn't allow this to happen. If I really cared about you, I would not let you do this. If I really cared about you, I would let you stay at my house. I would buy you a crib. I would buy you diapers."

"Obviously, you can't do that for everyone," I said.

"You can't," he replied. "But that's why the Christian church has failed. It's the Christian church that led blacks out of slavery in the

South, illegally. It's the Christian church that traditionally has fed the poor, clothed the naked, visited criminals in jail."

"In evangelical culture," I said, "I've noticed there's a lot of emphasis on individual responsibility, and not a lot on societal problems."

"Yeah," he said. "And you have someone like Mother Teresa who can do a lot of good things herself. Sure, she didn't change the world. But she started something. She couldn't change things overnight."

While I was researching this chapter, I Googled Pat Mahoney's name to find out more about him. One of the hits brought up a photo that I first viewed in my hotel room in Michigan, when I was at the Festival of Faith and Music. During the height of the Terri Schiavo controversy, a couple of local smartasses walked into the crowd of protesters in front of the Pinellas Park, Florida, hospice in which Schiavo was dying and hoisted signs that said, WE ARE IDIOTS. The photos, duly posted on the self-proclaimed idiots' website, flashed around the world instantly.

I don't know why Google considered this relevant to my search, since Mahoney's not pictured. But one of the middle-aged women who accompanied him to the Supreme Court protest I had just attended is there, leaning over the barrier, her expression a perfect conflation of anger, sadness, and disgust. But mostly anger.

What a strange way to live, I thought, recalling the way she conducted herself at the demonstration I attended, when fury filled the air around her like flop sweat—to be professionally enraged. I don't get that feeling from Erik Whittington. I'd seen him banter amiably with pro-choice protesters and even listen empathetically while one woman argued with him. He wasn't angry; he was even sort of peaceful.

During one of our interviews, I asked Whittington if he could be friends with someone who was pro-choice. He said it would be tough. Later, in front of the Supreme Court, he said to me, "I've been thinking a lot about your question." He hadn't arrived at an answer yet. But just that he was thinking about it makes me suspect he won't be at the barricades forever.

Mark Salomon

It's hard to think of questions for Mark Salomon, because his autobiography answers most of them. *Simplicity,* published by Relevant Books, is his adieu to Christian rock and details his life as the lead singer of '80s Christian hardcore icons the Crucified, which was hardly a blur of limousines and parties. The group toured econo, fought with one another, and struggled to keep jobs and apartments. Onstage, Salomon was a firebrand, preaching a militant, unapologetic Christianity; offstage, he struggled with premarital sex and crazy youth pastors who'd track him down at work to argue theological points with him.

One of the most fascinating parts of *Simplicity* is an account of Salomon's current band, Stavesacre, traveling to Europe to play a Christian festival. There they met Christians who smoked, drank, and made fart jokes. "At first it blew our minds. Then, when the reality of what we were learning caught up with us, it was just humbling," he writes.

These days, Mark Salomon is a very happily married guy living in Orange County, California, with no plans to ever darken the door of a youth-group show ever again. When we spoke, Stavesacre was recording its fifth studio LP, its second for a non-Christian label, and Salomon was trying to figure out how exactly to get a palm tree out of his yard. Apparently, casinos in Las Vegas will buy them and remove them for free—don't you just love the West Coast?

Do you have anything to do with the Christian music industry anymore?

MARK SALOMON: Not directly. Stavesacre came about as close to breaking up as you can, right about the time when I was writing that book. We were feeling caught between the Christian and the general market, which was not helping.

We decided when we wrote some new music, we weren't gonna be Christian market, general market, anything. We were just gonna be Stavesacre. So we just tried to reinvent ourselves, and part of it had to do with just completely disassociating ourselves with those kinds of labels. We didn't want to be considered a Christian band in the general market, 'cause we're not a Christian band. One of the guys in my band is not a Christian; that's kind of a false sort of thing anyway. And you've read the book; we don't feel like any kind of good can come out of that scene.

We're just a band, and we're not too worried about it. If we end up in a Christian distribution situation, it's not something we're gonna oppose. It's certainly not something that we're gonna pursue.

David Bazan told me that after he tried to desperately claw his way out of the Christian music industry, he was chagrined to find out that most of his fans were Christians.

Right. Yeah. It's kind of like you think the distinction is clearer than it really is.

How do you mean?

It really is this big, huge, involved decision, you know, where "I'm not doing this anymore," you make this declaration—

You write a book—

The book itself wasn't so much trying to get out of things as it was saying why we got out of it. I found myself at all these shows talking to all these kids. And sometimes getting in these massive debates as to why we didn't wanna do this anymore, and I always found out that it was never as easy as a ten-minute conversation, which is basically all you have time for when you load up the van!

So we just—on the way home from tour one time, I just started writing. And that was it. The distinction typically has way more to do with the individual band member than it really does with anybody else. You can make all these big declarations and big decisions and . . . no one cares!

Really?

[*Laughs*] Pretty much. The only people who care are the ones you don't want to talk to anymore anyway. So it's like, why try to convert these people to a way of thinking that you're simply not going to?

I've noticed American evangelicals can be quite argumentative.

Are you a Christian?

I'm not.

This is the lot that I've got. These are the people that I've picked. I believe that God chose me as one of his children. It's my faith. It's what I believe. And I love my savior very much. But this is America. America is a confrontational culture, and there's this chip on most Americans' shoulders about how they're being offended, and they'll stand up for their rights.

Some people would say, only in a place with this many creature comforts could someone feel so much conviction over such trivial stuff. Christian people are taught to be ready to fight for their faith at a moment's notice. And to a certain degree, that is right. The Bible does say to be ready to defend the faith, but it's very clear that you're not supposed to sit around and nitpick at each other. It's one of the few clear things about the way you're supposed to treat your fellow brothers.

And judgment is also one of those things—judgment and the fact that people try to hold people accountable. It's a bunch of crap, man! It's not from Christianity. It's not from the Bible. It's from American culture. People in America have to be right all the time.

I thought the part in your book where you go to Europe for the first time and find out that Christians there drink and smoke and swear was really fascinating.

Mind-blower. Mind-blower. My parents, as you read, are a little different. They declared Europe as "spiritually dead" before they'd ever gotten there. That's the way a lot of Christian people feel. I talk about it in the book a lot. You're raised the way that this is Christianity, and this is the way that Christians are supposed to be, and then you see people not acting that same way, and all of a sudden you're freaking out because they're bad or whatever.

So you work as a bartender?

Yeah. I work at this really bizarre steak house and martini lounge. We do a really big club business on Friday and Saturday nights. Not exactly the job that the Christian community would be all psyched up about.

Do you drink?

Yeah. I just believe in taking the Bible for what it says. I don't believe in cultural additions to Scripture. Christian people love to declare certain things as illegal. It's not scriptural. The very essence of the Holy Spirit, of the way that God changes your life, is that you don't need new rules to live by. Your heart is supposed to be different.

When Paul talks in the Bible about stumbling his brother, which is the main reason that Christian people say no one should drink, that's a pretty vague little standard. What is stumbling a person, and what are a person's own responsibilities, and where do those things meet in the middle? And I don't think that a Christian needs to declare anything as off-limits that God hasn't declared off-limits.

And the Bible just backs it up. In Colossians 2, I was given a huge breath of freedom when I read that such discipline has the appearance of godliness but, in the end, has no value in battling the temptations of the flesh. You can say, "Booze is off-limits forever, don't drink alcohol," and you could not ever drink it because the rules say so, and all your Christian brothers will whoop on you for doing it.

So does that really mean that you've made a change in your heart other than to just obey mankind? We're supposed to obey God, not man. But Christian people, because they're Americans, and that's what we do, they wanna please man more than they wanna please God.

I despise drunkenness, especially as a bartender. But there's a difference between getting drunk and having a drink, you know? For some Christian people, that's not a clear enough division of truths.

Do you ever see parallels between the hardcore punk scene you came out of, which has a lot of unspoken rules of behavior, and Christianity?

Yeah. Ultimately, the issues are the same. Pride, man. Ultimately, you're trying to please the pride of man, and it's impossible. I just don't think that a person can please all the people all the time.

In the Bible, Paul talks about not eating meat—I'll never touch meat again if it stumbles my brother. Was he trying to make a rhetorical statement, or was he making a specific statement? And if that was the case, was Paul a vegetarian? Because there were clearly people who were offended by him eating meat.

And, no, he wasn't. And dude, the Holy Spirit appeared to Peter when he was on a rooftop and said, Peter, arise, kill, and eat. Now,

God's not offended by meat eating—who are we to start making these kinds of rules? It's the same theory.

If I'm around a guy who's having a hard time with drinking, I'm gonna do my best to try and help that situation. I'm sure not gonna have a beer in front of the guy. At the same time, I can't be worrying about every single little thing that's gonna offend somebody, because offending somebody and stumbling them are two totally different things.

There are people who are offended by the fact that I'm a punk rocker. I'm not about to apologize for that. That was one of the biggest conflicts between my dad and I growing up, because there was that whole generation gap. Dad is this ex-hippie biker guy who's superbummed on me being involved in this new scene that he doesn't know anything about.

He probably saw that punk rock episode of Quincy.

Seriously. It was like an after-school special. It was ridiculous. But why did he feel that way? Because of personal taste, man, not because of any sin issues. And I actually said that to him in one of our big knockdown drag outs—"This is not a sin. I'm not stumbling you by being into this."

And his response was, "Yeah, but it's making me angry, so it's stumbling me." And as soon as it came out of his mouth, he couldn't admit it, but I could tell he knew how ridiculous that sounded.

What about this idea that you mentioned before about being caught between two worlds, in a weird limbo. Do you think that's always gonna be an issue for you? Do you feel you'll ever escape these kind of questions?

No, I don't expect that to happen. I also don't expect to answer them all the time. I know what I've experienced is just my own experience, but it's opened my eyes to a lot of things, not the least of which is the nature of man.

How do you mean?

People have their own opinions about everything, and everywhere you go, you're gonna find someone with a different one than yours. Is everyone entitled to their own opinion? No, I don't believe that at all. If I did, how far are you willing to take that? Is a guy who thinks it's okay to beat his wife okay to do that?

All these clichés we live by as Americans, you can put them on freaking bumper stickers, shit like that, those things to me are the reason why all these limbo situations are gonna exist, because there's just way too much ingrained dogma—it's impossible to shake it.

Even me, I'm a pretty liberal cat. But there are some things that I'll see other Christians doing that I don't dig on. I've also learned that I don't necessarily have to stop them right there and say it.

I am a punk rocker. I've been a punk my whole life. I despise the tendency in myself to be a cop. Back off, man. Mind your own freaking business. God changed me in lots of ways that nobody knows anything about, and it's nobody else's business, so who am I to assume that nobody else is gonna have the same thing happen to them?

It sounds almost like you're settling into your own skin. How old are you?

I'm thirty-five. I sure do wish I was settled into my own skin. You live with the expectations that you live with your entire life. They don't ever go away, just in case you're curious.

CHAPTER 10

To Be Mad for My King

A month after I went to GMA Week, Doug Van Pelt e-mailed me with a challenge.

If you're interested, I have some thoughts about a comment you made in Franklin, TN. You really pissed me off with that one, dude! Hahahahaha, just kidding (totally), but it has given me reason to stop and ponder. You mentioned going to some sappy worship concert while at GMA this year, stating that it was very "insider" or insulary to the point of being a real turn-off. I can understand the experience and the reaction, but for their sakes (no idea who the band or whatever was), you can't blame them.

Any people group or organization certainly has the right to get together and celebrate their cause or whatever. I would venture to guess that the only "agenda" this meeting had was to love on their god. Unlike many Christian events, there wasn't the underlying motivation or agenda to convert the non-believers. If there had been, then there would almost be an obligation to be sensitive to doubt, skepticism, and just a "welcome environment" to the "outsider." But, as long as another agenda, like "let's kill all the abortion doctors" or "Kill all the white people" or any such hatred, etc, wasn't there, you can't really knock 'em.

If a group of chihauha (i love the way that word is spelled) owners got together just to love on their dog and celebrate how cool they were, and there wasn't the underlying motive to get non-members to join their chihauha fan club, then it might be a big turn-off to the non-chihauha owning person.

Now, I'm not saying that being turned off by this is wrong. Even though I should, cuz that would be funny. "Andrew, that is so wrong that you felt turned off. You should be ashamed. You are like a whore unto the universe for even considering such a thought. How dare you. Your feelings are completely unvalidated and worth no consideration." hahaha That was fun. Imaginary and quite mean, but funny.

Anyway, this is just the ramblings of some guy who couldn't sleep the Saturday morning after a deadline, so there . . .

How 'bout them Nationals?

It was a good point. Not that the Nationals were doing unexpectedly well (the D.C. baseball team's inaugural season was yet young, and my hopes were as yet undashed), but that I was probably being a bit flip when I dismissed worship music altogether. I decided to spend a little more time looking into what a lot of people in Christian music are calling the "worship movement."

Juggernaut might be a better term. Praise-and-worship music, which began as a sleepy little subcategory of Christian music during the Jesus Movement, has turned into an economic powerhouse. Ten percent of the Top 100 bestselling albums in Christian music history are worship albums. Michael W. Smith's two worship albums have sold 2.25 million copies, and this past year, Amy Grant, Jars of Clay, Out of Eden, MercyMe's Bart Millard, Ashley Cleveland, and Beth Nielsen Chapman all made "hymn" albums, which recast old church standards for audiences with modern tastes.

And then, there's the Passion Movement. Organized by Atlanta worship leader Louie Giglio, Passion gatherings explore the limits of the term *corporate worship*, drawing tens of thousands of college students for several days of praise choruses and inspirational speakers. Chris Tomlin, Matt Redman, and the David Crowder Band are Passion's flagship acts, and all make records that sell extremely well for Giglio's joint venture with EMI, sixstepsrecords.

In fact, worship music has become such a part of modern Christian life that a company called Christian Copyright Licensing International exists to track the use of worship songs in churches, from whom it collects a licensing fee, which is then paid to music publishers, who in turn distribute royalties to songwriters.

That seemed like a good place to start. CCLI operates in a gray area of U.S. copyright law. You see, there's what's called a "religious service exemption" in the law that allows churches to use any religious-oriented music for free.

This is probably a good point for a quick tutorial on copyright and publishing. Anyone who writes a song gets a de facto copyright when the work is "fixed in a tangible form of expression"—written out or recorded. That's it. That satirical song I wrote in chapter 7? You'd have had to pay me to record it the moment I "fixed" its lyrics into my computer.

Songwriters collect royalties when their copyrighted works are fixed onto CDs or broadcast or performed publicly in clubs, stadiums, restaurants, what have you. Record companies pay the first kind of royalties, called mechanical royalties, and organizations such as BMI and ASCAP collect the second, called "public performance" royalties, from radio stations and venues and distribute them to writers.

Because the music industry was not created by people who were born yesterday, it created publishing companies to get a taste of those legally mandated payments. Basically the way a publishing deal works is that a songwriter gets an advance from a publishing company, which then is assigned ownership of the artist's copyrights for a defined period of time and collects all his or her mechanicals and half of his or her performance royalties until the advance is paid back (usually never).

Artists like publishing deals because they can get a big check up front, but I've always viewed them as betting against yourself, because even if you earn back the advance, you then have to split subsequent royalties with your publisher. (Full disclosure: I make upwards of $13 a year in performance royalties from some songs I cowrote in the early '90s, so aspiring songwriters should probably ignore my advice.) Companies love publishing deals because they are potential cash cows.

Now, not every artist has a publishing deal, but most of the artists you hear on the radio do. And to be fair, publishing deals can be really good for some folks—publishing companies plug your songs to other artists (this is particularly important in country music), try to get them on movie soundtracks and TV shows, and take care of a lot of financial details that cut into artists' valuable drinking time.

So what does this all have to do with singing songs in church? A lot, surprisingly.

I called CCLI's Paul Herman to learn why churches pay license fees when they don't seem, at first glance, to be required to do so. Herman confirmed my suspicion that the religious-service exemption applies when performing copyrighted religious works (most old hymns are in what's called public domain and require no license) and that there's a further exemption for displaying lyrics so congregants can sing along.

Where the law gets weird, Herman said, is when a church stores the lyrics on a computer so they can be projected on a screen, or broadcasts its service (either on radio or TV or via the Web), or prints the lyrics in a church bulletin. In all those cases, the church is entering or creating a copy, and to do so requires the permission of the copyright owner.

CCLI began as Starpraise Ministries in 1985 after FEL Publications, a small publishing company that collected and published songs for Catholic folk masses, sued the Archdiocese of Chicago and won a $3 million settlement after it discovered that churches were photocopying its songbooks and distributing them to members. A music pastor in Oregon named Howard Rachinski decided to make sure his church was covered and came up with something called a "permission of use," which he pitched to other churches—Rachinski would negotiate with all the major publishing companies, churches would pay one annual fee, and the companies would grant all license holders permission to use any of their works.

Today, CCLI has seventy employees in its U.S. office alone and has since branched out to Asia, Europe, and Africa. In the United States, about 138,000 churches hold CCLI licenses, the fees for which vary by congregation size. The fees are hardly onerous—a "Category B" church of fewer than 200 congregants pays $165 a year, going up to $999 a year for a "Category J" church of 20,000 to 49,999 congregants.

Every two and a half years, each church is required to keep track of the songs that it performs at worship services. Through what Herman calls "stratified sampling," CCLI creates a representative sample of worship songs in order of popularity and pays publishers accordingly. The company keeps a Top 25 chart on its website that is updated every six months.

I asked Herman how much a threat court cases actually are. "There certainly haven't been that many lawsuits," he said. "Most people—voluntarily, ethically, and morally—wanna do the right thing." And this is the crux of the issue, I think. Churches could probably tell the CCLI to go take a dip in the lake of fire and never have to worry about a lawsuit because it would be a rare artist or publishing company that would voluntarily walk into the propeller of criticism that would greet them suing a church.

But churches like having new music. And they want to keep the industry going. "People realize that songwriters deserve to be compensated for their work," Herman says. I called Duff Berschback, a copyright lawyer in Nashville, to ask him whether he thought churches paid the CCLI out of concern for the industry or as an insurance policy against being sued. "I think it's a combination," he said. "Here in Nashville, the churches are populated by the creators of most of this music, and there's a high level of sophistication when it comes to those people getting paid.

"Outside of Nashville," he continued, "it's more heavily weighted toward the insurance policy side."

But where did this never-ending demand for new worship tunes come from? David Di Sabatino is a historian who specializes in the early days of the Jesus Movement and was the editor of *Worship Leader Magazine* for five years, a post he recently left for a number of reasons, one of which was to make a documentary about Lonnie Frisbee, a charismatic youth pastor at Calvary Chapel in the early '70s whom Di Sabatino believes has been largely written out of the Jesus Movement's history because he died from complications of AIDS.

"You had a number of different things going on in the Jesus Movement, musicwise," Di Sabatino said. "One was these hard rock heavy bands that were used as this entertainment pull, so you'd get up in front of an audience, they went up there, played their Jesus rock, got the audience, and then the preacher came on. So they were kinda like bait, if you will. That was focused outward.

"Then you had music that was just between the person singing and God. And that was very worshipful. And that was, like, you were singing songs of praise to God, and they were slower songs, they were meant to be translated into the church songs, and that stuff got known as 'worship' because that's the stuff that was used for the times when you broke into this corporate time of prayer and praise to God. Which is the staple of a lot of church worship services in conservative evangelical churches."

A couple of people noticed this trend, Di Sabatino told me. David and Dale Garrett were music ministers from New Zealand who traveled the world, collecting songs into books and cassette compilations that they would sell to churches. They weren't the only ones: in 1974, Maranatha, Calvary Chapel's label, issued *The Praise Album,* which collected some of Calvary's best-loved praise songs, which were congregation tested and ready for export to like-minded churches around the country.

By the early '70s, the Christian music industry was coalescing, "which had this kind of notion like we have to go out and use this music as a vehicle of evangelism," Di Sabatino said. "That's a very external, outward focus. Worship is the inward focus of the church."

"So when did people figure out how to make money off of worship?" I asked him.

"That comes later," he said. "Maranatha had a coterie of bands, Love Song, the Way, all that stuff. From about 1971 to about 1979, they really tried to be a rock 'n' roll, A&M Records–type label."

"Now, depending who you talk to," he continued, "they made a shift. The powers that be will tell you they dispossessed themselves of all these rock bands because they decided that they were going to focus squarely on worship. God told them that this is what they were supposed to do. The people in the bands say it was easier for them to make money if they just hired people to come in and sing these songs. 'Cause they didn't have a band to take care of. You have to remember, that early kind of rock 'n' roll stuff, not everybody bought. And not everybody understood it. Now, worship, everybody bought that."

Praise was remarkably successful for the time, and Maranatha has since issued more than twenty volumes of *Praise* records. It also puts out compilations of each year's Top 25 worship songs (usually not performed by the original artists), theme-based worship compilations (for events such as Mother's Day), worship for kids albums, Promise Keepers–branded compilations, and so forth.

And Maranatha is now a small player in the worship field.

In the late '70s and early '80s, something called the Shepherding Movement took root in many charismatic churches. "In the Jesus Movement," Di Sabatino explained, "everything was very loosey-goosey. You had all these kids getting quote-unquote saved, but you had no external authority telling them what to do, so there was this void." He described Shepherding as "basically like an Amway thing, with a couple guys at the top and everybody underneath in a kind of pyramid structure of authority whereby you'd have to get permission to do anything from your shepherd, the person that was above you. If you wanted to marry, if you wanted to go and minister somewhere else, if you wanted to speak at an engagement down the street, you had to get permission."

The problem was that the shepherds were human.

"It got into a lot of abuse," Di Sabatino said. "It started out as a good idea, but when you have eighteen-year-olds taking spiritual authority over sixteen-year-olds, all of a sudden it's like, 'Go mow my lawn—*now!*' And it degenerates from there. But all the churches that were involved started a tape-of-the-month club. And that blossomed and just went through the roof and became Integrity Music."

Shepherding is more or less gone (though there's an interesting move back toward discipleship in today's church, especially among those influenced by Rick Warren's blockbuster book *The Purpose-Driven Life*), but Integrity remains as sort of the Microsoft of worship music. The company is now publicly traded and controls more than 60 percent of the worship-music industry. Many of the movement's most popular artists and writers—Paul Baloche, Sonicflood, Brian Doerksen—record for one of Integrity's three labels.

Integrity also distributes the Hillsong Music label—the record label of an Australian megachurch that serves 17,500 congregants *a week*—in the United States. Darlene Zschech is Hillsong's music pastor and wrote arguably the most popular worship song of all time, "Shout to the Lord," which has been in CCLI's Top 25 since it was released in 1998.

"They started just selling stuff out of the back of *Charisma* magazine," Di Sabatino said about Integrity. "Like, if you want these tapes every month sent to your place, send us five bucks. A church in Alaska wants to have worship music—well, the best stuff is being culled together by Integrity."

There was another movement, in the late '80s, that sprang from the Vineyard churches, themselves a more charismatic offshoot of Calvary Chapel. "Vineyard was a shift away from Scripture and song to more intimate, very passion-filled songs of praise *to* God, of personal intimacy," Di Sabatino told me. "It's almost like, in a crude way, you could say, 'Jesus is my girlfriend' songs."

I told Di Sabatino I thought there was an unsettling, near-sexual character to one of the worship services I'd been to.

"Nobody talks about it, but that's pretty much what's going on," he said. "They're having this intense, experiential experience with God. Very intimate, very private, very all-encompassing."

Di Sabatino is not a fan of most worship music. "How in the world, then," I asked him, "did you end up editing *Worship Leader* magazine?"

"The guy who owned the magazine [Chuck Fromme, who eventually bought Maranatha from Calvary] asked me to do it because I had a good understanding of the Jesus Movement and the history of that time, plus I knew theology," Di Sabatino said. "But I told him, 'I don't like this stuff.' I think worship music is horrible. It's crap! I listen to the lyrics, half the time I'm going, 'Hey, that's not theologically correct.' But he said, 'I want you *because* you're not a fan.'"

I asked him if he'd found any worship music artists he liked. He mentioned Capstone, a Canadian group, but said he found it hard to get excited about even relatively edgy worship music artists, such as Chris Tomlin.

"Yeah, it's upbeat, and everybody gets excited about it," he said, "but, really, when you put creativity next to U2—you wanna talk about worship music, I mean, beat 'One' as a worship song. They're writing worship music the right way, that is creative and brings the whole gamut of Scripture. The angry, deprecatory songs. The screaming-at-God, which is part of the Psalms as well. Well, worship music isn't like that at all. It's all happy-clappy."

"But if the Holy Spirit is what the Holy Spirit is," he continued, "which is anarchic, vibrant, enervating—that has nothing to do with worship music right now."

I was getting no closer to figuring out why Van Pelt thought I was being unfair to worship music. I began to wonder if I was having the same trouble understanding it that I did with the Grateful Dead. Back in the mid-to-late '80s, a fair number of my friends started following the Dead, traveling from show to show, living in parking lots, and getting by selling hippie wares to other Deadheads. When home, they'd lovingly catalog their bootleg cassettes and lists of set lists, all of which I found baffling for a band that has six good songs if you're feeling generous enough to count "Touch of Grey."

"You don't get it," they'd tell me. "You have to come to a show." What they really meant was, you have to be high to enjoy this music, and I didn't do drugs. So I went to a Grateful Dead show sober, which is really one of the worst ideas I've ever had.

This, I remember thinking, is what it must feel like to be insane. I was standing still while everyone around me twirled manically as the least interesting guitar solos and comically extended percussion breaks rattled on for what felt like hours. Actually, it *was* hours, and

I felt very lonely, because I just didn't get it. Later in life, during my occasional experiments with pot smoking, I tried listening to the band again. It couldn't hold a candle to watching TV.

Still, there had to be something to it that I was missing. You just don't get that many people to follow your band from town to town if you suck—otherwise, there would be a thriving subculture of Staindheads. I think the band's appeal wasn't so much its music though I'm sure there were other non-high people who liked it; to my ears, the band lacked the vocabulary that makes jazz improvisation, for instance, rewarding—but the carnival-like atmosphere of the parking lot outside its shows, the sense of community and acceptance the Deadheads felt in one another, a kind of fellowship to which the Grateful Dead was almost incidental.

I think that's why Deadhead culture adapted to the death of Jerry Garcia, the Dead's lead singer, so successfully, as Deadheads began to follow bands like Phish, Widespread Panic, and the String Cheese Incident in much the same manner. Because it wasn't about the Dead, per se. It was about tapping into the sense of freedom and adventure that the band represented, and other bands could take up that torch. I don't really like many jam bands, groups such as the above who've supplanted the Dead. But I love going to Bonnaroo, an annual festival held in Tennessee put on by a new generation of Deadheads, because it's really well organized, the festival also books bands I like a lot, like the Flaming Lips and the Allman Brothers, and, most important, it's just a real nice time, free of the atmosphere of uncorked aggression that burdens most rock festivals.

Ironically, the worship music I've connected with the most has a lot in common with a group that kind of dances on the line of jamband culture—the Dave Matthews Band, half of whose fans behave much the same as Deadheads (the rest have to get up and run the world the next morning). I kind of like Dave Matthews. He played a lot here in Richmond when I was in school, and there's something about his herky-jerky rhythms, medium-large choruses, and implied sense of humor that I dig—even if I'm not crazy about getting elbowed in the face by liquored-up ex–frat boys at his shows.

Subtract Dave Matthews' electric violinist, drummer with wind chimes, and the drunks in the cheap seats, add a whole lot of Jesus, and you're getting close to the work of David Crowder.

David Crowder does not look like the son of an insurance company owner from Texarkana, Texas. Tall and lanky with thick glasses, a billy goat beard, and '70s troll-doll hair that stands straight up, he suggests a botched genetic splice of Harry Potter, Gheorghe Muresan, and Don King. Clearly, he has come a long way from his fundamentalist Baptist childhood. Crowder's parents didn't allow him to listen to secular music, though he got around that by, for instance, convincing them that Queen's "Another One Bites the Dust" single was a Christian record.

"When MTV hit, holy cow," he said. "I wanted to spend the night at my friend's house every night of the week, and I would stay up all night long glued to the television, just in awe of the things I was hearing and seeing."

The Christian hair-metal band Stryper was likewise huge for Crowder because, finally, he had something that interfaced with his MTV-honed tastes and his parents' rules. "I think they were just glad that it was something I was doing in front of them," he said of listening to the band, "because I think they were pretty aware of the Walkman held closely to the chest at night."

Figuring he was going to join his dad's insurance company anyway, Crowder decided to major in music at Baylor University, a large Baptist school in Waco. He says he had a "pretty significant crisis of faith" during his years there.

"College is the kind of place where, if you've grown up within the faith, you're gonna have to think through all this stuff and figure out what's yours and what was your folks' or the environment that you're coming from," he said. "And at the same time, one of our family members, who was also really devout in faith, completely crumbled. He was very instrumental in what I thought to be the embodiment of following Christ."

"So, you stopped believing," I said.

"Yeah, it was like, 'This crap doesn't work!'" he said. "It was a pretty bleak number of years there in the middle of school."

And then, in the midst of his darkness, David Crowder had a chicken sandwich. In his book *Praise Habit: Finding God in Sunsets and Sushi,* Crowder tells a slightly difficult-to-re-relate story about how tearing out the bad part of a Chick-fil-A chicken sandwich reminded him that there was once only good in the world and that God had never intended there to be bad, and this discovery, on removing the lesser part of the sandwich, fired him up again.

I asked him about it. He swears it's true. Hey, Archimedes had his bathtub, Newton had his apple, Darwin had his finches. . . .

In 1995, Baylor surveyed its student population and found out that, like Crowder, more than half of its students didn't go to church anymore. "Really, the church had become completely irrelevant," Crowder said, speaking for himself but voicing a not-uncommon viewpoint among his peers. Post–chicken sandwich (and may I add that if any of my fellow nonbelievers wish to taste what heaven must be like, a Chick-fil-A #1 value meal is not the worst place to start), Crowder and some friends decided to, as he said, "provide a space to allow students to continue the journey of questioning without having to discard all their faith."

University Baptist Church (UBC) was the result. Crowder became music pastor, which meant that he was in charge of finding "words and sounds and such that would articulate faith for this particular group of folks that were somewhat outside of Christian culture but still in the middle of it."

The problem was, he couldn't find any music that did that. He went to a local Christian bookstore, bought as many records as the nascent church's budget allowed, and went home to plow through them. As he was doing so, a former roommate who'd introduced Crowder to Dave Matthews' music provided an unexpected epiphany.

"It's completely cinematic," Crowder said. "He comes into my apartment, and I'm going through the stack of CDs, and he's got his cigarette hanging out of his mouth, and the smoke's curling behind him, the sunlight's coming through the smoke, you know, and he takes a big drag and pulls it out, and he goes, 'What the—' you know, string of profanity comes out, 'is *that*?'"

"And then, he leaves," Crowder continued, "and there's this puff of smoke in the doorway. It was a brick to the head, going, 'Holy crap, *this* is who I'm trying to articulate this stuff for, and music's what we have in common—why don't *I* just try to say something for us?'"

So he started writing songs and performing them at UBC's worship services with a band of fellow congregants. Their first attempts were not particularly noteworthy, Crowder said, but eventually the "viral little thing here in Waco" took over, and students were taking tapes of David Crowder Band worship services home with them and playing them for their friends. Soon, the group was traveling to play for other churches whose youth groups were hungry for worship music that didn't make them want to ram their heads into concrete walls.

"It was a bizarre thing because we had created this space to provide something outside of the current Christian culture scene," Crowder said, "and the songs had found their way back in." Crowder signed with sixstepsrecords, the EMI-distributed label run by Louie Giglio, whom Crowder knew from a Bible study he used to attend at Baylor.

"He called and was like, 'Hey, we're doing a live recording, and we'd love to use this song,'" Crowder said, "and the conversation wound up just me really sensing in him a really similar heart for students." Giglio wasn't as concerned as Crowder was about attracting people from outside the church—his mission was to fire up youngsters. "We were still coming from two different places," Crowder said, "but he's just a great guy."

It was the beginning of a beautiful friendship. Crowder credits Giglio with helping him to trust the process of being inspired to do art. "My relationship with him has been a really healing thing for a lot of the baggage I've carried," Crowder said. "He's a really articulate person, he views his oration as art, and he's not sure where that moment when he starts talking is gonna end up."

The David Crowder Band has released four proper albums, a rarities collection, and a remix album. Crowder, as I mentioned, has written a book that artfully posits the existence of an intersection between making praising God part of your day and the habits worn by nuns. As I write this, I have an advance copy of the group's newest album, *A Collision,* which intersperses quotes from two guys named Ralph (Vaughan Williams—okay, he pronounced it "Rafe"—and Stanley) among trademark Crowder ecstatic praise and what he calls "just a bunch of noise junk." "Shout to the Lord" this is not.

The collision in question, Crowder said, is "divinity and depravity." I told him I would need definitions.

"Our fallen state and our maker's transcendence seem to be always entwined," he said. "Most of the record was born out of pain or contemplation of mortality. Every time I turn around, it's like somebody new in my proximity has cancer, and those things are long, slow battles, and most of the time you don't win."

"If you're a person of faith," he continued, "you have to figure out how to deal with that. Most of the record is very eschatological in orientation in that, despite our best efforts, our situation is still pretty bleak here. You still have to account for hurricanes"—we were speaking just after Katrina ravaged New Orleans—"and tsunamis."

Crowder had been unable to tear himself away from media coverage of the December 2004 tsunami in Asia that killed more than one hundred fifty thousand people. "You're watching this thing that comes from the ground in the middle of the ocean," he said, "carrying kids from mothers' arms. For me, it was a picture of the depth of our fall, you know, the ground under our feet's not even right.

"I feel like my writing has neglected, to some extent, the coming of God and things being set right and a new heaven, a new earth."

Hence the sample of the deeply religious Ralph Stanley speaking that precedes the techno-bluegrass version of Hank Williams' campfire chestnut "I Saw the Light" in *A Collision*'s midsection. Crowder draws a comparison between "heaven-oriented" American Christianity and bluegrass, whose pioneers didn't have "a lot of good to look forward to in life," he said. "All they had was something on the other side. It was all boll weevils and slavery."

"What that led to, I think, in American faith was a lot of room for neglect of social issues," he said. "I think when Jesus was talking about the kingdom of heaven, he's speaking of the here and now, and we've got to make a difference in the way we treat people, the way we're responsible with the societies that we live within. So in the process of reacting against our eternal-mindedness, I found my songwriting completely devoid of something to say to someone who just had an earthquake take from them everything that they own.

"So, this record has a lot to do with that as well. It's a rendering of our mortality as well. Immortality. The two things rolled together."

David Crowder, as best I can tell, does not smoke pot. But he thinks like a high person, which I mean as a compliment. People who get high are not terribly productive, but, man, can they ever draw connections between disparate stimuli. Maybe that "Another One Bites the Dust" single—which fundamentalist antirock crusaders in the '80s claimed contained the backward message "It's fun to smoke marijuana"—paid off!

Now, before you go chucking your Radiohead albums and head out to get deep into some Crowder, I feel the need to remind you that this is praise-and-worship music. As such, while Crowder's free to express doubt, struggle, and lament and does so impressively, he's bound by the form to end the journey in reconciliation, not rejection. Because, and Crowder knows it, this is not music for non-Christians.

"We play church music," he said flatly. "We play music that is for a corporate group of people to articulate their faith." To the extent that Crowder's band is out in "the world," it's to challenge the faithful to look at their faith in different ways. So, when the David Crowder Band plays in a nightclub or a bar, he has no illusions about whom he's reaching.

"I'm very aware of what we're doing," he said. "But what if you get a bunch of church kids in a club that has a bar, and it's open, and you wind up having church there? I think it shifts some of their paradigm of where God exists and where you can engage God, even through music."

"Music has become synonymous with worship, and I think that's a screwed-up thing," he said. "We started this church to try to blur the line between sacred and secular. We have this belief that there's not a moment that's happening that's outside of the presence of God. And I think that's not what has been verbalized by the church at large, because we're scared. We don't want kids to be running around having sex with each other, so we say, Don't ever go to an R-rated movie. We're scared of those."

"It's the same with the sacred/secular thing," he continued. "There's really disgusting things within the church. It's not out there; it's in here as well—'cause people are in here, just like they're out there. So that's why any chance we get to blur that line and make people scratch their heads, it's an opportunity for conversation."

After our interview, I e-mailed Crowder to ask him what kind of criticism he's gotten from within the church community. He told me one story of playing a show in L.A. at a club called the Avalon and seeing a guy in the front row getting visibly agitated, pointing and talking loudly to people around him. Here's what he wrote:

> i was starting thinking that the song we were in the middle of sucked. that it fell in a terrible spot in the setlist or we should just stop right there, never to make music again since we obviously couldn't hold the attention of people on the front row, when i turned to my left and caught sight of this girl on a balcony just off stage. her eyes were closed. her left hand was raised toward the ceiling in pentacostal-charismatic-praise-the-lord fashion. she was singing and swaying along with the song that i now thought to be completely brilliant. in her right hand was a budweiser. king of beers. i looked back at the four people on the front row and smiled watching them try to figure out where to put that image in their head.

He also told me about someone getting angry about him mentioning Jesus in the postscript of a mass holiday e-mail to fans, to which after some dithering, he decided to simply wish the critic grace and peace.

This is a man who knows his audience.

About six weeks after Crowder and I spoke on the phone, I was looking at an aggregation of "weird news" stories on the Internet and saw one about a pastor who'd died the day before while performing a baptism. It was Kyle Lake, thirty-three, who'd led University Baptist Church for three years.

Lake was in the baptismal pool and reached for a microphone, instantly grounding himself and sending thousands of volts of electricity through his body. He died a few hours later. Crowder left me a message on my cell phone two days later, responding to an e-mail I'd sent him saying that I'd try to make it to his band's Washington, D.C., show later that week. He sounded understandably scattered.

"It's just absolutely, you know, nuts," he said. "It's not often that a minister dies giving one of the sacraments, so it's definitely a newsworthy thing, and we made it back, and, man, our heads are a little messed up right now. I would love it if you'd be able to come up and hang and chat a bit."

Amazingly, Crowder's band hadn't missed a single show since their pastor's death. They'd decided to go ahead and play their scheduled concert in Orlando, Florida, the night Lake had died, then flown home to Waco for the funeral, which coincided with a couple of days off in their schedule. Then, they'd returned to the road.

Sitting in the band's tour bus outside George Washington University's Lisner Auditorium, Crowder told me why they hadn't just canceled the tour. Lake had had a big part in planning *A Collision,* he told me, offering suggestions and guidance to a Microsoft Word document the band members were passing back and forth while planning the album's narrative arc.

Referring to the album's themes of death, man's fall, and redemption, Crowder said they'd decided that, "We've been in this space for six months, and if we can't handle it in the art we've created, then we should just pack it in." I asked him if being away from Waco made it easier to deal with Lake's death, and he said it was actually worse, since touring gave them all many hours of nothing to do but dwell.

They were all holding it together pretty well, maintaining a fragile jocularity. Crowder nearly teared up a couple times when talking about the songs that had been hard to perform since Lake died— "We Win!" which was inspired by one of Lake's sermons, and "Amazing Grace," which Crowder had played at graveside at the funeral—but was friendly with fans who stopped him and asked to take photos with him when we walked down the street to get a cup of coffee.

Back on the bus, Mike Hogan, the band's violinist/keyboardist/DJ, announced that "the Asians are out tonight"—for some reason its members don't fully understand, the David Crowder Band is huge among Korean-Americans. They were due to play a large Korean church in New York City a few nights later and had recently played for a mostly Korean crowd of eleven thousand in Los Angeles.

I took my seat in the auditorium when it was time for the band to go on. The crowd was at least one-third Asian, which made it easily the most racially diverse crowd I'd seen at a Christian event so far. Crowder's opening band, Shane and Shane, closed with a sappy number about God being really freaking cool that had the guy next to me in tears. "Here we go again," I thought glumly.

Then, the lights went down, the crowd roared, and the David Crowder Band took the stage with a blast of low-frequency sound that I'm pretty sure shaved a few minutes off my life.

The reason I finally "got" worship music at this show wasn't that Crowder puts on an excellent show (which he does) or that the music was adventurous and fun and really, really loud (which it was) or even that, if I eyed my fellow spectators selectively, I finally got a glimpse of what it might have been like to see Cheap Trick at Budokan in 1979.

I didn't even fully get worship music (though I came close) when Crowder performed a song called "Undignified" toward the end of his set. "I will dance, I will sing, to be mad for my King," he sang as the audience members' last reservations melted away, and what seemed like the whole auditorium was jumping up and down in sweaty unison in a loud, inviting space the band had created where the crowd could be as goofy as they wanted, losing themselves in adoration. "And I'll become even more undignified than this!" they shouted with Crowder.

No, I got worship music during a sound collage during the last number, "Rescue Is Coming," when Crowder bent down and started fiddling with an effect pedal so that his guitar was feeding back in an interesting loop, so engrossing, in fact, that I didn't even notice that he'd disappeared completely for a minute or so.

And that, friends, marked my conversion to, or at least the end of my enmity to, worship music. Here's a guy surrounded by rabid fans who'd have done anything to get close to their worship leader (you should have heard some of the lines people laid on me to try to get my all-access pass after the show), consciously removing himself from the spotlight. There was only one star at that evening's show, and he hadn't been onstage at all.

"Okay, tough guy," I wrote Doug Van Pelt. "You like worship music so much, tell me why." It took him a while to respond, but when he did, it was a doozy, a long e-mail that compared Charismatic Christian worship with Shi'ite Islam and went deep into his own encounters with experiential worship.

Van Pelt confirmed my theory about worship music creating space where people can get goofy with God, and he also said he often worried about what he called the "emotional highs" of worship.

"One problem" with such highs, he said, "is that we measure our experience with God based on emotions, or how cool the last service 'felt,' and, thus, we deem not getting to that same level or beyond as a failure. Many churches are probably guilty of this."

"Even as Pentecostal/Charismatic churches might criticize the older denominations and their 'old, dry, dead worship,'" he wrote, "soon these 'spontaneous' and emotional charismatic meetings become just as predictable and just as humanly manufactured as the type of worship they might have despised or reacted against."

Keep a balance, Van Pelt urged. "During the real good worship times, I almost always engage my emotions in such a way that touches me deeply," he wrote. "I also value the worship in silence, of meditation. I try to measure my worship, if I do at all, upon whether the things I've said or done are true. That's easier and a lot more stable, in my opinion, than trying to match up to some experience or emotion from the past."

All in all, he said, the communication with God was worth the occasional mediocre song. "What about the hand-raising thing," I wrote back. "Do you do that?" Here's what he wrote back.

One thing that I personally do is I often lift my hands if the song says "I lift my hands to you." I do this mostly so that I can do what I sing and not have a cognitive dissonance thing going on, or, on a lower level, "be singing a lie." This might cause me to lose face or forget my pride and not care as much about what the people around me think as much as I care about what the invisible God I'm supposedly worshipping thinks.

I'm running out of battery. I'll send this now.

Peace out.

CHAPTER 11

Just Like Heaven

At Christian rock festivals, it's the adults who dress wacky—turning out in full kilt dress, for instance, or an Oompa Loompa outfit. These people are youth pastors, and I was more than slightly mortified when, upon entering the gates at the Orlando Fairgrounds to see the Florida franchise of the Cornerstone Festival, a well-scrubbed young fellow asked me if I was one.

You see, I have a standard outfit for when I cover outdoor rock events—cargo shorts (which sag with the weight of my tape recorder, cell phone, hand sanitizer, water bottle, sunblock, notebooks, and pens), T-shirt, floppy hat (to protect from the sun), and windbreaker tied around my waist in case of rain. It makes me look like an unmarried field anthropologist, but in the hip world, dressing so uncool has the odd effect of making me disappear altogether.

The reason that didn't work here is because looking ridiculous is often a prerequisite for relating to kids at Christian events. In fact, wackiness abounds in the evangelical subculture, whether it's a youth pastor in a snakeskin cowboy hat and a pink Snoopy backpack that says FEELIN' GROOVY or a rock band performing Justin Timberlake's "Cry Me a River" in—get this—alternative rock style! I used to think this goofiness was a symptom of a culture where humor is stifled by stricture, with much of life off-limits as subject matter. But now I suspect it's because being kooky is often the only way to express humor without it being analyzed to death. It's much easier to go with silliness, which seems to be considered unworthy of discussion. Plus, there's a freedom in embracing uncoolness, and Christian youth pastors are, by all appearances, extremely free.

But, hey, I didn't come here to whine. Or did I? Ten months into my look at Christian music, I'd had little luck getting phone calls and e-mails returned—publicists at Christian labels seemed to have a different view of their jobs than their secular counterparts, who at least have the courtesy to tell you no. I'd come to Florida with a dozen interview requests, most of which I'd made a month earlier, pending. I had no idea whether I was wasting my time.

It was hard not to feel like the wagons were circling. I had no evidence, and in retrospect, it sounds idiotic even to have considered otherwise, but people kept telling me artist X was "really into the idea" and then . . . nothing. Follow-up phone calls went unacknowledged. I remembered the trouble Brian Dannelly had when his film *Saved!*, a loving, gentle satire of evangelical youth culture, came under fire from religious conservatives while it was in production—suddenly, a Christian band called the Elms became unavailable to appear in the film, and no other Christian musicians would take the group's place.

Seeing as the Elms had read the movie's script, and I hadn't really written anything yet, I have to assume that the silence greeting me wasn't due to conspiracy. More likely it was because Christian music is a very small world, and knowing Doug Van Pelt really only gets you so far.

Later on, I discussed this phenomenon with an editor at Relevant Books, a publishing house associated with a Christian magazine called, appropriately, *Relevant*. He told me that he had been "absolutely astonished" when one of the magazine's editors had set up an interview with film director Cameron Crowe—"He just called his publicist, and they did the interview the next day." He said in the Christian world that would have taken weeks.

Anyway, here I was in another field, and there was even a little patch of corn—a display at the fairgrounds' agriculture exhibit—to remind me of Cornerstone in Illinois. The soundmen played Rage Against the Machine's "Killing in the Name Of" over one of the two main stages' P.A. systems, which seemed like a curious choice, seeing as the antiwar song starts with the line "Some of those that are forces are the same that bore crosses" and finishes with singer Zach de la Rocha repeatedly screeching, "Fuck you, I won't do what you tell me!"

Here's a list of T-shirts I noticed for sale in the first few minutes of walking around the merchandise tent:

CRUNK FOR CHRIST

NO HIGH LIKE THE MOST HIGH

HELL, NO

UNABORTED

JESUS IS THE (PICTURE OF A BOMB)

I'M IN LOVE WITH A MAN

That last slogan goofs on gay pride further by being printed over a rainbow stripe. The back, in case you hadn't guessed, says, HIS NAME IS JESUS.

It's a bit rich to see evangelical Christians detourning the symbols of other subcultures, especially when many Christians believe that discrimination and persecution against Christians is rampant in a country where, as of this writing, not just half the population describes itself as "born again," but the president, vice president, leaders of both houses of Congress, and all but two Supreme Court justices are Christians. The desire to make Christian kids revel in "outsider" status is understandable: it keeps kids fired up, ready to be soldiers of Christ.

In the documentary *Why Should the Devil Have All the Good Music?* Mark Nicks, the singer and drummer for the Christian band Cool Hand Luke says something I think is fairly spectacular in its lack of perspective:

> When kids make fun of us or are mean to us or cuss at us or whatever, like, it really sort of encourages us in a way, just because, I mean, Jesus told us, you know, if we're preaching the Word, He was persecuted, and we're gonna be persecuted. And it just kinda lets us know that we're doing something right.

Sorry, dude, but a drunken idiot shouting "Satan rules" when you play in a bar isn't quite the same thing as being *nailed to a tree.* A few months before, I'd asked David Bazan whether he'd felt persecuted as a young Christian. "Oh yeah," he said. "That's something that they really fostered growing up, the idea of being persecuted for your faith." Then, he told me a story about a youth group he used to go to in college, whose leader once told them, "You guys are always coming in here talking about being persecuted for your faith. Well, I'll tell you what: I bet the reason you're being persecuted is because you're a jackass. When you stop being a jackass all the time, you might be *able* to be persecuted for your faith."

Now, I happen to believe that Christians are often portrayed negatively in mainstream entertainment. And I've heard enough snippy comments from colleagues to say without a doubt that there's a clear bias against Christian musical artists in the mainstream music press, one I wouldn't be surprised to find carries over to radio and retail as well. (Imagine spending years carefully perfecting a cocktail of hip influences only to find your record filed under "Gospel" at Target!)

But the idea that there's some kind of widespread danger facing Christians in the United States of America in the early twenty-first century is ludicrous. Early Christians were stoned, fed to lions, and set on fire—hardly the equivalent of someone dubbing in fart sounds over a video of Robert Tilton preaching.

Okay. Sermon over. We now rejoin our music festival already in progress.

Think of the most embarrassing thing your parents ever did to you. Maybe your dad got drunk and leered at your date, or your mom hauled out some naked baby photos when she met your boss. Well, Jay Bakker can beat that. In fact, unless both your parents became national objects of derision after your dad got caught paying off his secretary to keep quiet about their affair and was later convicted of embezzling millions of dollars from the church business he founded, and your mom became an inspiration to drag queens everywhere, and the woman your dad had an affair with posed for *Playboy* as a result of her fame, and your mom went on to star in a reality show with Vanilla Ice, you may begin to feel like you had a model childhood.

Jay Bakker is the son of Jim and Tammy Faye Bakker, the televangelists whose fall from grace in the '80s was gleefully documented and satirized worldwide. But rather than change his name or attempt to quietly live out his life, Jay Bakker has taken on a mission: saving Christianity from religion.

Revolution Ministries, which Bakker cofounded in 1994, meets in a very secular Atlanta nightclub called the Masquerade (which has three levels: "Hell," "Purgatory," and "Heaven"). It's small, drawing about fifty people a week to services, and according to a profile of Bakker in the *New York Times*, that's just the way he likes it, remembering how his father's incessant drive to increase his flock led to his downfall.

Using a flight case for a lectern, Bakker began to address the crowd by talking about the idea behind his ministry. Of average height with piercings, a shaved head and arms absolutely covered in tattoos, Bakker looked like he knew what he was talking about when he said, "A lot of people feel rejected—not by the church but by Christianity in America."

Bakker's kind of a disaster as a public speaker. He trips over words, snickers at his own jokes, and fidgets. At one point in his presentation, he compared what he called his natural "nervousness" with that of Pedro the Lion's David Bazan. "Of course, if I swear, I don't get invited back," he said. Bakker's so awkward, he'd be kind of spellbinding even without a compelling message, which is really his only subject: love. "If you've ever seen me speak, you may have heard First Corinthians Thirteen: four through seven," he said with a snort of laughter. He reads through the famous verses about the character of love: not envious or boastful or arrogant, nor rejoicing in wrongdoing, but bearing all things, believing all things, enduring all things.

"I just ate a big Moe's burrito," he said, parenthetically. "So I might get sick up here," then said his sermon "was basically on these points: what does love look like?"

It's human nature to be judgmental, he said. "But when it becomes arrogant and rude is when we start calling people perverts and murderers and immoral."

"I might be stepping on some toes right now," he continued, "but the point is, that's not love." Bakker said he was worried about a great divide growing in the church between liberals and conservatives. "It seems like they're getting into little camps," he said. "And if you remember what Jesus said, a kingdom divided will fall. And I think we've gotta get to a point where we're loving each other, we're agreeing to disagree, and we're not so arrogant and rude that we think we know it all."

Bakker said he'd just turned down a speaking gig at a Christian rock festival that required him to sign a contract stating that he hadn't committed "any unbiblical activity for three years."

"I was like, 'Well, my assistant pastor offended me, but I killed him in front of the altar, but that's cool right, because it's biblical? And there was this girl that I really thought was hot, but she was married, but I killed her husband—is that cool?' You followin' me? David? Yeah, David, man after God's own heart."

"Sometimes God's gonna call you to places that aren't morally great," he said, talking about how Revolution encourages its congregants to spend time in bars, "loving people."

"You start to see things differently," he said.

Bakker described an encounter with a bike-shop salesman who shrank from him when he told him he was a pastor. The guy automatically assumed he didn't like gay people, voted a certain way, etc. "It made me really sad that this twenty-year-old kid is scared of someone saying he's a pastor," he said. "We're missing the point. We can come to our festivals, [speaking in a sarcastic voice] get all high on Jesus, take a hit off the Bible."

But people outside the Christian world, he said, are afraid of Christians. They're afraid we'll be arrogant, rude, insist on our own way, he said. "People have an idea of what Christianity represents, and it's not living the love. When did it become about being a Republican?"

Take the stickers off your cars, he advised. Put aside your political agendas. "I'm not anti-Christian," he said, summing up. "I'm antireligion. We've created a monster. I don't know what to do. Do you?"

I'd love to tell you that the reason Bakker's talk resonated with me was because, in the course of researching my book, I'd come to many of the same conclusions, but I have to make a confession. Remember back in chapter 1, when I said that religion was something I didn't have much experience with? I lied.

Here's something even my closest friends don't know: I have two fathers. The man I call Dad isn't my biological parent. My "real" father is a disgraced Episcopalian priest whose life I watched fall apart twice—first, after he was forced out of his church once his affair with a congregant became known and, second, after he embezzled from the church that he landed in next. I've seen firsthand the mess humans can make while supposedly attending to God's work and how much their failures hurt the people who believed in them, congregants and families alike.

Don't go shouting "aha!" just yet—I was done with religion long before my father was convicted of his crimes. I'd spent a lot of my youth trying to convince myself that there was something I should have been feeling in church but wasn't. I always figured I was doing something wrong. One day, after reading Friedrich Nietzsche and Herman Hesse in rapid succession, I wondered, What if there were no God? I decided to see if living as if that were the case changed anything for me. It didn't. As far as I'm concerned, death is the end of life—lights out, game over, don't forget to rewind, please. I'm okay with that.

This is the kind of talk that makes my Christian friends unbearably sad, and that's what I love about them—they really, really, really don't want anyone to die, and that's why they can sometimes be such a raging pain in the ass. So next time a Christian tries to save you from the fate that awaits you, don't get irritated—remember that it's because they care about you. Seriously. If you take nothing else away from this book, remember that.

A few weeks before Cornerstone Florida, I'd gone down to Alley Katz, a nightclub near my home in Richmond, to see Mute Math. A couple of people I'd met—Ken Heffner at Calvin College in particular—had recommended I check the band out. I'd heard their single, "Control," which I thought was just okay, but Mute Math's live show completely blew me away. A four-piece from New Orleans,

Mute Math is the rare Christian rock band that doesn't settle for simply not sucking but actually reaches for greatness. Onstage, the band members really stretch out sonically, feeding their instruments through delays, creating new rhythms, jamming—jamming! As the jazzmen say, these cats really take it *out*. I can pay them the highest compliment I know for a band that records for an imprint of Word Records—I wouldn't have had any idea they were Christians unless I'd read their lyric sheet.

Mute Math's manager turned down my request to follow the band on tour for a couple of days—probably for the best as I'd have ended up begging them to let me stay on as a roadie just so I could see them every night—but agreed to an interview, which took place on the band's bus after they played a sweaty set on the main stage.

They were something of a sorry lot. Paul Meany, the band's vocalist and electric piano torturer, had a cold. Guitarist Greg Hill had injured his foot playing basketball. Only drummer Darren King and bassist Roy Mitchell were in relatively good shape, and everyone but Hill, who'd met up with friends after the show, joined me in the band's swanky bus.

Before Mute Math, Meany and Mitchell played in a band on Sparrow Records called Earthsuit, which Meany said, was a group that "couldn't make up its mind between sincerity and being cerebral." Despite some success on Christian radio, Earthsuit never made much of a dent commercially, and Meany said that "most people didn't care when we broke up!"

King had briefly been a part of Earthsuit, after the band's original drummer left. He'd been collaborating with Meany on some new songs (which would eventually become Mute Math numbers) through the mail, but he leaped at the chance to join his favorite band the day after he graduated high school. What he hadn't counted on was that his hypermilitant Christian identity would be a little hard to take.

"I was having the time of my life," he said. "I was a loose wire. And after a month and a half of that, they sent me home. Now the way that they tell the story is that I did an internship," he said to laughter from his bandmates. "And that softens the blow. Really what it was, was a monthlong failed audition."

But a funny thing happened to the kid from southwestern Missouri who'd alienated most of the kids at his school (praying solo at the flagpole each morning, accusing the drama team of being "hypocrites"), seriously tested his relationship with his mother (hectoring her for listening to Garth Brooks and dating a non-Christian), and burned all of his Christian records for not being "Christian enough." In fact, King listened to only worship music for over a year, which I'm pretty sure qualifies him for sainthood.

Looking through the CD collections of his temporary bandmates, King discovered Beck. And DJ Shadow. And Björk. And the Beastie Boys. And Sigur Ros. "I couldn't believe it," he said about the world of music he had stumbled into. "I just became an audiophile. I just made sound effects in my bedroom."

When Meany reactivated their postal side project as his new band, King was ready to try again. The new band's mission, in King's words, would be "to make complex music with very simple lyrics." "Control," the Dove-winning single from the group's debut EP, is an ode to submission that has odd echoes in Meany's approach to playing live. "Take control of the atmosphere," he sings. "It's such a beautiful surrender."

"When we do our show," Meany said, "all we can control is that everyone's comfortable, no one feels alienated, and I think this comes from an atmosphere we can create as musicians. Whether you get it or not, whether this is blatantly Christian or not."

Paul Meany grew up in Chalmette, Louisiana, a blue-collar suburb of New Orleans, in what he calls a "very legalistic family where all we could listen to was Christian music. And not even Christian rock. It pretty much had to be Southern gospel, Sandi Patty."

"I remember the first time I got to hear the radio," he said. "This sounds like a nineteenth-century story, but we didn't believe in going to doctors, we didn't believe in celebrating Christmas, definitely not Halloween. We had to turn the lights off and pray inside while the demons were walking around outside!"

The small church Meany grew up in wasn't associated with any denomination. "It was just weird," he said. "If you're from New Orleans, [the fact that the church was in Chalmette] makes perfect sense."

Still, his dad was the music minister of the church, and as far back as Meany can remember, he's always played piano. "I was just never really exposed to good music," he said.

When Paul was twelve, his parents divorced, and suddenly, all bets were off. "We didn't go to church anymore," he said. "I was kinda still searching. I got hooked up with this really cool youth group, so I was exposed to the Christian music scene at that point. I idolized it."

Young Paul fell hard for artists like D.C. Talk and Tim Miner. Because of his prodigious keyboard skills, his new church asked him to be in charge of the music for a Christian coffeehouse it was starting on Bourbon Street. "That's how I met a lot of Christian musicians in the New Orleans scene," he said. He started writing with a couple of them, and the result was Earthsuit.

"You start making music, playing out. You start networking, calling other churches and Christian coffeehouses, and there's this kind of scene," he said. They didn't consider trying to work outside of the Christian market. "It never crossed our minds," he said. "I talk to a lot of young bands now, and, you know, it's all about keeping a healthy distance from anything Christian—they wanna come up like a real rock band."

When Mute Math began, Meany, King, and Hill (Mitchell joined later) decided there was no point in denying their background. "See, we all met through church, and the one thing we had

in common was we were all brought up in a Christian church,"
King said. "And though we've all been through various attitudes
and responses to being brought up in church culture, that imper-
fect, at times very quarantined church culture—at times we've
been very bitter, at times disappointed, at times hurt, but we've
reached a point where we're proud to embrace it, aren't ashamed
of it, but at the same time see that there's lots more to experience
than just that culture."

"I think you have the choice of whether or not to feed it as it is,"
Meany said, "which we don't. We don't really want to give it the finger, either, because there are good things that happen in it. We're
hoping that we can expand it."

Mute Math are signed to Teleprompt, a label started by a producer who goes by the name Tedd T. and made his bones in the
Christian music biz by helming Rebecca St. James and Stacie Orrico
records. The idea behind the label, which is funded by Warner Bros.'
Word division, is to "screen out the ugly stuff," Meany said. I asked
what he meant.

"Of the industry," he clarified. "Through the record-making
process, when it's all about these executives coming in, telling you
you need to change this lyric, this lyric, this lyric, rearrange the song
here so we can get it to Christian radio."

"Is that the 'Jesus-per-minute' factor I've heard decides whether
a song gets on Christian radio or not?" I asked.

"Exactly," Meany said. "That part is real disheartening when
you're in the Christian music industry. And that's why I really sym-
pathize with a lot of bands who are just like, 'I don't want anything to
do with that.'"

Mute Math didn't mean to snub the Dove Awards when they
weren't present to accept their statuette for Modern Rock Recorded
Song of the Year. They just figured they had no chance of winning.
"We were just down the street, recording," King said.

What's so funny about the award, Meany said, is that "Earthsuit was a little more geared toward catering to Christian-ese culture. But it seems like Mute Math is gaining even more attention from the Christian side."

And while all the gentlemen of Mute Math say they'd be fine if the band never catches on beyond the confines of Christian music, Mitchell says that "the one thing that draws me to Mute Math and its music is that it does have an aspect to it that's universal. It might not be too blatantly Christian. But a Christian or someone who might be spiritually minded can tap into it, which I think is cool. What I love about what we do onstage—we just do our thing, and the music, the performance, speaks for itself. If what's going on between us four on-stage can translate to people in the crowd, I think we've done our job. Because the way we live, I think, reflects the music."

Jesus fatigue settled in pretty early for me on the second day of Cor-nerstone Florida. With a few exceptions, the bands were just so hopelessly mediocre that I found myself wandering out to the park-ing lot, calling home just to see how things were going, which, as an inveterately unemotional Virginia male, I *never* do.

It was during one of these phone calls to my increasingly less-amused wife that I found out our son had just stood up on his own for the first time. "Great," I thought. "Here I am in a stinkin' field in Florida, watching a bunch of bands who won't talk to me, just so I can miss milestone after milestone." Over the course of writing this book, I later missed his first word and first steps as well. Now, I real-ize just how incredibly lucky I am to listen to rock music for a living, but I was having a hard time remembering that as I watched a singer from a folk-rock duo say he writes "a lot like Psalm 13." Yeah, you and King David, dude, I thought. Peas in a pod.

That touches on something I'd been noticing in Christian music—the assumption of God's voice in song. "I will wait for you,"

I heard one band singing. "Just call my name," sang another. I don't want to be too flip about this. Poetic license is a real thing, and sometimes the best way to communicate such an intensely personal experience as conversion is to step outside of a narrative and just say what you heard when you were called. Still, it does seem a little overconfident, if not downright presumptuous, to communicate such a holy mystery as God himself taking time out of running the universe to speak to you by setting what you think is His thought process to a riff you ripped off from Green Day.

That morning, I met up with Glenn Kaiser from Jesus People USA, which puts on the Cornerstone Festival in Illinois and franchises this one to a local promoter. Kaiser, a real gentleman, walked me through the early days of Christian rock, which he experienced with his trailblazing rock group the Resurrection Band. Then, he went off to get ready to play with his eponymous blues-rock group, and I split to find Aaron Weiss of Mewithoutyou.

When I interviewed Brandon Ebel, Mewithoutyou's label head, he made a joke about Aaron Weiss's curious devotion to making sure nothing went to waste. And sure enough, within seconds of meeting Mewithoutyou's singer, I saw him eat trash.

"Oh!" he exclaimed, spying a couple of McDonald's bags in a trashcan as we walked to the shore of the fairgrounds' lake to do an interview. He pulled out two half hash browns and a ketchup packet. "I usually rip the bitten part off, but not always," he said.

"Are you a vegetarian, Aaron?" I asked.

"Sorta," he said. "Not strict. I mean, I'll eat meat out of the trash."

That must not happen too often: Weiss, twenty-six, is vegan-skinny, with a scraggly beard and dark, searching eyes. The son of a Jewish father and an Episcopalian mother who both converted to Islam's mystical Sufi sect ("bringing all the Abrahamic religions together," he jokes), Weiss grew up in Philadelphia loving poetry, cheese steaks, and the Smiths. He was completely unaware of the Christian subculture until he converted to Christianity around the time he graduated high school.

"I went to a church with our bass player, Greg," Weiss said. "He would always tell me about Jesus: 'You know, people are gonna go to hell, and the only way not to go to hell is to accept Jesus as your savior, so you have to say this prayer.'"

"So, after a few times, I was like, 'Okay, I'll say this prayer,'" he said. "But nothing really changed in my life." He stopped going to that particular church ("there were some weird things that were going on behind the scenes," he said), got serious with a Christian girl, and "just forgot about God, you know?"

Weiss had been playing drums in a band called Operation, but he really wanted to sing, so his bandmates gamely rearranged the lineup to let him do just that and called the resultant band Mewithoutyou. "It just picked up more momentum," Weiss said, "so the other band just kind of fizzled out."

Around the same time, Weiss broke up with his girlfriend and decided he "needed to really pursue God" instead. "Whatever I believe," he remembers thinking, "I need to take it seriously and confront this question of who God is and what are my responsibilities as a creation of Him?"

He describes his eventual recommitment to Jesus as a "life-wrecking experience. Not one of those stories of, 'I was hooked on drugs and down in the dumps and in prison.' More like, I felt all right, I had my friends, I had my girlfriend. But then I met Jesus, and He kinda knocked me down."

Actually, that's kind of how I felt when I first saw Mewithoutyou at Cornerstone in Illinois the previous summer. Weiss, wearing a velvet jacket in the ninety-degree heat, stomped a stage strewn with flower petals. He doesn't really sing per se—he kind of just talks emphatically, shouting on the choruses as the other musicians find grooves informed as much by the "math rock" of groups like Helmet as by the Beatles and Sunny Day Real Estate. Mewithoutyou also reminded me of two of my favorite bands when I was a teenager—Rites of Spring and Honor Role, generally obscure D.C. and Richmond post-punk bands, respectively—not so much in sound but in spirit. Weiss was here to tell you a story, demanding your empathy till you were right there with him. Mewithoutyou was the first excellent Christian band I saw and was still among the best I'd heard a year later.

"Is Mewithoutyou a Christian band?" I asked Weiss.

"I don't think so," he said. "I don't know. We've never been clear on that one. I don't even know if I'm a Christian. I hope I am. I have to be afraid of making bold claims of who I am and how faithful I am. I don't have very much faith. As little faith as I have in God, I have much less faith in this world. So I have to go with the lesser of two passions."

Weiss's Christianity comes from possibly the most emo book of the whole Bible, Acts, whose second chapter talks about "Divided tongues, as of fire"[1] descending on the apostles, who were suddenly able to speak the languages of all people, before Peter exhorted them, "Save yourself from this corrupt generation,"[2] and they settled into communal living where "they would sell their possessions and goods and distribute the proceeds to all, as any had need."[3]

Weiss lived in a Philly Christian commune called the Simple Way for a while but finally moved his stuff to his parents' house when Me-withoutyou began touring extensively with the release of its second album, 2004's *Catch for Us the Foxes*. He clearly misses communal life. "When you see how the early Christians lived," he said, getting excited, "they shared everything. When people were in need, Christians would sell all they had, sell their house and land and say 'distribute this as there's need.' So, nobody went hungry."

"It's like, if I have two jackets, and this person doesn't have one jacket," he said, "I give them my extra one. That's just pure common sense. Our conscience tells us that, our Scripture tells us that, our reason tells us that. The only thing that doesn't tell us that is our greed, and the Devil, and the powers of this world who say, What's mine is mine."

Weiss says Christianity can basically be reduced to two commandments. "That's kind of the Good News," he said, referring to a common translation of the Old English word that became *Gospel.* "All I'm saying is, we need to love God with all of our heart, all of our mind, all of our soul, all of our strength, and to love our neighbor as ourselves. Jesus said, 'This contains everything else.' You don't need to know the coolest bands coming out, you don't need to wear the right outfit or have any amount of money—you don't even need to read the Bible to understand that. God's put that in our hearts, I think."

The obvious question, I asked him, is why his band records for a Christian record label and plays Christian festivals.

"I don't feel very comfortable in the Christian subculture environment," he said. "I don't feel a lot of authenticity. I don't connect with a lot of people. Not that I'm authentic, and they're not, but somewhere in my heart is longing for something honest and eternal, and all I see is fads and corny T-shirts and young kids who were mostly raised and taught what they should think and haven't had a chance to question it."

"So why play?" I asked. "Nothing's stopping you from only playing nightclubs." He said they don't play churches and do no other Christian events but the Cornerstone Festival's and another in Pennsylvania called Purple Door. Like David Bazan, Weiss considers Mewithoutyou's ventures into the Christian world almost as missionary ventures.

"The main reason I can try to justify even being in a band is to communicate to the people who are gonna come to these kind of gatherings or listen to our band just because we're on Tooth & Nail Records and say to them, 'You know what Jesus called us to do is to

come and die, suffer and sacrifice, lay down our lives for other people. Not try to live the most comfortable life we can or have a whole
lot of fun or look a certain way.'"

Weiss took me on a tour of Mewithoutyou's bus, an old Grey-
hound coach they purchased off eBay and retrofitted with a biodiesel
system that Weiss paid for himself (the band is slowly paying him
back). "This is my baby," he said, snapping on a pair of long rubber
gloves and demonstrating how the used fryer oil they siphon off from
restaurants (with permission of course) is filtered four times between
two seventy-gallon tanks and warmed by antifreeze. As a result, Mewithoutyou tours with almost no fuel costs whatsoever.

On the bus, Weiss showed me a volume of the Sufi poet Rumi
that his mom had sent him. "If you read that, you'll recognize a lot of
our lyrics," he said. He told me he often felt stranded between the
ecstatic mysticism of Sufism and conservative evangelical Christianity. "I'm very much divided," he said. "I have a thousand different
loves and distractions. But there's nothing as powerful as the desire
in my heart for unity and worship with others. We worship God together in peace. That would be the greatest thing in the world—
work together and love each other. That's stronger than my desire for
sex or for recognition of the band or money and comfort, things like
that. It's like there's all that, and it's there, and I can't deny it, and I
ask for forgiveness, and I ask for help, but, man, to really love God
and to really have unity in the world with others, to make peace in
the world and to worship God together would . . . be greater than
anything. No doubt."

"God put us here to know him," he continued. "I wanna search
for him. And, as it says in the Scriptures, we live by the spirit, not by
the letter. And the feeling I have is that we can read the words in the
Bible and use them for most anything. So I just have to believe the
truth that's behind it, the reality that's being brought to us *through*
the words on the paper.

"You know, you can read about Jesus saying 'Forgive them father, they know not what they do,' and go and repeat that to someone else. But Jesus is forgiving the people who crucified him. And here, we're not usually able to forgive our parents for screwing up here and there. I feel like we could take this one alone out of the Scriptures, and that would be enough for me to live the rest of my life without memorizing John 3:16 or something. Forgiveness is really at the essence of all of this."

Weiss insisted on hugging me before I left, and I really didn't mind. On my way out the door, I asked him what the Hebrew words tattooed on his wrists said. "It says, 'Blessed are the poor in spirit, for theirs is the kingdom of Heaven,'" he told me.

The Indoor Stage was the place to be this evening, not only because it was air conditioned (central Florida gets humid early in the year) but because it boasted the best lineup of the festival: John Davis, Denison Witmer, David Bazan, and Mewithoutyou. I was particularly interested in Davis because I used to love his old band, Superdrag, which had a modern rock hit in the '90s called "Sucked Out." (I just put the song on and spent three minutes playing air guitar in my office after typing that.) Davis had a life-changing experience while recording the final Superdrag album, 2002's *Last Call for Vitriol*. Now he's a Christian recording artist, and Superdrag is no more.

There's a bit of Brian Wilson about the John Davis of 2005—the skinny young man who shredded his throat on "Sucked Out" now boasts the slightly gone-to-seed look Christian audiences seem to demand of their front men, and he exhibited a quiet naïveté, switching from guitar (on which he is a freaking *monster*) to piano, singing sweet songs of getting saved while his suit-clad band, augmented by Sixpence None the Richer's Matt Slocum, nailed four-part harmonies, ably navigating the course Davis set through gospel music, British Invasion pop, and the Beach Boys' *Pet Sounds*. It didn't seem to matter to Davis that the cavernous Indoor Stage pretty much

remained that way during his set—he still played like his life de-
pended on it. And judging by lyrics like "I want You to tear me
apart," I get the feeling it does.

At the end of Davis's set, I sneaked around to the "Masada Tent"
to catch the last songs by a group called Psalters. I'd seen members
of the group clomping around the festival both days, dressed like a
troupe of mutant Morris Dancers in black pirate gear, flowing pants
and skirts, and jingle bells affixed to their ankles. They lived and
toured in a black-painted school bus festooned with banners that
said FREE STATE OF PSALTERS, which they'd parked on the festival
grounds on day one. One imagines that on the highway, cops pull it
over on principle.

Onstage, Psalters had incense pots burning, a Bible on a table,
and enormous drums that were being pummeled by the eight-
strong ensemble's burlier members. Their jingle bells jangled in
time as the group—its members furiously pumping accordions,
electric guitars, bouzoukis, and ouds—worked itself into an ecstatic
frenzy of Middle Eastern harmonies and indie rock shouting. The
crowd was going nuts, too—this was simply like nothing else. When
the song ended, the soundman cut on the lights, and the group and
the crowd started stomping and yelping until he relented and let
Psalters do one more song.

Back at the Indoor Stage, Denison Witmer set up. When I saw he
was going to perform with just an acoustic guitar, I got ready to go
see whether Psalters had set the restrooms on fire because I'd had
my fill of Christian folk-rock. But Witmer won me over with his bare-
bones, low-key songs. I happen to think writing simple songs is the
hardest thing in the world to do, and Witmer excels at finding five-
note melodies that stay with you for days. Also, he looks a little bit
like Timothy McVeigh, which makes for an interesting juxtaposition.

During Witmer's set, David Bazan called my cell phone, and he
and I and Tim Walsh went outside to catch up. I told Bazan I'd

missed my kid standing up for the first time, and he said, "Oh man, I'm sorry." We had a brief pity party about spending too much time away from our kids. (Walsh, who, unlike Bazan and me, has more than one child, seemed to have gotten over this inconvenience.)

When Bazan took the stage, the room quickly filled to the back. It never ceased to amaze me how these kids who supposedly couldn't think for themselves were drawn in such numbers to a guy who couldn't have been more out of step with evangelical culture.

During the first of his three question-and-answer sessions that evening, a kid in the audience asked him why he cursed on Pedro the Lion songs.

"Why do I curse on Pedro the Lion songs? Why don't I curse on more?" he asked. He added that he probably wasn't going to curse that night. Then, someone requested the song "Backwoods Nation," Bazan's song about how mindless violence permeates American culture. "I don't want J.D. [Herrin, one of Cornerstone's promoters] to sift through 150 e-mails about this performance," he warned, then began the song.

"Calling all rednecks to put down their sluggers," he sang. "Turn their attention from beating the buggers/Pick up the machine guns and kill camel—" he sang the word *fuckers* off-mike.

Most non-Christians look at evangelical Christianity and see a monoculture, a place where the nail that sticks out is mercilessly hammered down, so to speak. But over two days in a field in Florida, I'd watched the O.C. Supertones present their version of Jesus, a muscular advocate of banning abortion and gay marriage, staying pure till marriage, and beating the crap out of Satan.

But contrast that with Bazan, who told a rapt crowd he didn't consider himself a Christian, because "I wouldn't want my identity to infer that I voted for George Bush [to cheers] or against gay marriage [to boos]." Or with Mewithoutyou, whose hippie-ish, dervish-flavored

Christian worldview harkens back to the early days of the Jesus Movement and calls them to meet with, as a recent Web posting implored, "friends, your enemies, your parents, your pets, strangers, saints and scumbags. Especially the scumbags!"

Or the sound-heads of Mute Math, trying to find a way to challenge Christian or mainstream culture with their outer-space sounds. Or the aficionados of handmade music I met in Michigan, trying to be salt and light in the kingdom of death. Or the shiny, happy people of the Christian music industry in Nashville, constructing an ever-more-impregnable fortress in which Christians can amuse themselves while waiting out the apocalypse. Or any of the believers I'd met doing this book, all of whom were trying their best to figure out how their convictions fit in with the culture at large.

It's truly fascinating, I thought, how music is the public square of evangelical Christianity, a place where all these visions of Christ get a hearing. Most everyone seems to agree that the current Christian culture needs to change, and, slowly, a dialog is emerging. And this evening, in this blowsy fairground in Orlando, as Bazan sang, "I need a miracle/Someone to help me help myself," a thousand people sang along, every single one of them reading off the same page, feeling every word, waiting breathlessly for the hallelujah that may or may not follow.

AFTERWORD

"Christian *rock?*"

"That's right."

"*Christian* rock?"

"Seriously."

It was a year and a few days after I started this project, and I was back in Illinois, this time for a "normal" assignment: reviewing Eminem and 50 Cent's Anger Management tour on its Chicago stop.

Except I wasn't in Chicago—I was in Tinley Park, Illinois, twenty-five miles south, in the parking lot of the Tweeter Center. It was almost midnight, and I was giving a stranger a ride home. Now, I was raised not to do such things, but during the show, I'd started talking with a few other people in the press seats, and that's when I met Markus Larsson, the pop music critic for *Aftonbladet*, Sweden's biggest newspaper. To get to the show, Larsson had taken the El as far south as he could, then walked for an hour before happening on a cab in the parking lot of a seedy motel.

It was all a bit *Planes, Trains and Automobiles*, and seeing as I was heading back to the city anyway, I gave Markus a ride home. Karma and all that. And as we waited—courtesy a long streak of nasty South Suburbs types—for a break in the traffic exiting the parking lot, we talked about our current projects. He couldn't believe such a thing as Christian rock existed.

269

"But why do they need their own music?" he asked.

I'd spent the past year trying to answer that question, I guess, and I wasn't totally sure myself. Maybe it's just an American thing, something foreigners couldn't possibly grasp, why Marion Barry got re-elected after getting caught smoking crack with a prostitute, or why our sandwiches are so big.

But the thing is, I could have had essentially this same conversation with someone from New York City, the only difference being that he or she wouldn't be shocked, as Markus also was, that maternity leave in the United States is usually unpaid.

Evangelical Christian culture is all around us. Since the 2004 presidential election, we've heard a lot about the two Americas, red and blue, exurban and citified, but I think it's important to note that the two largest markets for both Christian music and NASCAR are New York and Los Angeles. You might not meet a lot of people in Williamsburg or Silverlake who could pick Michael W. Smith or Mark Martin out of a lineup, but someone who could is just a cab ride away.

It's way too easy for those of us outside evangelical culture to dismiss Christian rock as clumsy proselytizing or a cynical attempt to convert people's devout beliefs into cash, and while those motivations probably exist for some people on some level, I haven't met anyone that manipulative while working on this book. I've met lots of critics and cynics—people sincerely concerned or even angry about the way the Christian music industry conducts itself and what the music's saying—and not a few Pollyannas, but no evil genius pushing hot buttons from behind a curtain.

That said, you lose perspective after working on a project for as long as I have done with this one. Part of it is looking back on yourself a year earlier—I can't believe I used to not know the difference between Pentecostals and Baptists. I really like some of the music I've learned about, and even some of the stuff I dislike has grown on me. Lately, I've found myself singing "Awesome God" and "If We

Are the Body" while doing household chores, a development my wife regards as ominous.

When I started this book, she was concerned that I was going to become a Christian. That didn't happen. But I have become a fan, not just of the music, but of Christians, and of Jesus himself. To me, the message of the Gospel is love one another, look out for the less fortunate, and try to walk gently on the earth. And I *love* that. I think evangelical Christians tie themselves in ontological knots trying to make the whole Bible jibe, which is simply impossible with a collection of historical texts written over more than a thousand years. To anyone struggling with Christianity, my advice (and I realize how little this is worth, coming from someone who doesn't believe in God) is to try to keep your eye on the big picture, not a verse here and there. Love God, if you're so inclined, and one another. Sort out the rest using those principles as a lens.

Which leads me to the end of this book, and my answer to Markus's question. In chapter 1, I said there was something quintessentially American about Christian rock, and I couldn't put my finger on it. I think I may have it now—it's that fusion of swagger, winging it, and production values that fascinates some people about Americans and drives others completely bonkers. Swagger because sincerity gives it confidence. Winging it because theologically, a lot of Christian music is the product of heartfelt beliefs and self-guided education. And production values because it sounds good and has an awards show.

As long as Americans continue to try out identities till they find one that suits them, they're going to need maps, if you will, of whatever path they've chosen. The tessellated world of Christian music is really just a guide to the many ways to navigate the muddled, mottled landscape of just one of those choices. Here's to never stopping seeking, to never stopping rocking, to never stopping shopping. No, there doesn't need to be Christian rock. But I'd hate to live anywhere that didn't give people enough hope to think the opposite.

NOTES

Chapter 1

1. "The ultimate source of Whitefield's astonishing power over the multitudes was the great timbre and sonority of his 'magical voice.' . . . [T]he Great Awakener could be heard, without shouting, by 30,000 at one time. David Garrick, the actor, noticed that Whitefield could convulse an audience merely by pronouncing the word 'Mesopotamia'; actually, he could get this effect with other less exotic words, too. . . . He began flights of fancy frequently with the phrase, 'Me-thinks I see'. . . and favored surprise endings. . . . His taste was vulgar but his wit was ready. When a clergyman in Boston Common told him, 'I'm sorry to see you here,' he replied, 'So is the Devil.' When he raised emotions to a high pitch, Whitefield was usually a casualty himself, weeping more or less openly as he preached" (Cowing 1972, 59).

2. Cowing 1972, 73.

3. "Evangelicals in America," Greenberg Quinlan Rosner Research, Ltd., April 2004. *greenbergresearch@com/index.php?ID1230.*

4. All figures from "Evangelicals in America."

5. Acts 2: 44–45.

Chapter 2

1. Powell 2002, 875.

2. Thu Phan, "Christian Bookstores Reject Carrying P.O.D.'s Album," *The Christian Post*, December 29, 2003.

3. Alfonso 2002, 29.

4. Powell 2002, 375.

5. See av1611.org/amysalut.html. Accessed 1/13/06.

6. Stockman 2004, 26.

7. Stockman 2004, 30.

8. Alfonso 2002, 25.

9. Powell 2002, 240.

Chapter 3

1. Jon Richards, "New Releases," *Seattle Weekly,* January 27, 2000.
2. Howard and Streck 1999, 209.

Chapter 4

1. Trae Cadenhead, "Achilles Heel," *The Phantom Tollbooth*, May 24, 2004.

Christian Rock Lifers #2

1. Powell 2002, 933.
2. Powell 2002, 931.

Chapter 5

1. Janet I. Tu, "Pastor Mark Packs 'Em In," *Pacific Northwest: The Seattle Times Magazine,* November 30, 2003.
2. 1 Corinthians 11:3.
3. 1 Corinthians 11:10.
4. 1 Corinthians 11:14.
5. Grace Driscoll, "Is the Biblical View of Women Applicable in Our Culture Today?" at acts29network.org.

Chapter 6

1. 1 John 2:15–17.
2. Ballmer 2000, 34–35.
3. Schaeffer 1981, 44.
4. Schaeffer 1981, 27–28.

Chapter 7

1. Ballmer 2000, 106.
2. Farias, Andree, "Yearning for Diversity," *Christianity Today,* October 25, 2004.
3. Farias, Andree, "A House Divided," *Christianity Today,* July 12, 2004.
4. Ronald J. Sider, "The Scandal of the Evangelical Conscience," *Christianity Today* (January/February 2005).

Chapter 8

1. Ballmer 2000, 24.

Chapter 11

1. Acts 2:3.
2. Acts 2:40.
3. Acts 2: 44–45.

BIBLIOGRAPHY

Note: Bible verses, when quoted, are taken from the New Revised Standard Version (NRSV), specifically the *HarperCollins Study Bible*, ed. Wayne A. Meeks (HarperSanFrancisco, 1993). I realize there is great debate within the Christian community over the best translation; many evangelical Christians favor the New International Version, and the NRSV has been criticized (sometimes by people profiled in this book) for its "political correctness" because it strives to eliminate what it calls "the inherent bias of the English language toward the masculine gender, a bias that, in the case of the Bible, has often restricted or obscured the meaning of the original text." I understand the objections to this attempt. Nonetheless, I defer to the Bible scholarship of my friend Jim Coe, who holds a master's of divinity from Union Theological Seminary in Richmond, Virginia, and maintains that this is the clearest, most accurate translation currently available. All I can add to his recommendation is that I, a chronic nonbeliever, have enjoyed reading this edition, especially its copious footnotes, and sometimes even pick it up when I'm not working.

Alfonso, Barry. *The Billboard Guide to Contemporary Christian Music*. New York: Billboard Books, 2002.

Ballmer, Randall. *Mine Eyes Have Seen the Glory: A Journey into the Evangelical Subculture in America*. 3rd ed. New York: Oxford University Press, 2000.

Cowing, Cedric B. *The Great Awakening and the American Revolution: Colonial Thought in the 18th Century*. Chicago: Rand McNally and Co., 1972.

Horton, Michael S. *Where in the World Is the Church? A Christian View of Culture and Your Role in It*. Phillipsburg, N.J.: Presbyterian and Reformed Publishing Co., 2002.

Howard, Jay, and John Streck. *Apostles of Rock: The Splintered World of Contemporary Christian Music*. Lexington: University Press of Kentucky, 1999.

Joseph, Mark. *Faith, God & Rock 'n' Roll*. London: Sanctuary Publishing, 2003.

Powell, Mark Allan. *Encyclopedia of Christian Contemporary Music*. Peabody, Mass.: Hendrickson Publishers, 2002.

Saloman, Mark. *Simplicity*. Orlando, Fla.: Relevant Books, 2005.

Schaeffer, Franky. *Addicted to Mediocrity: 20th Century Christians and the Arts*. Westchester, Ill.: Crossway Books, 1981.

Stockman, Steve. *The Rock Cries Out: Discovering Eternal Truth in Unlikely Music*. Lake Mary, Fla.: Relevant Books, 2004.

————. *Walk On: The Spiritual Journey of U2*. Lake Mary, Fla.: Relevant Books, 2003.

Thompson, John J. *Raised by Wolves: The Story of Christian Rock & Roll*. Toronto, Ontario: ECW Press, 2000.

Van Pelt, Doug. *Rock Stars on God: 20 Artists Speak Their Minds about Faith*. Lake Mary, Fla.: Relevant Books, 2004.

INDEX

A&M, 28
ABC, 27, 180
Abortion, 3, 5, 15, 65, 99, 187, 188,
    189–217, 267
    and contraception, 195, 211–212
"Abortion Is Murder," 3
Achilles Heel, 85–86
ACME (Alternative Christian Music
    Enthusiasts) fanzine, 49
Acts 29 (organization), 109, 112
*Addiction to Mediocrity: 20th
    Century Christians and the Arts*
    (Schaeffer), 122–123
"Adeste Fideles," 152
Adrenaline Circus, 155
Africa, 148
Aftonbladet (newspaper), 269
Against the Law, 40
Agence France Press, 15
Age to Age, 33
AIDS, 135, 158, 230
Alan Guttmacher Institute, 195
Alcorn, Randy, 202
Alfonso, Barry, 33, 37
ALL. *See* American Life League
Allegory, 87
Alley Katz (nightclub), 254
Allman Brothers, 235
All That You Can't Leave Behind, 134
Altar Boys, 39, 40, 61
Altar calls, 83

"Amazing Grace," 159, 243
Americana, 136
American exceptionalism, 87
American Life League (ALL), 187,
    188, 189, 191, 192–193,
    202–204
    boycotts proposed by, 203–204
American Medical Association,
    195
Americans of Faith, 205
Americans United for Church, 209
"Ammunition," 13
Anoraks, 134
"Another One Bites the Dust," 236
Antichrist, 76
Apologetics, 38, 41
*Apostles of Rock: The Splintered
    World of Contemporary
    Christian Music* (Howard and
    Streck), 62, 65
Arcade Fire, 103
Art, 52, 53, 122, 123, 239
Assisted suicide, 192
Asthmatic Kitty (label), 116, 117,
    125, 133
Astralwerks, 182
Atheism, 2
Australia, 99, 102, 172, 233
Avalon, 42
Awaiting Your Reply, 32
aWAKE project, 140, 147, 148

"Awesome God," 177, 270
Azitis, 21

"Backwoods Nation," 267
Bakker, Jay, 251–253
Bakker, Jim, 37, 251
Baldwin, Stephen, 155, 156–157
Ballmer, Randall, 121, 122, 161–162,
    171
Baloche, Paul, 232
Baptisms, 106
Barnes and Noble, 28
Barr-Jeffrey, Anthony, 31, 35, 154,
    160, 166, 167
Barry, Marion, 270
Baylor University, 236, 238
Bazan, Ann, 75, 92, 93
Bazan, Dave, 1–2, 34, 38, 75–94, 125,
    126, 131–133, 218, 250, 252,
    263, 265, 266–267, 268
  on moral issues, 91–94
Bazan, David, Jr., 76–77, 78, 79,
    117–118, 129, 136–137
BBC Ulster radio, 134
Beach Boys, 265
Beatles, 78, 81, 85, 262
Beautiful Letdown, The, 11, 13
BEC (label), 62, 164
Becker, Margaret, 139
Bedhead, 82
Believer, 142
Benson (distributor), 40
Bereit, David, 189–190, 196, 197,
    209, 210–211
Bernardo, Wuv, 4
Berschback, Duff, 230
Best Buy, 59–60
Bible, 7, 9, 15, 22, 28, 39, 53, 77, 87,
    97, 98, 109, 110, 132, 171, 219,
    220, 221, 264, 271
  Acts 2, 14, 262
  audiobook version of, 154–155
  biblical law, 36, 93, 111–112
  Book of Exodus, 208

Book of Genesis, 80, 111
Colossians 2, 221
First Corinthians, 111, 112, 252
First Letter of John, 121
Letter to the Philippians, 155
Matthew 28:19, 121
Proverbs, 78
Psalms, 234
  second chapter of Timothy, 132
  Sermon on the Mount, 63
"Big Trucks," 85
Bierman, Denver, 171
Billboard albums chart, 34
Billboard Guide to Contemporary
    Christian Music (Alfonso), 33
Black, Frank, 22
Black Eyed Peas, 101
Black Sabbath, 65
"Blessed Be Your Name," 159, 175
Blessitt, Arthur, 20
Blink-182, 62
Blogs, 144
Bloodgood, 40
Bluegrass, 240
Bobby Jones, 153
Bob Jones University, 162
Body decorations, 1, 12
Bogut, Andrew, 172
Bonnaroo festival, 235
Bono, 35, 36–37, 60, 86, 135, 140,
    146–148
Born-again Christians, 6, 8, 249
Born Again Lesbian Music (BALM),
    23
Bound for Life, 200
Boycotts, 203–204
Briner, Bob, 146
Brother Danielson, 127–128
Brown, Judie, 192
Bryan, William Jennings, 8
Buchanan, Pat, 66
Building 459, 154
"Bullfrogs and Butterflies," 26
Burgess, Rick, 174

Burlap to Cashmere, 96, 143
Bush, George W., 66, 136, 170,
  192–193, 204, 206, 267
Byrds, 24

Caedmon's Call, 120
Calvary Chapel church, 20, 23, 50,
  230, 231, 233
Calvin College's Festival of Faith,
  115, 116, 117–120, 126–128,
  129, 136–137
Calvinism, 7, 116, 136
Camp, Jeremy, 62–63, 173, 174
Canada, 85
"Candy," 120
Capitalism, 86, 88
Capitol (label), 21, 39
Capstone, 234
Card, Michael, 139
Carman (singer), 77
Caroline (distributor), 62
Carter, David "Dad," 173
Carter, Marsha and Wendy,
  22–23
Cash, Johnny, 24, 47
Cassidy, Shaun, 61
Casting Crowns, 172, 178
Catch for Us the Foxes, 262
Caviezel, Jim, 150, 153
CBS, 27
CCLI. *See* Christian Copyright
  Licensing International
CCM *See* Contemporary Christian
  Music
CCM magazine, 31, 139–140, 141,
  144–146, 154, 156
Centers for Disease Control, 195
Cetera, Peter, 34
Chaffee, Jim, 157–158
Chagall Guevara, 96
"Champion, The," 77
"Change the World," 166
Chapman, Beth Nielsen, 226
Chapman, Gary, 176

Chapman, Steven Curtis, 38, 146,
  172
Charisma magazine, 233
Chavez, Hugo, 97
Cherone, Gary, 156
Chevelle, 6, 42, 63, 96, 101, 143–144
Chicago, 14
Children of the Day, 22–23, 24
Choi, Jae, 168
Chomsky, Noam, 87
Christ-a-Go-Go, 124
"Christian and Art, The" (column),
  53
Christian Booksellers Association,
  28
Christian bookstores, 28–29, 60
Christian Coalition, 162
Christian Copyright Licensing
  International (CCLI), 151, 227,
  228, 233
Christian Defense Coalition, 198
Christian Goth, 16–17
Christianity Today, 163–164
Christian music sales, 9, 179, 226
Christian Post, 29
Christianpunks.com, 88–89
Christian radio, 185, 186
Christian rock music, 9–10, 71, 110,
  231, 255, 269
  early days of, 19
  first album of, 20–21
  rock stars, 165–166
  and safety factor for kids, 49–50,
    53
  strictures of, 59
  use of term, 71, 72
Chuck Wagon Gang, 173
"Church Is One Foundation, The,"
  159
Circus magazine, 47
Clash, 96, 98
Clawson, Cynthia, 29
Cleveland, Ashley, 226
Clinton, Hillary, 211

Clothes, 157, 247, 261, 266. *See also* T-shirts
Cohen, Leonard, 130
Coldplay, 65
Coleman, Paul, 139
Collins, Bootsy, 163
Collision, A, 239, 240, 243
Columbia House, 81
"Come Thou Fount," 137
Come to the Waters, 23
Communes, 262
   communal living experiments, 19–20
Communism, 33
Compassion International, 158
Complex Infrastructure of the Female Mind, The (Relient K), 171
Concrete Rubber Band, 20
Conservatives, 5, 33, 66, 122, 252
Contemporary Christian music (CCM), 24, 26, 33, 34, 123, 125, 139, 154, 158, 164, 178
   three camps of, 62–63
Contraception, 192, 195, 207, 211–212
Control, 86–87, 88–89
"Control," 254, 256
Conversions to Christianity, 5, 7, 8, 23–23, 26, 27, 40, 47–48, 67–68, 84, 99, 108–109, 201, 260, 261
   celebrity converts, 155, 156
   and personal testimonies, 161
Cook, Tim, 5
Cool Hand Luke, 250
Coolidge, 82
Cooper, Alice, 156
Cornerstone Festival, 1, 11, 12–16, 45, 46, 57, 67, 89, 92, 187–188, 193, 261, 263
   Florida franchise of, 247–253, 259, 260, 265–267
Corporate culture, 88
Corporate worship, 227
"Cosmic Cowboy," 25

Counterculture, 20
Counting Crows, 151
Country music, 182–183, 228
Crabb, Kemper, 53
Crabb Family, 172–173
Creed, 70
Creem magazine, 47
Crisp, Quentin, 158
Cross Movement, 161
Crouch, Andraé, 24, 141
Crowder, David, 39, 151, 153, 175, 227, 236–245
Crowe, Cameron, 249
Crucified, 39, 61, 217
Crumbs from Your Table (Stockman), 134
Cure, 81
Cynicism, 85–86

Dancing, 30
Daniel Amos, 35, 61, 141
Daniels, Charlie, 179
Daniels, Traa, 5
Dannelly, Brian, 248
Darby, John Nelson, 121
Dark, David, 117–118, 122, 123, 126, 130–131, 136
Darwin, Charles, 132. *See also* Evolution
DATA organization, 140, 146–147, 148
Dating, 56, 107, 165
Dave Matthews Band, 235–236
David (King), 132
David Crowder Band, 227, 243, 244–245. *See also* Crowder, David
Davis, John, 265–266
Day of Fire, 154
D.C. Talk, 40–41, 147, 156, 163, 175, 257
Death Cab for Cutie, 110
Debt relief. *See* Third World debt
Decca (label), 26

Deep Purple, 47
DeepSpace5, 163
Degarmo and Key, 32
de la Rocha, Zach, 249
DeLorean, John, 139
Demon Hunter, 63, 183
Denver and the Mile High
    Orchestra, 171
Deuce, 161, 162
Dion, Celine, 62
Di Sabatino, David, 230–231, 233
Disciples, 24
Dispensational premillennialism, 121
Divorce, 31, 59
Doerksen, Brian, 232
Doe v. Bolton, 191, 192
Dolan, Jon, 188
"Don't Take the Girl," 54
Doppelganger, 35
Dove Awards, 13, 68, 169, 173, 176,
    258–259. *See also* Gospel Music
    Association, Gospel Music
    Awards
Downhere, 160
Drinking alcohol, 1, 39, 52, 68, 110,
    129, 135, 154, 160, 209, 217,
    220–221, 222
Driscoll, Grace, 112–113
Driscoll, Mark (Pastor), 106–112
Drugs, 23, 39, 65, 154, 166, 209, 234,
    270. *See also* Drinking alcohol;
    Heroin; Marijuana
"Drugs or Jesus," 182
Duluth News Tribune, 205–206
Dupree, Bishop Kenneth H., 171
Dying of Thirst, 166
Dylan, Bob, 27, 129

Earthsuit, 255, 257, 259
"Easter Song," 26
Ebel, Brandon, 40, 55–56, 57–60,
    60–61, 63, 64, 66–73, 129,
    153–154, 260
  conversion story of, 67–68

Ebel, Dale, 60–61, 66
Economic issues, 122, 124, 150. *See
    also* Money issues
Eddy, Phil, 190, 196, 198–199, 208,
    209
Edge, the, 35
Edwards, Jonathan, 7
Elms, 160, 248
"El Shaddai," 33
Elsinore Theatre (Salem, Oregon), 22
Elwood, Joey, 146
EMI (label), 37, 62, 64, 179,
    181–182, 227
Emo rock music, 76, 86, 183
*Encyclopedia of Christian
    Contemporary Music* (Powell),
    23, 95
English, Michael, 176
Enigma (label), 39
Enoch, 80
E.R.A.C.E. foundation, 163, 166
Eschatology, 21
Euthanasia, 95
Evanescence, 5
Evangelicals, 6, 8–9, 20, 21, 29, 30,
    33, 36, 37, 38, 40, 41, 48, 86,
    87–88, 90, 93, 97, 108, 112, 113,
    121, 132, 135, 150, 158, 159,
    161, 170, 171, 219, 249, 268,
    270, 271
  and being in the world, 176
  and celebrity, 155–156
  genesis of Evangelicalism, 28
  and personal vs. social problems,
    65, 122, 159, 163, 215, 240
  and "planting" churches, 123
  secular stereotypes of, 9
"Eve of Destruction," 25
*Everyday Apocalypse: The Sacred
    Revealed in Radiohead, The
    Simpsons and Other Pop
    Culture Icons* (Dark), 126
Evie, 141
Evolution, 8, 88, 121, 132

Exit (label), 28, 35
Explo 72, 24, 31, 47
Extreme, 156

Fagg, J. Elmo, 173
Fair Trade products, 135, 140
Falling Up, 164
Falwell, Jerry, 36–37, 40, 192
Farias, Andree, 163–164
Feldman, Wayne, 124
FEL Publications, 229
Feminist Majority, 209
Fenholt, Jeff, 65
"Filler," 39
"Find a Way," 34
Finney, Charles Grandison, 8
First Amendment, 190
First Call, 176
"Fish, The" (radio format), 62, 156
Fisher, Claire, 6
Flaming Lips, 235
"Flood," 42
Floodlight (label), 110
"Fly, The," 36
Flying Burrito Bros., 24
Fontamillas, Jerome, 12
Forefront (label), 53, 183
"Foregone Conclusions," 2, 92
Foreigner, 156
Foreman, Jonathan, 10, 11–12, 13,
    173
Foreman, Tim, 42
Forgiveness, 265
4 Him, 42
4th Avenue Jones, 163
"For Those Tears I Died," 23
Foster, Stephenie, 197
Franklin, Benjamin, 171
Free at Last, 41
"Freedom Fighter," 4–5
Frisbee, Lonnie, 20, 230
Fromme, Chuck, 233
Frontline (label), 40, 61
Fugazi, 79–80, 87

*Fundamental Elements of Southtown,
    The*, 29
Furler, Pete, 172
Further Seems Forever, 6

Gaither, Bill and Gloria, 173
Galloway, Glen "Galaxy," 123
Gallup Poll, 194
Garcia, Jerry, 235
Garrett, David and Dale, 231
Gaylord Entertainment Company, 37
G8 Summit, 140, 148
Gender roles, 110–113
General market, 10, 11, 28, 34, 38,
    42, 59, 62, 63, 71, 72, 80, 96,
    156, 175, 183–184, 218
Giglio, Louie, 151–153, 226, 227,
    238–239
Gill, Vince, 176
Glue, 167
GMA. *See* Gospel Music Association
    Week
Godsmack, 46
Golden Republic, 182
Gold records, 33
Goode, Paul, 116, 117, 124
Gordon, Nina, 6
Gospel According to America, The
    (Dark), 118
Gospel Music Association (GMA)
    Week, 149–168, 169–178, 225
  crowds divided by dress at, 157
  Gospel Music Awards, 62, 168,
    169–178. *See also* Dove Awards
  rules for Christian recordings, 177
Gotee records (label), 144, 163, 183
Graham, Billy, 24
Gramm, Lou, 156
Grand Ole Opry House, 169, 170
Grand Rapids, Michigan, 115, 116,
    125
Grant, Amy, 33–34, 63, 147, 154, 176,
    226
Grant, Natalie, 172

Grateful Dead, 234–235
Great Awakening(s), 7, 8, 162
Great Commission, 121
Green, Keith, 26–27, 179
Green Day, 5, 62
Grits, 144, 163, 164
Grohl, Dave, 5
Guilty, 82

Haase, Eben, 82
Hagar, Sammy, 46
Half-Baked (film), 157
Half-Handed Cloud, 136
Hall, Mark, 172, 178
Hardcore music, 183, 217
Harris, Josh, 56
Harris, Larnelle, 174
Hawk Nelson, 164
Hearn, Bill, 24–25, 35, 38, 179–186
Hearn, Billy Ray, 24, 25, 26, 179
Heaven, 119, 240, 265
Heaven's Metal magazine, 45–46,
    48–49
Heavy metal, 39, 45, 49, 59, 142
Heffner, Ken, 118–120, 126–127,
    128, 129, 130, 136, 254
Helmet, 262
Heretics, 90
Herman, Paul, 228, 229–230
Heroin, 82–83
Herrin, J. D., 267
Hesse, Herman, 254
Hetrick, Amy, 206–208
Hill, Fatih, 62
Hill, Greg, 255, 257
Hillsong Music (label), 233
Hip-hop, 40, 41, 101, 161, 163, 165,
    166, 175
    battle rapping, 162
Hippies, 20
HM: The Hard Music Magazine, 45,
    46, 48–49, 53, 150
Hogan, Mike, 244
Holm, Dallas, 29

Holy Hip-Hop, 161, 162
"Holy Worldliness—Culture and the
    Problem of Evil" (workshop),
    118–120
"Honestly," 40
Honesty, 94
Honor Role, 262
Hootie & the Blowfish, 151
Horizontal aesthetics, 124–125
Houghton, Israel, 171
House of Acts (community), 19, 20
Howard, Jay, 62, 65
"How Great Thou Art," 152

"I Blew Up the Clinic Real Good,"
    99
"I Can Only Imagine," 119–120
"If We Are the Body," 178, 270–271
Illect (label), 168
"I Love a Lonely Day," 33
I Love You, 21
"In Christ Alone," 176
"Indescribable," 152
Indie rock, 84–85, 110, 123, 127, 142
In God We Trust, 39
Insiderz, 144
Integrity Music, 232–233
In vitro fertilization, 192
iPod Shuffle, 153
"I Saw the Light," 240
Islam, 245. *See also* Sufism
Island (label), 28, 35
"I Still Haven't Found What I'm
    Looking For," 36, 86
It's Hard to Find a Friend, 84, 86, 91
"I Want to Be a Clone," 37, 95
"I Wish We'd All Been Ready," 21

Jackson, Josh, 129
Jacobs, Peter, 23
Jade Tree (label), 59, 76, 86
Jam bands, 58, 235
Japan, 40, 183
Jars of Clay, 42, 147, 226

Jefferson, Thomas, 171
Jesus Christ, 4, 7, 8, 9, 20, 29, 34, 46,
    48, 53, 60, 63, 65, 76, 87, 88, 93,
    97, 106, 119, 131, 159, 252, 261,
    263–264, 267, 268
    and being in the world, 110, 119,
    120–121, 135, 240, 264, 265,
    271
    Jesuses-per-minute factor,
    184–185, 258
Jesus Freak, 41, 43
Jesus freaks, 20, 43
Jesus Movement/People, 19–20, 21,
    22, 25, 30, 226, 230, 232, 233,
    268
Jesus People USA (JPUSA), 14, 30,
    260
J Moss, 174
John Paul II (Pope), 116, 133–134
Johnson, Chad, 58, 70
Johnson, Daniel, 127
Joint ventures, 28, 227
Jones, Denise, 154–155
Jordon, Marabeth, 176
Joshua Tree, The, 35, 123, 134
J3, 164
Jurado, Damien, 82
Jurassic 5, 204
"Just Between You and Me," 41, 156

Kaiser, Glenn, 29–32, 33, 42, 260
Karate, 110
Katrina hurricane, 239
Kaufmann, Mike, 117, 123–125, 133,
    136
Keaggy, Phil, 160
Kemper, Bryan, 202, 203
Kerouac, Jack,, 118
Kerry, John, 5, 28, 66, 205, 207
KEXP radio station, 64, 84
Kid Rock, 12
"Killing in the Name Of," 249
King, Darren, 255–256, 257, 258
King's X, 51

Kiss, 203, 205
"Kiss Dating Good-bye" (seminar),
    56
"Kiss Me," 96, 176–177
KJ-52, 165
Kolosine, Errol, 182
Korean-Americans, 244
Korn, 3, 5
Kristofferson, Kris, 24, 47

Lacey, Rob, 15
LaHaye, Beverly, 154
Lake, Kyle, 242–243
Larkin, Patti, 130
Larsson, Markus, 269–270
Last Call for Vitriol, 265
Last Days Ministries, 27
L.A. Symphony, 96, 101, 143, 144,
    163
Led Zeppelin, 47, 48, 51
LeFevre, Myron, 21
Legend of Chin, The, 143
Lesbians, 23, 154, 190, 209
Le Tigre, 204
"Letter to the President," 164–165
Lewis, C. S., 38
Liberals, 5, 22, 66, 252
Liberation theology, 87
Liberty University, 40
Life chains, 201
Lighthouse Ranch (community), 19
Lightning Bolt, 124
Lil' Flip, 126
Lilith Fair, 190
Limp Bizkit, 4
Linkin Park, 3
Living Sacrifice, 142
Livin' It (video), 155
Liz (Christian Goth), 16
London Calling, 96, 98–99
"Longer I Lay Here, The," 85
Long's Christian Music, 141
Love, 252, 253, 263, 264, 271
Love, Courtney, 6, 67

Love Song, 23–24, 231
Low, 82
Luis Palau Ministries, 155
"Lullaby," 82, 83
Luther, Martin, 21, 28, 93, 171

Mac, Toby, 144, 146, 163, 166, 170,
    175, 178
McCartney, Bill, 112, 162
McCorvey, Norma, 191, 197
McGraw, Tim, 54, 182
McGuire, Barry, 25–26, 179
Macho, 166, 167
MacKaye, Ian, 39
McKeehan, Toby "Toby Mac," 41
MacKinnon, Adam, 56–57
MacKinnon, Amanda, 56–58, 64, 68,
    70, 72
Mad at the World, 40, 61
Made in Mexico (label), 84, 91
Madison (film), 150
Madison, John, 168
Mahoney, Reverend Patrick, 198,
    199–200, 210, 215
Mallonee, Bill, 136
Maniacs, 143
Manning, Steve, 64
Maranatha (label), 20, 23, 231–232,
    233
March for Women's Lives, 189, 194,
    202
Marijuana, 67, 91, 235, 240
Marilyn Manson, 123
Maroon 5, 62
Marshall Tucker Band, 180
Martin, Chris, 65
Masen, Sarah, 136, 143
Masquerade (nightclub), 251
Matos, Michaelangelo, 64
Matrix, The (film), 131
Matthews, Randy, 25
MCA (label), 27, 29, 96, 100
"Meant to Live," 11
Meany, Paul, 255, 256–259

Media, 9, 49, 210, 240
Medieval reenactments, 16
Meltdown at Madame Tussaud's, 96
Men at Work, 140, 141
MercyMe, 6, 119, 226
Mercy Ministries, 154
Merritt, Stephin, 84
Metallica, 40
Mewithoutyou, 63, 73, 260, 261–262,
    263, 265, 267–268
MGM, 150
Millard, Bart, 226
Miner, Tim, 257
Mine Eyes Have Seen the Glory
    (Ballmer), 121, 161–162
Minor Threat, 39, 61
Misfits, 46
Mitchell, Roy, 255, 257, 259
Modest Mouse, 5, 110
Mommy Don't Love Daddy Anymore,
    31
Money issues, 69–70, 79, 153–154,
    181, 231. *See also* Christian
    music sales; Economic issues;
    Royalties
Monogamy, 93, 176
Moore, Mandy, 11
Moral issues, 91–94, 95
    morality clauses in contracts, 176
Morello, Tom, 46
Morelos, James, 84
"More Than Words," 156
Motown, 24
Mr. Del, 166
MTV, 71–72, 236
    Video Music Awards, 5
Mullen, Larry, Jr., 35
Mullins, Rich, 177
Multiculturalism, 41
Mute Math, 254–255, 257, 258, 259,
    268
MxPx, 40, 62
"My Place in This World," 34
Myrrh (label), 24, 25, 179, 181

Nader, Ralph, 66, 199
NARAL Pro-Choice America, 192
Nashville, Tennessee, 142, 146, 168, 182. *See also* Gospel Music Association Week
National Organization for Women, 209
National Right to Life Committee, 192
Nevermind, 79
Newsboys, 96, 100, 172
New York Times, 251
"Next Time I Fall, The," 34
Nicks, Mark, 250
Niemyjski, Josh, 168
Nietzsche, Friedrich, 254
Nirvana, 5, 79, 81
No Compromise, 26
Norful, Smokie, 174
Norma Jean, 57
Norman, Larry, 21–22, 24, 28–29, 47, 49, 148
Norquist, Grover, 192
"Nothing," 82
Nugent, Ted, 47
Number One Gun, 69, 70
Nu Thang, 41
NY Underground, 165

O.C. Supertones, 40, 56, 267
"Of Up and Coming Monarchs," 85
"One," 234
ONE campaign, 135, 140, 148
Onetruth.com, 15
"One Way," 21
"On Fire," 13
Operation, 261
Operation Rescue, 198, 201
Opie and Anthony, 203–204
Orange County, California, 38–39
Orrico, Stacie, 6, 42, 183, 258
"Our God Reigns," 127
Out of Eden, 147, 226
Owen, Tim, 59, 86

Palmer, Dave, 146
Paolotti, Tyson, 70
Passion movement, 151, 226–227
Passion of Christ, The (film), 150, 172
Paste magazine, 129
Pastor Skip, 108
Patillo, Leon, 77
Patty, Sandi, 34, 77, 154, 175–176, 256
Paul (Apostle), 108, 111, 155, 220–221
Payable on Death, 29
Peacock, Charlie, 10, 35, 140, 142, 143, 146, 147
Pearl Jam, 133, 204
Pedro the Lion, 1, 34, 63, 82, 83–84, 85, 89, 90, 91, 98, 267
Pentecostals, 8, 76, 78–79, 181
People, 21
People for the Ethical Treatment of Animals (PETA), 198
Permission of use, 229
Petra, 2, 32, 33, 77
Pet Sounds, 265
Pet the Fish, 61
Pettis, Pierce, 136
Phair, Liz, 6
Phantom Tollbooth, 86
Philly Soul, 24
Phish, 235
Pixies, 22
Plankeye, 61
Planned Parenthood, 189, 190, 192, 195, 196–197, 199, 209, 210
Please Let Me Live, 201
P.O.D., 3–5, 29, 39, 42, 63
Point of Grace, 42, 154
Poison, 40
Pokinatcha, 62
Police, 140
Poor Old Lu, 38, 68–69
Populism, 8
Posthardcore, 90

Postmodernity, 125
Poverty, 135, 148
Powell, Mac, 178
Powell, Mark Allan, 23, 32, 34, 95
Praise Album, The, 231
Praise Habit: Finding God in Sunsets and Sushi (Crowder), 237
Prince Paul, 101
Priority (label), 27
Problem of evil, 119
Profanity, 2, 60, 68, 92, 135, 166, 220, 238, 267
Progressive economics, 124
Prohibition, 8
Pro-Life Answers to Pro-Choice Questions (Alcorn), 202
Promise Keepers, 112, 162, 232
Promise Ring, 86
Prosperity theology, 79, 88
Prostitutes, 158
Proverbs 31 Ministries, 112
Psalters, 266
Publishing companies, 227–228, 229
Punk scene, 221–222
PunkVoter.com, 204–205
Puritans, 119
Purple Door, 263
Purpose-Driven Life, The (Warren), 232

Queen, 236

Race issues, 95, 97, 162–164, 174, 199–200
Rachinski, Howard, 229
Radical Reformission, The: Reaching Out without Selling Out (Driscoll), 109
Radio and Retail ECHO awards, 154
Rage Against the Machine, 46, 130, 249
Raised by Wolves: The Story of Christian Rock & Roll (Thompson), 25–26

Rap music, 41, 166. *See also* Hip-hop
Rapture, the, 21, 76–77, 87, 121
Rattle and Hum, 36
RCKTWN (club), 164
RCRC. *See* Religious Coalition for Reproductive Choice
Reagan, Ronald, 29
Reborn, 40
"Reclamation," 87
Redman, Matt, 151, 175, 227
Red Rocks (Colorado), 3
Reed, Ralph, 162, 192
Relativism, 125
Relevant magazine, 248–249
Relient K, 90, 144
Religious Coalition for Reproductive Choice (RCRC), 192, 206, 207
R.E.M., 173
Remixing, 96
Renaissance Nashville Hotel, 150, 155, 166. *See also* Gospel Music Association Week
Republican Party, 9, 253
"Rescue Is Coming," 244–245
Respect Life Month, 201
Resurrection Band (Rez Band, Rez), 29–32, 35, 49, 141, 260
re:think (label), 10, 143
Revisionism, 171
Revolution Ministries, 251, 253
R.E.X. (label), 142, 143
Reynolds, Heather, 150
Reynosa, Dax, 166–167
Rhythm Kitchen (Nashville club), 167–168
Rhythms of Redemption (rock show), 134
Rick & Bubba, 174
Ringhofer, John, 117, 133, 136
Rioux, Jeff, 129
Rites of Spring, 262
Roaring Lambs (Briner), 146
Roberts, John, 189, 197
Robertson, Pat, 97, 192

Rock, Chris, 203, 205
Rock for Life, 15, 187–188, 189, 190,
    191, 193, 194, 195, 196–197,
    202, 205, 209, 212, 213
Rock Stars on God (Van Pelt), 46
Roe v. Wade, 191–192, 197, 206
Rogers, Mark, 146–147
Rolling Hills Community Church
    (Portland, Oregon), 61
Rolling Stone, 40, 42, 175
Rollins, Henry, 46
Royalties, 227–230
Rumi, 264
Ryman Auditorium (Nashville),
    157–160

Sacred/secular issues, 241
St. James, Rebecca, 154, 155, 171,
    174, 177, 258
Salem, Oregon, 22
Salem Communications, 156
Salt Company (community), 19
Same-sex marriage, 165, 267
Samuel Adams beer, 203–204, 205
San Diego, 4, 10, 39
Sandoval, Sonny, 4, 5
San Francisco, 20, 107
Sanger, Margaret, 200
Santorum, Rick, 146
Saved! (film), 108, 248
"Savior," 178
Scandals, 23, 37, 59, 176
Schaeffer, Franky, 122–123
Schenck, Paul and Rob, 208
Schiavo, Terri, 115–116, 136, 215
Seattle, Washington, 55–56, 61, 64,
    67, 81, 112, 199
    Mars Hill Church in, 105–108,
    109, 113
Seattle Times, 109
Sebadoh, 82
Second blessing, 78–79, 80
Second Chance, The (film), 96, 104
2nd Chapter of Acts, 25, 26, 179

"Secret of the Easy Yoke," 85
Seinfeld, 6
September 11 attacks, 87, 88
Seven Swans, 116, 128
Seventy Sevens, 35, 141
Sex, 9, 39, 65, 87, 92, 110, 158, 159,
    175–176, 200, 204, 205, 217,
    233, 241, 267
Sexton, Martin, 120
Shalom, 36
Shane and Shane, 244
Shepherding Movement, 232
She's All That, 96
Shirley, Andrew, 11
"Shout to the Lord," 172, 233
Simple Way (commune), 262
Simplicity, 217
Simpson, Jessica, 175
Sims, Tommy, 166
"Sin for a Season," 78, 98
Six Feet Under, 6
Sixpence None the Richer, 6, 96, 101,
    142–143, 147, 176, 265
Sixstepsrecords (label), 151, 227, 238
Six: The Mark Unleashed (film), 157
Skillet, 169, 178
Slain in the Spirit (worship rite), 79
Slavery, 214, 240
Slocum, Matt, 265
Slowcore (subgenre), 85
Smith, Chuck, 20
Smith, Daniel "Brother Danielson,"
    116, 127–128, 133
Smith, Kevin "Kevin Max," 41
Smith, Lenny, 127
Smith, Michael W., 34, 96, 147, 155,
    158, 164, 178, 226
Smoking, 60, 68, 135, 217, 220
Snake King, The (film), 157
Snuff the Punk, 3
Soap Opera Awards, 67
Social Distortion, 46
Social justice, 36, 98, 134, 135, 140,
    158, 207

Solid Rock (label), 22
Solid State (label), 62
Solomon, Mark, 39, 217–223
So Long Ago the Garden, 28–29
Something Sacred, 15
Sometimes Sunday, 202
Sonicflood, 232
Soul Junk, 123
SoundScan, 179
Sounds Familyre (label), 116
Sound systems, 109
South Africa, 135
Soviet Union, 33
So You Wanna Go Back to Egypt, 27
Sparrow (label), 10, 11, 26, 27, 37,
    53, 143, 179, 181, 183, 184, 255
Speaking in tongues, 79, 80–81, 90
Spin magazine, 3, 73, 118, 127, 189
Spiritual Youth for Reproductive
    Freedom (SYRF), 206, 207, 208
Springsteen, Bruce, 5
Sprinkle, Aaron, 68–69, 70, 82
Squint, 96, 101
Squint Entertainment (label), 96,
    101, 143–144, 176
Stafford, Dr. Wess, 158
Stafford, Virginia, 189, 190–191
Stand True, 203
Stanley, Ralph, 239, 240
StarFlight (radio show), 141
Starflyer 59, 61, 63, 65
Starpraise Ministries, 229
StarSong, 32
Stavesacre, 217, 218
Stay, 173
Stem cell research, 192, 193, 205
Stevens, Russ and Marsha, 23
Stevens, Sufjan, 116–117, 125, 127,
    128, 133, 136
Stipe, Michael, 173
Stockman, Steve, 36, 129, 134–135
Streck, John, 62, 65
String Cheese Incident, 235
Stryper, 2, 39–40, 42, 65, 236

Subculture, 32, 33, 43, 50, 53, 125,
    156
Sub Pop (label), 61, 64, 82
"Sucked Out," 265
Sufism, 260, 264
Sullivan, Andrew, 211
Sunny Day Real Estate, 262
Superdrag, 265
Supreme Court, 5, 189, 191, 196, 215
Swaggart, Jimmy, 37, 39, 40
Swartzendruber, Jay, 41, 42,
    139–148
Sweet, Michael and Robert, 40
"Sweet Sweet Song of Salvation," 21
Switchfoot, 6, 10–13, 42, 63, 143,
    147, 173, 174, 178, 184
SYRF. *See* Spiritual Youth for
    Reproductive Freedom

Taff, Russ, 78
Tait, Michael, 170
Take6, 175
Talbert, Bishop Melvin, 208
Talbot Brothers, 179
Taxes, 66
Taylor, Steve, 37, 78, 95–104, 139,
    141, 142, 143, 144, 146, 147,
    176, 178
    and political issues, 97–98, 140
Taylor, Terry, 35
Tedd T., 258
Teen Mania, 15
Teleprompt (label), 258
Terrorism, 9
They're Only Chasing Safety, 71
Third Day, 147, 172, 178
Third World debt, 135, 140
"This Little Light of Mine," 174
"This Theatre," 38
Thomas More Law Center, 194
Thompson, John, 25–26
Time magazine, 211
Time Warner, 144
To Hell with the Devil, 39

Tomlin, Chris, 151–152, 175, 227, 234
Tonex, 173–174
Too Small to Ignore: Why Children Are the Next Big Thing (Stafford), 158
Tooth & Nail (label), 40, 53, 56–60, 61, 62, 63, 64–65, 71–72, 82, 83, 84, 127, 164, 183, 263
  and charity work, 66–67
  studio, 68–70
Topanga Community House, 19
To the Bride, 25
"Touch of Grey," 234
Tragedy Ann, 202
Travis, Randy, 182
Trent, Tammy, 155
Truman's Water, 123
Truth, 52, 132, 264
T-shirts, 1, 15, 161, 174, 187, 188, 193–195, 197, 212, 214, 249
  Pro-Life T-Shirt Day, 193–194
Tsunamis, 239–240
Tunnel Rats, 162, 166
Twin Sister, 202
Tyler, Steven, 47

"Ugly Truth about Christian Rock, The" (Van Pelt), 46
Under God (Mac and Tait), 170–171
Underoath, 6, 57, 63, 71, 72
"Undignified," 244
Unguarded, 34
Union Gospel Tabernacle (Nashville), 157
Unitarian Universalist Church, 207
University Baptist Church (UBC) (Baylor University), 237, 242
Upon This Rock, 21
Usual Suspects, The (film), 156–157
U2, 35–37, 86, 123–124, 125, 129, 134–135, 142, 234

Values, 118, 152, 171, 174, 207
Van Halen III, 156

VanLiere, Donna, 155
Van Pelt, Charlotta, 150
Van Pelt, Doug, 27, 45–54, 149, 150, 164, 225–226, 234, 245, 248
Vaughan Williams, Ralph, 239
Vector, 35
Vegetarianism, 221–222
Velasquez, Jaci, 175
Village Voice, 124
Violence, 9
Virgin (label), 183
"Voice of Harold," 173
Voting, 205

Walk On: The Spiritual Journey of U2 (Stockman), 36, 134
Walk to Remember, A (film), 11
Walsh, Tim "TW," 91, 125, 129, 137, 266, 267
War, 36
Warner Music Group, 37, 101
Warren, Rick, 232
Washington City Paper, 116
Washington Post, 149, 187, 209
Way, 231
Webb, Derek, 120
Weiss, Aaron, 260–265
Welch, Brian "Head," 5, 156
Welcome to Diverse City, 163, 175
Well, Chris, 139
We Need a Whole Lot More of Jesus and a Lot Less of Rock and Roll, 21
West, Matt, 154
"We Win!," 243
WFMU radio station, 127
What? Records, 28
Whitefield, George, 7–8
WhiteHeart, 32, 33
Whittington, Erik, 188, 189, 190, 191, 193, 194, 195, 196, 199, 200–206, 208, 209, 211–216
Whittington, Tina, 190
Whole, 82, 83, 86

*Why Should the Devil Have All the
Good Music?* (documentary),
250
Widespread Panic, 235
Williams, Hank, 240
Williams, Joy, 175
Williams, Pharrell, 89
Williams, Ricky, 67
Wilson, Brian, 265
Wilson, Matt, 189, 196, 208
Wilson-McKinley, 21
Winans, CeCe, 147, 174, 175
Wish for Eden, 61
With Footnotes, 26
Witmer, Denison, 63, 265, 266
Word (label), 24, 25, 27, 33, 37, 96,
180, 182, 255, 258
Word Becomes Flesh (audiobook),
154–155, 158
Word on the Street, The (Lacey), 15

Worship Jamz, 151
Worship Leader Magazine, 230, 233
Worship music, 10, 109, 124, 151,
158–160, 175, 225, 226,
230–246, 256
and emotional highs, 245–246
Worship Together Collection, 10, 151
*Wow #1s: 31 of the Greatest
Christian Music Hits Ever,* 176
WVFJ radio station, 141

Yeager, Angela, 22
Yellow and Black Attack, The, 39
Yellowcard, 6
Young, Neil, 100
Young, Shawn, 123
Young Life, 2

Zschech, Darlene, 171–172, 233
ZZ Top, 180